Adapted Physical Education National Standards

National Consortium for Physical Education and Recreation for Individuals with Disabilities

Luke E. Kelly
Project Director

Human Kinetics

Library of Congress Cataloging-in-Publication Data

National Consortium for Physical Education and Recreation for
   Individuals with Disabilities (U.S.)
      Adapted physical education national standards / National
   Consortium for Physical Education and Recreation for Individuals
   with Disabilities ; Luke E. Kelly, project director.
         p.   cm.
      Includes bibliographical references (p.   ).
      ISBN 0-87322-962-2
      1. Physical education for handicapped children--Standards--United
   States.   2. Physical education teachers--Certification--United
   States.   I. Kelly, Luke.   II. Title.
      GV445.N38   1995
      371.9'04486--dc20   95-3492
                                                                    CIP

ISBN: 0-87322-962-2

Federal Disclaimer: This manual was developed as part of the National Standards for Adapted Physical Education Project, which was funded by the United States Department of Education, Office of Special Education and Rehabilitation Services, Division of Personnel Preparation: #H029K20092. The views expressed herein are those of the grantee, the University of Virginia. No official endorsement by the U.S. Department of Education is intended or should be inferred.

Acquisitions Editor: Richard D. Frey, PhD
Special Projects Editor: Dawn Roselund
Assistant Editor: Julie Marx Ohnemus
Proofreader: Karen Bojda
Typesetting and Text Layout: Sandra Meier
Text Designer: Judy Henderson
Cover Designer: Jack Davis
Printer: Versa Press

Printed in the United States of America

10   9   8   7   6   5   4   3   2   1

Human Kinetics
P.O. Box 5076, Champaign, IL 61825-5076
1-800-747-4457

Canada: Human Kinetics, Box 24040, Windsor, ON N8Y 4Y9
1-800-465-7301 (in Canada only)

Europe: Human Kinetics, P.O. Box IW14, Leeds LS16 6TR, England
(44) 532 781708

Australia: Human Kinetics, 2 Ingrid Street, Clapham 5062, South Australia
(08) 371 3755

New Zealand: Human Kinetics, P.O. Box 105-231, Auckland 1
(09) 309 2259

CONTENTS

Standard 4   Measurement and Evaluation   59

Standard 5   History and Philosophy   73

Standard 6   Unique Attributes of Learners: Considerations for Professional Practice   80

Standard 7   Curriculum Theory and Development   113

Standard 8   Assessment   118

Standard 9   Instructional Design and Planning   128

ACKNOWLEDGMENTS

This manual is the culmination of thousands of hours of work by hundreds of volunteers. The standards presented in this manual could not have been developed without the leadership and support provided by the National Consortium for Physical Education and Recreation for Individuals with Disabilities and United States Department of Education, Office of Special Education and Rehabilitation Services, Division of Personnel Preparation. Special recognition is given to the practicing adapted physical educators who completed the job analysis survey that provided the basis for the standards and to the adapted physical educators who served on the Evaluation and Review Committee and validated the final standards.

Thanks are extended to the representatives from the other professional organizations who shared both their time and experience with us: Ms. Patricia Tice, representing the American Physical Therapy Association; Ms. Maureen Plombon, representing the American College of Sports Medicine; and Mr. Paul Grace, representing the National Athletic Training Association and the National Organization on Competency Assurances.

In all projects of this magnitude, some individuals are called upon to make extraordinary contributions. Special recognition is given to Martha Bokee of USDE, OSERS, DPP for her support, guidance and patience working with the project. Special thanks is given to the members of the Steering Committee who were called upon to contribute an inordinate amount of their time and to comply with extremely tight time lines and did so with enthusiasm and conviction. Special appreciation is also extended to Bruce Gansneder who served as the project's research consultant and to the graduate students at the University of Virginia who rallied on many occasions to allow the project to meet deadlines.

Finally, special thanks is given to the spouses, children and significant others of the volunteers for their assistance and patience in allowing the volunteers who worked on this project to devote the time and effort needed to make this project a reality.

OVERVIEW

Introduction

The standards presented in this report represent the culmination of two years of work by over 500 adapted physical educators nationwide. These standards are the first product of a five-year federally funded project to develop national standards and a national certification examination for the field of adapted physical education. The need for this project evolved from the mandates of Federal legislation, including Public Law 101.476, Individuals with Disabilities Education Act (IDEA), which mandates that physical education services, specially designed if necessary, must be made available to every child with a disability receiving a free appropriate education. Unfortunately, the rules and regulations stopped short of defining who was "qualified" to provide these services. Qualified was defined:

> As used in this part, "qualified" means that a person has met State educational agency approved or recognized certification, licensing, registration, or other comparable requirements which apply to the area in which he or she is providing special education or related services (Section 121a.12, Federal Register, 1977).

The definition of who was "qualified" to provide physical education services to individuals with disabilities was left to the individual states and their respective certification requirements based on the assumption that these currently existed. Unlike other special education areas (teachers of individuals with mental retardation, learning disabilities, etc.), most states unfortunately do not have defined certifications for teachers of adapted physical education. While 14 states subsequently defined an endorsement or certification in adapted physical education, the majority of states and eight territories (n=44) have not defined the qualifications teachers need to provide adapted physical education services to their students with disabilities (Cowden & Tymeson, 1984; Kelly, 1991).

In the Spring of 1991, the National Consortium for Physical Education and Recreation for Individuals with Disabilities (NCPERID) in conjunction with the National Association of State Directors of Special Education (NASDSE) and Special Olympics International conducted an "Action Seminar" on adapted physical education for state directors of special education and leaders of advocacy groups for individuals with disabilities (NASDSE, 1991). This conference had two goals:

1. identify the barriers that were preventing full provision of appropriate physical education services to individuals with disabilities; and
2. establish an action agenda for addressing and resolving these problems.

Although numerous barriers were identified by the group, the most significant for state education leaders were that they did not know what adapted physical education was, how individuals with disabilities could benefit from appropriate physical education programming or what competencies teachers needed to deliver appropriate physical education services to students with disabilities. In response to this need, it was recommended that the NCPERID develop professional standards and a means for evaluating these standards. These products could then be used by state and school administrators as well as parents to communicate the need for adapted physical education and to evaluate who was qualified to provide physical education services to students with disabilities.

The "Action Seminar" recommendations were presented to the NCPERID Board in the Summer of 1991. The NCPERID Board voted unanimously to assume responsibility for developing national standards for the field (NCPERH, 1991). A committee was created, with the NCPERID President as Chair, and charged with developing a plan for creating national standards. To this end, the president of the NCPERID prepared and submitted a special project proposal (Kelly, 1992) to the United States Department of Education (USDE), Office of Special Education and Rehabilitative Services (OSERS), Division of Personnel Preparation (DPP) in the Fall of 1991. This grant was funded in July of 1992 and provided funding for five years to develop national standards and a national certification examination for the profession.

Project Purpose

The purpose of this project is to ensure that physical education instruction for students with disabilities is provided by qualified physical education instructors. This purpose was designed to be achieved by addressing two goals:

1. Develop national standards for the field of adapted physical education, and
2. Develop a national certification examination to measure knowledge of the standards.

The first two years of the project focused on developing the national standards. These standards will serve as the foundation for creating a national certification examination in years three and four which will be administered nationally during the last year of the project. It is important to note that what was proposed and funded was a dynamic process for achieving these goals. This process served as the initial framework and has been continuously shaped and refined by input from a variety of constituencies and the ongoing evaluation process.

Committees

The work force for this project is composed of four committees and the project staff. Each of the major committees is briefly described below in terms of its membership and responsibilities.

Executive Committee (6 Members)

Project Director and Past President of NCPERID —Luke Kelly (Chair); the President of the NCPERID—Jeff McCubbin; two members from the NCPERID Board of Directors, appointed by the NCPERID Board—Patrick DiRocco, University of Wisconsin–La Crosse (official liaison between the project and the American Alliance for Health, Physical Education, Recreation and Dance [AAHPERD]) and Hester Henderson, University of Utah (official liaison between the project and the Council for Exceptional Children [CEC]); one member representing NASDSE—Smokey Davis; and one member representing USDE/OSERS/

DPP—Martha Bokee. This committee is responsible for insuring that the project is implemented as intended, for making all policy decisions, and for approving all materials and products produced by the various committees.

Steering Committee (7 Members)

The Chair is the Project Director Luke E. Kelly. Members: John M. Dunn, Oregon State University; G. William Gayle, Wright State University; Barry Lavay, California State University—Long Beach; Monica Lepore, West Chester University; Michael Loovis, Cleveland State University; and Janet A. Seaman, California State University—Los Angeles. The members of this committee applied for these positions and were reviewed and selected by the Executive Committee. The responsibilities of the Steering Committee are to: develop credentialing procedures and criteria for selecting the members of the Standards Committees and Evaluation/Review Committee; develop, implement and monitor the development of the standards and the exam; chair one of the Standards Committees; and report progress on a regular schedule to the Executive Committee.

Standards Committees (72 Members)

There are six Standards Committees each chaired by a member of the Steering Committee. The members on these committees applied for the positions and were selected by the Steering Committee and assigned to a Standards Committee based upon their area(s) of expertise and experience. The responsibilities of the Standards Committees are: delineate the scope and sequence of the content in the standards they are assigned; revise the content based upon the Evaluation/Review Committee's feedback; develop test items to measure the standards; and revise the test items based upon the Evaluation and Review Committee's feedback. The members of the Standards Committees are shown in Figure 1.1. Fifty-four percent of the committee members were female and 46% were male. The committee members were from 26 different states and from both K-12 schools (45%) and colleges and universities (55%).

Evaluation/Review Committee (300+ Members)

Members volunteered for the Evaluation/Review Committee (ERC) and were appointed by the Steering Committee based upon credentials. For evaluation tasks, multiple sub-evaluation groups

APE National Standards: Standards Committee Members

Judy Alexander	Bernadette Ascareggi	James Ascareggi	Ted Baumgartner
David Bermann	Nick Breit	Sandy Brungardt	Ellen Campbell
Alana Campbell	Judy Chandler	Charlie Daniel	John Downing
Gail Dummer	Charles Duncan	Peter Ellery	Steven Errante
M. Rhonda Folio	Sheri Folsom-Meek	Taralyn Garner	Georgia Frey
Michael Gerick	Wanda Gilbert	Mike Haeuser	Constance Hayes
John Herring	Ric Hogerheide	Mike Horvat	Cathy Houston-Wilson
Joseph Huber	Charlotte Humphries	Daniel Joseph	Monica Kleeman
Ellen Kowalski	Karen Leightshoe	Lauren Lieberman	Dwayne Liles
Patrice Manning	Nancy Markos	Deborah Maronic	Elaine McHugh
Robert Merrifield	William Merriman	Sue Ellen Miller	Duane Millslagle
Thomas Murphy	Kathy Omoto	Michael Paciorek	Gloria Palma
Jan Patterson	Vicki Vance	Thomas Pennewell	Virginia Politino
Lynda Reeves	Jim Rimmer	Catherine Schroeder	Cindy Slagle
Stephen Butterfield	Christine Stopka	Perky Stromer	Christine Summerford
Paul Surburg	Ric Tennant	Kathleen Tomlin	April Tripp
Terri Troll	Garth Tymeson	Dale Ulrich	Paul Vogel
Bill Vogler	Tim Wallstrom	Robert Weber	Andrea Williams

Figure 1.1 Standards Committee members.

composed of 30 members each were randomly formed from the pool of ERC members. The Project Director is responsible for instructing and monitoring the work of this committee. The ERC's responsibilities included validating the draft content of the standards and test items developed by the various Standards Committees. A total of 977 professionals expressed interest in working on the ERC. From this pool, 300 were selected to evaluate the draft standards based upon their willingness to perform this task and evidence that they were in fact practicing adapted physical educators with one or more years teaching experience. See Appendix A for the names of these ERC members. Descriptive data on the ERC are shown in Figure 1.2. Review of the data in Figure 1.2 reveals that 90% of the committee members were K-12 adapted physical educators. They had a mean age of 40.36 years, an average of 11.28 years teaching experience, and represented 40 of the 50 states.

Project Staff

The Project Staff is composed of the Project Director, a Research Consultant, a Project Assistant and a Clerical Assistant. The Project Director is Luke E. Kelly, Past President of the NCPERID and Director of the graduate adapted physical education programs at the University of Virginia. The Research Consultant is Dr. Bruce Gansneder from the Bureau of Educational Research, Curry School of Education, University of Virginia. The Project Assistant responsibilities have been distributed

ERC Demographic Data

Variables	n	%
Gender		
Male	90	30
Female	210	70
Training		
Bachelors	279	93
Masters	210	70
Doctorates	45	15
Teaching level		
K-12 schools	269	90
University	31	10
States represented	40	80

Variables	n	Min	Max	Mean
Age	300	22.0	66.0	40.36
Years teaching	300	1.0	30.0	11.28
% time teaching APE	300	10.0	100.0	80.54

Figure 1.2 Demographic data on the Evaluation/ Review Committee members used to validate the draft standards.

across four doctoral students at the University of Virginia during the first two years of the project: Ms. Katie Stanton, Mr. Jim Martindale, Mr. Morris Pickens and Mr. David Striegel. The Clerical Assistant responsibilities have been distributed across a number of graduate students during the first two years of the project, most notably: Ms. Karen Etz, Ms. Alyssa Watkins, and Ms. Jennifer Williams.

Standards Development Process

The first year of the project was devoted to achieving three objectives. The first of these objectives was to review and compare our proposed procedures with those of other professional organizations that have already gone through the process of developing standards and national exams. The second objective was to identify the roles and responsibilities adapted physical educators were being asked to perform in our nation's schools as well as the perceived needs of these educators. The final objective for year one was to interpret the job analysis data to determine the content that adapted physical educators need to know to perform their roles and responsibilities and to create a means of organizing this content.

Since a number of other professional organizations have already developed national standards and certification exams, it seemed prudent to contact these organizations to see what could be learned from their experiences. To this end, the Executive Committee identified six professional organizations that were viewed as having elements of similarity to adapted physical education. Some of these elements were size, focus, need and purposes for creating their standards and exams. These six organizations were the: American College of Sports Medicine, American Occupational Therapy Certification Board, American Physical Therapy Association, National Athletic Training Association, National Council for Therapeutic Recreation Certification, and National Organization on Competency Assurances. Extensive phone interviews were conducted with key members of these associations who had been involved in the standards and/or exam development processes of their respective organizations. The results of these interviews were compiled and reviewed by the members of the Executive Committee. Based upon the review of the phone interviews, the Executive Committee decided to invite three representatives to a two-day work session to discuss the proposed procedures for our project. These representatives were Ms. Patricia Tice, representing the American Physical Therapy Association; Ms. Maureen Plombon, representing the American College of Sports Medicine; and Mr. Paul Grace, representing the National Athletic Training Association and the National Organization on Competency Assurances. Prior to the work session, each representative was sent a complete copy of the proposed project and the five-year project management plan. At the work session, the proposed procedures for developing the adapted physical education national standards and certification examination were confirmed by the representatives. They also provided a number of helpful suggestions, particularly related to developing and administering the exam, that have subsequently been added to the project management plan.

Determining the current roles, responsibilities and perceived needs of practicing adapted physical educators required:

1. the creation of an appropriate tool to collect this information; and
2. the identification of a representative sample of practitioners to supply the needed information.

The first step in this process was to review previous needs assessment instruments that had been used in the profession and to solicit input from the Executive and Steering Committees. With this information, the project staff developed a draft survey using the total design method (Dillman, 1978). The draft survey was reviewed by the Executive and Steering Committees and revised accordingly by the project staff. The revised draft was field tested using small groups (total n=36) of adapted physical educators identified by members of the Steering Committee. The field test results were compiled and reviewed by the Steering Committee and final revisions made to the instrument.

The second task related to the job analysis was to identify a representative sample of practitioners to receive the survey. The initial plan had been to use the AAHPERD Adapted Physical Activity (APAC) membership list as the pool and to sample from this by region for the job analysis survey. However, a survey performed by the project director (Kelly, 1991) using this method revealed a number of limitations with this sampling plan. For example, the APAC membership list did not distinguish between K-12 and college/university adapted physical educators nor did it distinguish between members interested in adapted physical education versus those who were actually practitioners. Kelly (1991) drew a random sample of 600 from the membership list of 1500+ members. Based upon a return rate of 81% (n=491), only 22% of the respondents were full time adapted physical educators at the K-12 level. Since it was essential that the job analysis be completed by teachers who were actually practicing adapted physical educators, a more appropriate sampling plan was needed. Based upon the recommendation of the Steering Committee, it was ultimately decided to identify K-12 adapted physical educators in each state and then to use this group as the sample. A stratified sampling plan was developed. For more detail, see the summary report (Kelly, in press). Each member of the Steering Committee was assigned several states. The Steering Committee members then contacted key leaders in adapted physical education in each of their assigned states. Depending upon the size of the state, the initial contact in a given state may have been asked to identify other leaders within the state to ensure the entire state would be represented. The contacts in each state were asked to collectively provide a specific number (based on state size) of names and addresses of adapted physical education practitioners in the state. The sample size obtained by state is illustrated in Figure 1.3. This process resulted in a total sample size of 585 with each state contributing a weighted number of subjects based upon the population of the state. Two states were unable to produce the requested number resulting in the final sample size of 575.

The results of the job analysis are contained in a separate report (Kelly, in press). The final return rate was 55% (316/575). These results were reviewed by the Steering Committee and the content

needed by practicing adapted physical educators divided into the 15 broad standard areas shown in Figure 1.4. The members of the Steering Committee were then assigned 2-3 of these standard areas for which they were responsible for delineating the content with their Standards Committee.

One of the key decisions the Steering Committee had to make early on was the degree to which the content should be delineated. For example, should the standards be limited to just the unique content that adapted physical educators should know or should they include the prerequisite content that regular physical educators would be expected to know? In making this decision, the Steering Committee considered the following factors:

1. delineation of what regular physical educators should know relative to the proposed 15 standards does not exist;
2. the standards developed would be used by parents, state department officials and others who probably would not have the training to deduce the prerequisite content; and

Job Analysis Sample Distribution by State

State	Sample	State	Sample
Alabama	10	Montana	5
Alaska	5	Nebraska	5
Arizona	10	Nevada	5
Arkansas	10	New Hampshire	5
California	40	New Mexico	5
Colorado	10	New York	30
Connecticut	10	New Jersey	20
Delaware	5	North Carolina	15
Florida	25	North Dakota	5
Georgia	15	Ohio	25
Hawaii	5	Oklahoma	10
Idaho	5	Oregon	10
Illinois	25	Pennsylvania	25
Indiana	15	Rhode Island	5
Iowa	10	South Dakota	5
Kansas	10	South Carolina	10
Kentucky	10	Tennessee	10
Louisiana	10	Texas	20
Maine	5	Utah	5
Maryland	10	Vermont	5
Massachusetts	15	Virginia	15
Michigan	20	Washington	10
Minnesota	10	West Virginia	5
Mississippi	10	Wisconsin	10
Missouri	15	Wyoming	5

Figure 1.3 Weighted number of teachers targeted by state to receive the national job analysis survey.

Adapted Physical Education National Standards

Standard	Title	Chair
1	Human Development	John M. Dunn
2	Motor Behavior	Michael Loovis
3	Exercise Science	Willie Gayle
4	Measurement and Evaluation	Janet A. Seaman
5	History and Philosophy	Monica Lepore
6	Unique Attributes of Learners	Monica Lepore
7	Curriculum Theory and Development	Michael Loovis
8	Assessment	Janet A. Seaman
9	Instructional Design and Planning	B. Lavay/W. Gayle
10	Teaching	Barry Lavay
11	Consultation and Staff Development	Willie Gayle
12	Student and Program Evaluation	Janet A. Seaman
13	Continuing Education	Michael Loovis
14	Ethics	John M. Dunn
15	Communication	Barry Lavay

Figure 1.4 The 15 standard areas and the Steering Committee member who was responsible for chairing the development of each standard.

3. what is defined as the minimum standards to be qualified may be interpreted by others as the absolute criteria.

Based upon these considerations it was decided that the delineation should include both the prerequisite content a regular physical educator should know and the content an adapted physical education specialist should know. As a result, the content in each standard area was divided into five levels. Figure 1.5 shows the five levels and their corresponding descriptions.

The first three levels of each standard represent content that should be known by all physical educators. These levels were developed by the Steering Committee and reviewed and validated by the Standards Committees. The level 4 content represents the additional content adapted physical educators need to know to meet the roles and responsibilities of their positions. Level 5 contains example applications of the level 4 content that adapted physical educators would be expected to be able to demonstrate.

The majority of the work during year two of the project has been devoted to delineating and validating the level 4 and level 5 content for each standard. The following process was used to create and validate the content:

1. The Steering Committee members developed an example for each of their standards illustrating the five levels of content. The Steering Committee

Illustration of the Five Levels

Level 1	Standard number and name (e.g., 2. Motor Behavior)
Level 2	Major components of the standard (e.g., Theories of motor development, principles of motor learning, etc.)
Level 3	Sub-components, dependent pieces of knowledge of fact or principle related to the major component that *all regular physical educators* would be expected to know (e.g., stages of learning, knowledge of types of feedback, etc.)
Level 4	Adapted physical education content—additional knowledge regarding the sub-components that teachers working with individuals with disabilities need to know (e.g., common delays in development experienced by individuals with severe visual impairments)
Level 5	Application of adapted physical education content knowledge from level 4 to teaching individuals with disabilities (e.g., can identify and interpret motor performance delays in children with disabilities)

Figure 1.5 Illustration of the five levels used to delineate each standard.

members then provided their Standards Committee members with the first three levels of the standard and an example of how to delineate the specific content they were being assigned to develop.

2. The Standards Committee members delineated the content they were assigned and returned this information to their Chair. Each Chair then edited and compiled the results into a draft document which was submitted to the Project Director.

3. The Project Staff entered the draft standard content into a database and produced an ERC evaluation instrument. See Figure 1.6 for an example of one page of an ERC instrument. The typical ERC instrument was 8-10 pages in length and contained 50-60 content items to be evaluated. For some of the larger standards, the content was divided into two or more ERC instruments to keep the amount of content reviewed in any given evaluation reasonable.

4. The Project Staff randomly drew a sample of 30 ERC members from the database of 300+ and sent them the ERC instrument. The ERC members were asked to complete and return the instruments as soon as possible. When the ERC instruments were returned, the Project Staff entered the ERC ratings into an SPSS data file. Summary statistics were computed and entered into the database for each content item. A summary statistics report was generated and sent to the appropriate member of the Steering Committee. See Figure 1.7 for an example of the first page of a typical ERC summary statistic report.

5. The Steering Committee members reviewed the summary statistics for their standards and decided what revisions were warranted. This information was sent to the Standards Committee members with the request to revise and/or expand the content as indicated by the evaluation data.

The above process was repeated for the level 4 and 5 content of each standard until the Steering Committee as a group agreed it was acceptable. At this time, the Steering Committee identified and defined any terms they felt should be included in the Glossary and added cross references within the standards.

Dissemination

Given the goal of this project, to ensure that all students with disabilities received appropriate physical education services delivered by a qualified physical educator by developing national standards, a plan was included in the original proposal to disseminate the products of this project. Complimentary copies were sent to:

1. all state directors of special education;
2. all state directors of physical education;
3. all members of the National Consortium for Physical Education and Recreation for Individuals with Disabilities;
4. all identified directors of college/university adapted physical education programs;
5. members of the Executive, Steering and Standards Committees; and
6. the executive directors of select professional and advocacy groups associated with physical education and/or serving the needs of individuals with disabilities.

These databases were combined and sorted to remove duplicates.

After the creation and distribution of the complimentary copies of the standards document, the rights were transferred to NCPERID.

Disclaimers

While significant progress has been made in defining the scope and sequence of the content that adapted physical educators should know, the current standards are viewed as only the initial steps of what will be an ongoing evolutionary process. It is anticipated that at the end of this funded project, the NCPERID will create a certification board that will be charged with managing, evaluating and regularly updating the standards and the examination. Professionals interested in becoming involved with this process should complete and submit the ERC application form at the back of this document. Professionals who are not interested in becoming involved at this time, but would like to submit feedback on the standards can do so using the feedback form at the back of this manual.

It was accepted as a limitation at the start of this project that measuring an individual's knowledge via a paper and pencil test was no guarantee that the knowledgeable individual would correctly apply this information when delivering services to individuals with disabilities. However, it was also clear that if teachers did not know what should be done or why, there was little likelihood that they would do it correctly. Therefore, it appeared reasonable, given the financial and time constraints

ADAPTED PHYSICAL EDUCATION
NATIONAL STANDARDS PROJECT

ID#: _____

Directions: Please rate the degree to which each piece of content listed below needs to be known by adapted physical educators to do their jobs. Use the 4 point scale to indicate whether you think the content is (1) Essential, (2) Desirable, (3) Optional or (4) Not Needed. If it is unclear what is meant by a content statement, put a check in the space provided.

Standard: 15. Communication

Major Component: Parents and Families: Communication with parents and families

Subcomponents APE Content APE Applications	1=Essential 2=Desirable 3=Optional 4=Not Needed
Subcomponent: Understand the importance of parent and family intervention *APE Content: Understand the importance of family support during the Individualized Education Program (IEP) and Individualized Family Service Plan (IFSP) and other parent/teacher conferences/meetings*	
Explain the motor components of the IFSP plan to family members	1 2 3 4 _____
Assist family members with the transition of the motor component from the IFSP to the IEP	1 2 3 4 _____
Explain physical education service plan (IEP) to family members	1 2 3 4 _____
Subcomponent: Understand the importance of parent and family intervention *APE Content: Understand the management skills needed to encourage families to participate in play, sport and physical activity for individuals with disabilities*	
Develop a management plan specific to family's needs	1 2 3 4 _____
Train families in the specific management skills needed to implement a play, sport or physical activity program	1 2 3 4 _____
Provide families with strategies and teaching techniques to increase their effectiveness as instructors	1 2 3 4 _____
Subcomponent: Be a family advocate and counselor of physical activity *APE Content: Understand the importance of family advocacy meetings where parents can meet and learn about physical activity programs for individuals with disabilities*	
Advocate for programs by working closely with the press and media such as writing in newsletters	1 2 3 4 _____
Volunteer to be a speaker at parent advocacy meetings	1 2 3 4 _____

Figure 1.6 Sample ERC evaluation instrument.

of this project, to delimit this project to creating the initial version of the standards and a written test to measure knowledge of this content. It is anticipated that in the coming years, the standards will be expanded and the examination revised to include measures of knowledge, application and demonstration.

The standards described in this document were developed in response to the roles, responsibilities and perceived needs of practicing adapted physical educators. While many faculty from institutions of higher education (IHE) were involved, there was no attempt to limit the standards to either what was currently being offered by IHEs or to what higher education faculty felt could be easily accommodated. As a result, it is possible that many IHEs may need to revise their training programs to adequately address these standards.

ADAPTED PHYSICAL EDUCATION
NATIONAL STANDARDS PROJECT

Directions: Please rate the degree to which each piece of content listed below needs to be known by adapted physical educators to do their jobs. Use the 4 point scale to indicate whether you think the content is (1) Essential, (2) Desirable, (3) Optional or (4) Not Needed. If it is unclear what is meant by a content statement, put a check in the space provided.

Standard: 15. Communication

Major Component: Parents and Families: Communication with parents and families

Subcomponent: Understand the importance of parent and family intervention	Data Summary						
	F1 (%1)	F2 (%2)	F3 (%3)	F4 (%4)	F5 (%5)	n sd	Avg
Understand the importance of family support during the Individualized Education Program (IEP) and Individualized Family Service Plan (IFSP) and other parent/teacher conferences/ meetings							
Explain the motor components of the IFSP plan to family members	16 66	7 29	1 4	0 0	0 0	24 0.6	1.38
Assist family members with the transition of the motor component from the IFSP to the IEP	11 45	5 20	4 16	0 0	4 16	24 1.4	1.65
Explain physical education service plan (IEP) to family members	24 100	0 0	0 0	0 0	0 0	24 0.0	1.00
Develop a management plan specific to family's needs	7 29	15 62	0 0	0 0	2 8	24 1.0	1.68
Train families in the specific management skills needed to implement a play, sport or physical activity program	5 20	10 41	8 33	0 0	1 4	24 0.9	2.13
Provide families with strategies and teaching techniques to increase their effectiveness as instructors	8 33	9 37	6 25	1 4	0 0	24 0.9	2.00
Understand the importance of family advocacy meetings where parents can meet and learn about physical activity programs for individuals with disabilities							
Advocate for programs by working closely with the press and media such as writing in newsletters	2 8	10 41	10 41	1 4	1 4	24 0.9	2.43
Volunteer to be a speaker at parent advocacy meetings	0 ***	0 **	0 **	0 **	0 **	0 0.0	*****
Design family home-based physical activity programs	4 16	13 54	6 25	1 4	0 0	24 0.8	2.17

Figure 1.7 Sample summary ERC statistic report.

Any implications for change emerging from this project are intended to be positive and proactive and not as threats or criticisms of current training programs.

It may also be the case that the standards presented in this document vary from the standards in the 14 states that have established state certifications or endorsements for teachers of adapted physical education. The current standards were not developed with the intent of challenging or interfering with state requirements. In fact, states that have credentials should be acknowledged for their initiative and proactive compliance with the mandates of IDEA. Hopefully these states can take advantage of the up-to-date and national representation involved in the current standards and use these standards as a basis for evaluating, and if needed, updating their state standards.

Finally, the standards were developed and reviewed independently by many professionals using all available resources. Any specific mention in the standards to any specific products, projects, programs, terms, resources, or references should not be interpreted as endorsements. Rather, these references should be viewed solely as illustrative examples.

Introduction to the Standards

The purpose of this section is to explain how the content of the standards has been organized. While it is anticipated that this document will be used by a number of different groups for a variety of purposes, the content was organized with practicing teachers and IHE faculty as the primary audiences. Given the background of these groups, the content for each standard was delineated into five levels as illustrated in Figure 1.8.

The first line of each section indicates the Level 1 content, which is the standard number and the standard name (e.g., Standard 15: Communication). There are a total of 15 standards and each standard is presented in a separate section.

The Level 2 (major component) and Level 3 (subcomponent) contents are presented inside a box. The Level 2 content represents the major content categories or divisions covered under the standard. In Figure 1.8, the first Level 2 content presented is "Parents and Families: Communication with parents and families." The Level 3 content represents dependent pieces of knowledge of fact or principles related to the major component. In Figure 1.8, the first Level 3 content presented is "Understand the importance of parent and family intervention."

The Level 4 and 5 contents pertaining to each Level 3 statement are listed immediately below each box. The Level 4 and 5 contents represent the unique knowledge and applications adapted physical educators are expected to know and be able to demonstrate. In Figure 1.8, the first Level 4 statement presented is "Understand the importance of family support during the Individualized Education Program (IEP) and Individualized Family Service Plan (IFSP) and other parent/teacher conferences/meetings." The Level 5 content pertaining to each Level 4 knowledge statement is listed under the Level 4 content. The Level 5 content represents example applications of the Level 4 knowledge that adapted physical educators would be expected to be able to demonstrate. In Figure 1.8, the first Level 5 statement presented is "Explain the motor components of the IFSP plan to family members."

Each statement is preceded by a number that codes its position in the standards in terms of the five levels. Each level within the number is separated by a period. To decode a number, start at the end and work backwards. For example, the number 15.01.01.01.02 indicates that this is the second level 5 statement for the first APE knowledge statement (Level 4), for the first subcomponent statement (Level 3) for the first major component statement (Level 2) for the 15th standard—Communication. The primary purpose of these numbers is to serve as a reference system for future project activities such as test item development and the eventual creation of a study guide.

Given the diversity of terms and the common use of abbreviations and acronyms in the field, a Glossary has been provided at the end of the manual to assist the reader. Although not coded to each statement, a summative list of references that were used by the various committees in developing the standards is also included at the end of the manual.

Standard **15** COMMUNICATION

15.01	***Parents and Families: Communication with parents and families***
15.01.01	Understand the importance of parent and family intervention

15.01.01.01   *Understand the importance of family support during the Individualized Education Program (IEP) and Individualized Family Service Plan (IFSP) and other parent/teacher conferences/meetings*

15.01.01.01.01   Explain the motor components of the IFSP to family members

15.01.01.01.02   Assist family members with the transition of the motor component from the IFSP to the IEP

15.01.01.01.03   Explain physical education service plan (IEP) to family members

15.01.01.02   *Understand the management skills needed to encourage families to participate in play, sport and physical activity for individuals with disabilities*

15.01.01.02.01   Develop a management plan specific to family's needs

15.01.01.02.02   Train families in the specific management skills needed to implement a play, sport or physical activity program

15.01.01.02.03   Provide families with strategies and teaching techniques to increase their effectiveness as instructors

15.01	***Parents and Families: Communication with parents and families***
15.01.02	Be a family advocate and counselor of physical activity

15.01.02.01   *Understand the importance of family advocacy meetings where parents can meet and learn about physical activity programs for individuals with disabilities*

15.01.02.01.01   Advocate for programs by working closely with the press and media such as writing in newsletters

15.01.02.01.02   Volunteer to be a speaker at parent advocacy meetings

15.01.02.02   *Knowledge about already developed home-based physical activity programs such as Data-Based Gymnasium*

15.01.02.02.01   Design family home-based physical activity programs

15.01.02.02.02   Teach parents to implement a plan that includes long range goals, behavioral objectives, lesson plans, teaching cues, and strategies for charting child progress

15.01.02.02.03   Provide homework assignments or home-based activity programs

15.01.02.03   *Knowledge of national agencies, organizations and community programs to assist families in play, sport and physical activity such as Special Olympics, United States Association for Blind Athletes, and American Occupational Therapy Association*

15.01.02.03.01   Assist families in contacting and getting involved in such national agencies, organizations and community programs

15.01.02.03.02   Assist families in appropriate assessment procedures for placement in play, sport and physical activity

Figure 1.8   Sample standard page.

NCPERID

National Consortium for Physical Education and Recreation for Individuals with Disabilities

For Membership Information
Contact:

Dr. Hester Henderson, Treasurer
Dept. of Exercise & Sport Science
HPER N-255
University of Utah
Salt Lake City, UT 84112

or

Dr. Manny Felix, Membership Chair
Dept. of Exercise & Sport Science
University of Wisconsin–La Crosse
115 Wittich Hall
La Crosse, WI 54601

Standard 1 — HUMAN DEVELOPMENT

1.01	**_Understand Cognitive Development_**
1.01.01	Explain the theory of cognitive development as proposed by Piaget

1.01.01.01   *Understand the implications of Piaget's theory for the development of infants and individuals with disabilities*

1.01.01.01.01   Apply Piaget's theory to the development of infants and individuals with various disabilities

1.01.01.01.02   Recognize the strengths and limitations of Piaget's theory as applied to individuals with disabilities

1.01	**_Understand Cognitive Development_**
1.01.02	Define perception, attention, memory, and the relationship to participation and learning in physical education

1.01.02.01   *Explain the impact of mental disabilities on perception, attention, and memory for learning in physical education*

1.01.02.01.01   Develop programs that sequence materials appropriately for individuals with disabilities, recognizing unique attention deficits and perceptual disorders

1.01.02.01.02   Create environments that enhance instruction in physical education by reducing external stimuli as needed

1.01.02.02   *Understand the difference between short-term and long-term memory capacity as applied to individuals with selected disabilities (see Standard 2.03)*

1.01.02.02.01   Recognize the implications of long- and short-term memory in the learning process, specifically among individuals with disabilities

1.01.02.02.02   Adapt the learning environment to compensate for long- or short-term memory deficits for individuals with disabilities such as mental retardation, traumatic brain injury

1.01.02.03   *Explain the impact of physical and sensory disability on perception, attention, and memory for learning in physical education*

1.01.02.03.01   Appreciate and understand that individuals with selected disorders such as cerebral palsy and spina bifida, may have other disabilities such as a hearing disorder or mental retardation

1.01.02.03.02   Adjust programs to respond to the challenges associated with disabilities such as dwarfism and arthritis, on the ability of the individual's perceptual skills

1.01.02.04   *Explain the impact of emotional disability on perception, attention, and memory for learning in physical education*

1.01.02.04.01   Adapt programs to respond to the needs of individuals with various forms of emotional disturbance and behavior disorders including autism, depression, and mental illness

1.01.02.04.02   Develop programs to respond to the unique needs of individuals with clinical mental disabilities including psychosis, neuroses, and personality disorders

1.01.02.04.03   Recognize that some individuals with behavior disorders have the ability to excel in physical activity

1.01.02.04.04   Emphasize that repetitive activity with consistent rules and structure is essential for individuals with behavior disorders

1.02	**_Demonstrate knowledge of the development of language and cognition through the lifespan_**
1.02.01	Describe the effect of limited verbal language on participation in physical education

1.02.01.01   _Understand the impact of limited expressiveness and receptive language on participation in physical education_

1.02.01.01.01   Develop programs that respond to the expressive and receptive language needs of individuals with selected disabilities such as autism, congenitally deaf

1.02.01.01.02   Provide programs that respond appropriately to the needs of individuals with language disorders

1.02.01.02   _Understand the need to employ alternative/augmentative communication in physical education (see Standard 9.04)_

1.02.01.02.01   Use alternative forms of communication such as American Sign Language, Signing Exact English

1.02.01.02.02   Apply technology so that individuals with selected disabilities such as visual disabilities can be successful in physical education

1.02.01.02.03   Recognize that the teacher must not only know how to express him/herself in the mode of communication utilized by the students, but must also know how to receive information from augmentative communication such as signs

1.03	**_Understand essential concepts related to social or affective development_**
1.03.01	Understand and define important terms such as socialization, social roles, and social norms

1.03.01.01   _Recognize that individuals with disabilities are often excluded and/or inappropriately portrayed in discussions of social roles and social norms_

1.03.01.01.01   Advocate for individuals with disabilities and their right to be included in programs of physical education and sport sponsored by schools and communities

1.03.01.01.02   Include individuals with disabilities in all aspects of physical education and sport programs

1.03.01.01.03   Utilize examples of individuals with disabilities that highlight their successes in physical education and sport activities

1.03.01.01.04   Recognize students with and without disabilities who do well in physical education

1.03	**_Understand essential concepts related to social or affective development_**
1.03.02	Appreciate the social influences present during infancy (e.g., attachment to objects, recognition of touch, and involvement with the environment)

1.03.02.01   _Understand that some individuals with selected disabilities experience significant sensory deprivation_

1.03.02.01.01   Create programs that emphasize the individuals' strength and limit situations that could frustrate some individuals such as deaf/blind

1.03.02.01.02   Utilize alternative forms of interaction to insure that individuals with sensory disorders are not unnecessarily excluded

1.03	**_Understand essential concepts related to social or affective development_**
1.03.03	Recognize the role that the family plays in social development

1.03.03.01 *Understand the stages of grief (denial, guilt, rejection, anger) experienced by parents at birth and the early stages of development of the child with a disability*

1.03.03.01.01 Create programs and opportunities for parents and guardians and their infants and toddlers to participate in movement programs

1.03.03.01.02 Cooperate with other professionals in developing support programs and activities for parents and guardians of individuals with disabilities

1.03.03.01.03 Continually inform parents and guardians of curricular innovations, special programs and progress of the student

1.03.03.02 *Appreciate the impact of the presence of an infant/child with a disability on the structure and function of the family*

1.03.03.02.01 Communicate with parents about the services provided in adapted physical education and the commitment to assist the development of their child (see Standard 15.01.02)

1.03.03.02.02 Listen to parents and guardians recognizing their needs to express concerns and frustrations about various issues, including the need for and value of physical education

1.03.03.03 *Understand the unique needs, concerns, and worries experienced by many siblings of individuals with disabilities*

1.03.03.03.01 Create opportunities for siblings to observe their brother or sister successfully participating in physical activity and sport related movement experiences

1.03.03.03.02 Share information, as appropriate, with siblings that helps to reduce anxiety and improve understanding about the long-term outlook for individuals with disabilities

1.03.03.04 *Demonstrate knowledge of the role that the family plays in promoting health and physical fitness throughout the lifespan of individuals with a disability*

1.03.03.04.01 Develop programs that promote social interaction between family members and the individual with a disability

1.03.03.04.02 Structure programs to assist caregivers to play and interact with an individual with a disability

1.03.03.05 *Identify behavioral indices of an individual with a history of abuse and neglect*

1.03.03.05.01 Structure programs to respond to the possible special health, fitness, movement, and play needs of individuals with a history of abuse and neglect

1.03.03.05.02 Accept responsibility according to state and professional standards for reporting suspected cases of abuse and neglect

1.03 1.03.04	**_Understand essential concepts related to social or affective development_** Demonstrate knowledge of diversity of American families including child kinship patterns of never-married, single-parent families, remarried, and two-parent families

1.03.04.01   _Describe the impact of diverse child kinship patterns on the physical activity development of the child with a disability_

1.03.04.01.01   Create programs that encourage parents, caregivers, and advocates to be involved in play and related movement experiences of their child without inhibition or concern as to social norms

1.03.04.01.02   Respect parents, caregivers, advocates, and others for their willingness to actively participate in physical education programs for individuals with disabilities

1.03 1.03.05	**_Understand essential concepts related to social or affective development_** Demonstrate knowledge of and appreciation for cultural diversity of American families

1.03.05.01   _Understand the importance of cultural heritage, including games and sports, toward development of the individual with a disability_

1.03.05.01.01   Employ various forms of play, sport, and games enjoyed by individuals with diverse cultural backgrounds

1.03.05.01.02   Adapt games that can be enjoyed by individuals with disabilities from various cultural backgrounds (see Standard 10.0)

1.03 1.03.06	**_Understand essential concepts related to social or affective development_** Understand the important and unique role of play in the development of the individual

1.03.06.01   _Know the various stages (independent, parallel, small group, group) of play experienced by infants and children as they develop_

1.03.06.01.01   Plan programs that respond to the developmental play needs of infants, toddlers, and children

1.03.06.01.02   Provide play experiences wherein infants, toddlers, and children with disabilities have the opportunity to engage in positive social interaction

1.03.06.02   _Understand the importance of group play to the process of socialization between infants and children with and without disabilities_

1.03.06.02.01   Plan physical education programs that maximize opportunities for integrated group play

1.03.06.02.02   Conduct physical education and sport programs that promote group interaction for individuals with and without disabilities

1.03.06.03   _Understand the value of play interaction between individuals with and without disabilities_

1.03.06.03.01   Promote opportunities that support integrated play experiences

1.03.06.03.02   Create integrated play experiences based on the concepts of full inclusion

1.03.06.04   _Understand the effect that various developmental delays and disabilities can have on the individual's successful participation in play activities_

1.03.06.04.01	Describe play behavior through the lifespan (infant, toddler, youth, adolescent, young adult, adult, middle age, aged) within and between individuals with disabilities
1.03.06.04.02	Adapt programs such that individuals with disabilities can be successful in play experiences
1.03.06.04.03	Recognize that individuals with various disabilities will need modifications requiring teachers to individualize instruction

1.04	**_Understand theories of moral development in children_**
1.04.01	Understand the role and impact of social institutions on the moral development of individuals with disabilities

1.04.01.01	_Understand the unique opportunities within the physical education curriculum to promote appropriate values for individuals with disabilities_
1.04.01.01.01	Create opportunities in the physical education curriculum that allow individuals with disabilities to exercise choice
1.04.01.01.02	Utilize instructional strategies that emphasize the importance of fair play, sportsmanship, and teamwork

1.04	**_Understand theories of moral development in children_**
1.04.02	Appreciate the role of schools in the moral development of individuals with disabilities

1.04.02.01	_Understand the sensitive nature of moral development and the vulnerability of some individuals with disabilities to exploitation_
1.04.02.01.01	Apply moral development concepts in the teaching of sport, play, and physical activity for individuals with disabilities
1.04.02.01.02	Model acceptance of individuals with disabilities, emphasizing the person rather than the disability
1.04.02.01.03	Emphasize that individuals with disabilities are to be treated respectfully and viewed as people rather than objects

1.05	**_Understand the outcome different theories of personality have on human behavior_**
1.05.01	Understand that field or ecological theory of personality describes the psychosocial interdependence of individuals in a community, taking into account the physical environment and the systems that operate in the environment

1.05.01.01	_Understand that there is a reciprocity between the actions of an individual with a disability in a physical education class and the effect of the class on the person with a disability_
1.05.01.01.01	Model acceptance and inclusion of the individual with a disability in the physical education class
1.05.01.01.02	Create physical education environments that emphasize the capability of the individual with a disability
1.05.01.01.03	Include individuals with disabilities in planning physical education programs and related sport experiences

1.05.01.02   *Understand the role of the physical environment from which they came (where they live, what school they attend) and the subsystems (social, economic, societal, home, day care) affecting the individual*

1.05.01.02.01   Review records and interview primary care provider to assist in creating successful physical education experiences

1.05.01.02.02   Accept individuals with disabilities, recognizing that their prior experience and background may require a sensitive and empathetic teacher

1.05.01.02.03   Avoid establishing predetermined limits on students because of background, culture, or socio-economic status

1.05.01.03   *Understand the importance of assessing students with disabilities by accounting for the environmental conditions under which activity can be performed, the attributes of the performer, and the interaction of that environment and performer*

1.05.01.03.01   Utilize an ecological task analysis approach in teaching adapted physical education

1.05.01.03.02   Change the instructional environment as appropriate to insure that the relationship among the performer, task, and conditions leads to success

1.05.01.04   *Describe how an individual's actions affect the environment and the environment affects the individual*

1.05.01.04.01   Obtain desired skill level and behavior performance by utilizing various approaches, including applied behavior analysis, and task analysis

1.05.01.04.02   Structure the environment such that it responds to needs of selected students such as increase or decrease amount of stimuli, size of movement space, number of cues

1.05

1.05.02

> **Understand the outcome different theories of personality have on human behavior**
> Understand that self-actualization theory emphasizes that individuals are constantly striving to realize their full inherent potential

1.05.02.01   *Understand the importance of meeting basic physiological, safety and security, love and belonging, and self-esteem needs before an individual can be self-actualized*

1.05.02.01.01   Plan programs in cooperation with others, including related personnel such as therapists, psychologists, parents, and as appropriate, persons with disabilities

1.05.02.01.02   Implement programs that focus on the whole child, acknowledging the importance of incremental success

1.05.02.02   *Understand the importance of unconditional positive regard of the individual with a disability*

1.05.02.02.01   Emphasize strengths of the individual in order to build on the needs that will generate self-actualization

1.05.02.02.02   Create a physical education setting that allows the individual "to dare to be one's self"

1.05.02.02.03   Select assessment and learning tasks that allow the individual with a disability to perceive the teacher and peers as supportive in the learning process

1.05 1.05.03	**_Understand the outcome different theories of personality have on human behavior_** Understand that self-efficacy theory of personality development emphasizes that belief in one's ability and personal resourcefulness will allow one to successfully achieve desired outcomes

1.05.03.01 — *Understand that a child with a disability will experience a sense of personal mastery that can generalize to new situations*

1.05.03.01.01 — Create opportunities for students with disabilities to succeed using an incremental approach with positive reinforcement

1.05.03.01.02 — Encourage and facilitate individuals with disabilities to transfer skills learned in physical education to other activities and life experiences

1.05.03.02 — *Understand levels of cues/prompts that will foster an individual with a disability taking credit for learning new behaviors*

1.05.03.02.01 — Utilize cues/prompts that are appropriate to the instructional and/or behavioral needs of the individual with a disability

1.05.03.02.02 — Recognize the importance of withdrawing cues/prompts to the least intrusive level for an individual with a disability

1.05.03.02.03 — Recognize in every learning situation that the individuals are learning about their own level of competence

1.05 1.05.04	**_Understand the outcome different theories of personality have on human behavior_** Understand that normalization theory emphasizes that individuals with disabilities should live and function as closely as possible to the normal living, learning, and working conditions of people in society

1.05.04.01 — *Understand procedures and techniques in physical education classes that enhance the image of individuals with disabilities*

1.05.04.01.01 — Structure the learning environment to create full integration of individuals with and without disabilities

1.05.04.01.02 — Incorporate examples of successful athletes with disabilities within instruction in physical education

1.05.04.02 — *Recognize the importance of selection of appropriate services to support inclusion of individuals with disabilities in regular physical education settings*

1.05.04.02.01 — Work cooperatively with other professionals to maximize integrated experiences for individuals with and without disabilities

1.05.04.02.02 — Support other professionals who provide motor experiences for individuals with disabilities

1.06 1.06.01	**Factors Influencing Development** Understand that many forms of disabilities are directly attributable to genetic, medical, and environmental factors

1.06.01.01   *Explain the impact of infections and intoxicants as related to mental retardation and subsequent participation in physical education*

1.06.01.01.01   Explain the impact of infections such as rubella and syphilis on performance in physical education

1.06.01.01.02   Explain the impact of postnatal cerebral infections such as meningitis and encephalitis on performance in physical education

1.06.01.01.03   Explain the impact of hemolytic blood diseases such as Rh incompatibility or poison from lead, mercury, drugs, and narcotics on performance in physical education

1.06.01.02   *Understand that developmental disabilities can be caused by metabolic, nutritional, endocrine, and mineral dysfunction*

1.06.01.02.01   Explain the impact of genetically determined metabolic disorders such as phenylketonuria (PKU), Tay-Sachs disease, cretinism, and Prader-Willi syndrome

1.06.01.02.02   Appreciate that dietary imbalances in the infant or expectant mother can seriously impede cognitive development which, in turn, impedes performance in physical education

1.06.01.03   *Understand that developmental disabilities can be caused by heredegenerative disorders*

1.06.01.03.01   Check medical records and be aware of current medical status and medications

1.06.01.03.02   Plan proper safety precautions during physical activity as these types of disorders can cause problems such as seizures (see Standard 9.02.03)

1.06.01.04   *Understand that the cause of some disabilities is not well understood*

1.06.01.04.01   Consult with physicians and medical experts regarding such disabilities with unknown causes

1.06.01.04.02   Identify national, state, and local agencies that have information on the causes of these disabilities (see Standard 9.02.03)

1.06.01.05   *Recognize that some disabilities can be caused by aberrations of chromosomes*

1.06.01.05.01   Explain the incidence of common chromosomal aberrations

1.06.01.05.02   Explain the impact of common chromosomal disorders on motor performance, such as Down syndrome

1.06.01.06   *Appreciate that some disabilities are related to gestational disorders*

1.06.01.06.01   Explain the impact of premature delivery on learning and performing motor skills

1.06.01.06.02   Explain the impact of postnatal complications during delivery on learning and performing motor skills

1.06	**Factors Influencing Development**
1.06.02	Understand that several causes of mental retardation are attributed to environmental influences (e.g., sensory deprivation, trauma, or physical agents)

1.06.02.01   *Understand the impact of environmental influences as related to mental retardation and subsequent participation in physical education*

1.06.02.01.01   Appreciate that a lack of experience can impede development and delay physical activity performance

1.06.02.01.02   Provide a variety of success-oriented physical activity experiences

2.01	***Understand Motor Development***
2.01.01	Understand neuromaturational/hierarchical models

2.01.01.01   *Understand sensory integration*

2.01.01.01.01   Recognize the relationship between sensory integration and ataxia (motor awkwardness)

2.01.01.01.02   Identify factors in intersensory and intrasensory integration related to movement control and coordination

2.01.01.01.03   Select and design activities to stimulate the development of intersensory and intrasensory integration

2.01.01.02   *Understand neurodevelopmental theory*

2.01.01.02.01   Structure tasks and activities to inhibit abnormal movements

2.01.01.02.02   Structure tasks and activities to stimulate and facilitate normal postural responses

2.01	***Understand Motor Development***
2.01.02	Understand dynamic systems theory

2.01.02.01   *Understand the diversity and influence of rate limiters such as body size and proportions, gravity, cognitive development, and biomechanical constraints on motor experiences of individuals with disabilities*

2.01.02.01.01   Apply knowledge of dynamic systems theory to program planning and implementation

2.01.02.01.02   Develop individual program plans that diminish or accommodate for the effects of rate limiters

2.01	***Understand Motor Development***
2.01.03	Understand factors (including prenatal and postnatal influences) affecting motor development such as nutritional status, genetic makeup, and environmental opportunities for practice & instruction

2.01.03.01   *Understand how these factors could influence the rate and sequence of development for individuals with disabilities*

2.01.03.01.01   Identify characteristic behaviors related to factors which impact rate and sequence of development

2.01.03.01.02   Implement a program of activities specifically designed to minimize factors affecting motor development and to maximize developmental potential

2.01.03.02   *Synthesize information on physical, cognitive, and psychological changes and their implications for skill acquisition and use by individuals with disabilities*

2.01.03.02.01   Develop programs that maximize individuals' strengths and diminish and/or accommodate for weaknesses in specific domains of motor behavior

2.01.03.02.02   Maintain an integrated programmatic approach based on knowledge of the individual's cognitive and social development and its relationship to motor development

---

2.01

Understand Motor Development

2.01.04   Understand normal sensory development such as the visual, auditory, tactile, vestibular, and kinesthetic systems

---

2.01.04.01   *Understand common deviations in the development of the visual system among individuals with disabilities*

2.01.04.01.01   Recognize deficits in refractive and orthoptic vision including accommodation and tracking in individuals with disabilities

2.01.04.01.02   Describe the relationship between the development of visual functions such as constancy, figure-ground perception, and depth perception to movement control in motor activities

2.01.04.01.03   Apply knowledge of visual functioning deficits in selecting and designing activities

2.01.04.01.04   Develop and implement programs that strengthen orthoptic visual abilities such as visual fixation, pursuit, and search behaviors

2.01.04.01.05   Modify activities to accommodate visual deficits

2.01.04.02   *Understand common deviations in the development of the auditory system among individuals with disabilities*

2.01.04.02.01   Recognize and assess deficits in auditory recognition, discrimination, and localization

2.01.04.02.02   Select and design activities to help accommodate deficits in auditory functioning

2.01.04.02.03   Modify activities to accommodate auditory deficits

2.01.04.03   *Understand common deviations in the development of the tactile system among individuals with disabilities*

2.01.04.03.01   Recognize behaviors associated with hyperresponsive (tactile defensive) and hyporesponsive (tactile seeking) tactile disorders

2.01.04.03.02   Select and design activities to help remediate hyper- and hyporesponsive tactile disorders

2.01.04.03.03   Develop and implement programs to enhance individuals' abilities to tolerate various levels of tactile stimuli

2.01.04.03.04   Develop and implement programs that enhance individuals' abilities to accurately discriminate from among various tactile stimuli and use the information profitably

2.01.04.04   *Understand common deviations in the development of the vestibular system among individuals with disabilities*

2.01.04.04.01   Recognize behaviors associated with vestibular functioning deficits

2.01.04.04.02   Recognize signs of vestibular over-stimulation

2.01.04.04.03   Conduct basic screening to assess vestibular function

2.01.04.04.04   Select and design activities to help remediate balance problems related to deficits in vestibular functioning

2.01.04.04.05	Develop and implement programs that stimulate the vestibular system for integration with visual, kinesthetic, and tactile inputs
2.01.04.05	*Understand common deviations in the development of the kinesthetic system among individuals with disabilities*
2.01.04.05.01	Recognize behaviors associated with deficits in the kinesthetic system
2.01.04.05.02	Conduct basic screening to identify possible deficits in kinesthetic system functioning
2.01.04.05.03	Select and design activities to help remediate deficits in kinesthetic functioning
2.01.04.05.04	Develop and implement programs that stimulate efficient use of kinesthetic inputs and integration with vestibular, visual, and tactile input systems

2.01	**Understand Motor Development**
2.01.05	Understand patterns of cognitive, perceptual, and perceptual motor development and the factors that influence those patterns

2.01.05.01	*Understand the influences of perceptual motor programs that emphasize cognitive and perceptual abilities among individuals with disabilities*
2.01.05.01.01	Develop and implement programs that afford individuals opportunities to formulate and execute motor plans
2.01.05.01.02	Implement opportunities for augmented feedback when students are involved in activities that enhance motor planning abilities

2.01	**Understand Motor Development**
2.01.06	Understand the development of postural control and the components and mechanisms of balance and equilibrium

2.01.06.01	*Understand the significance of developmental delays (throughout the lifespan) on balance and related tasks*
2.01.06.01.01	Develop and implement programs that stimulate vestibular, visual, and proprioceptive senses
2.01.06.01.02	Develop and implement programs that increase the strength and endurance of postural muscle groups

2.01	**Understand Motor Development**
2.01.07	Understand the influence of the development of reflexes on normal motor development and the implications on skill acquisition

2.01.07.01	*Understand the relationship between lack of persistence of primitive reflexes and disabling conditions*
2.01.07.01.01	Identify the difference between primitive and postural reflexes
2.01.07.01.02	Describe the influence of weak or persistent primitive reflexes on the rate and sequence of motor development and voluntary motor control in individuals with disabilities

2.01.07.02   *Understand reflexes and reactions observed in individuals developing normally and abnormally*

2.01.07.02.01   Recognize the differing patterns of reflex behavior among persons with disabilities such as persistent primitive reflexes in cerebral palsy

2.01.07.02.02   Identify behaviors associated with persistent or weak primitive residual reflexes

2.01.07.02.03   Select and design activities that inhibit primitive reflexes through positioning and stimulation of voluntary responses (see Standard 9.05.01)

2.01.07.02.04   Select and design activities to help stimulate the development of postural and equilibrium reactions

2.01.07.02.05   Modify activities to accommodate residual primitive reflexes

---

2.01

Understand Motor Development

2.01.08   Understand the development and emergence of locomotion including prone progressions, assumption of an upright gait, and walking

---

2.01.08.01   *Understand variance in "motor milestones" such as typical or average age of achievement for individuals with disabilities*

2.01.08.01.01   Identify behaviors associated with lack of attainment of "motor milestones"

2.01.08.01.02   Implement activities that stimulate upright postures and control of head, neck, and trunk

2.01.08.01.03   Implement activities that strengthen postural muscles and extremities necessary for support of locomotion

---

2.01

Understand Motor Development

2.01.09   Understand the development and emergence of manipulation including reaching, grasping, and releasing

---

2.01.09.01   *Understand variance in manipulation associated with individuals with disabilities*

2.01.09.01.01   Identify the impact of developmental delays in reaching, grasping, and releasing on the ability to perform functional motor skills, sport, and life-time recreational activities

2.01.09.01.02   Select and design activities that stimulate visual fixation, enabling the visual to motor match needed for reach-grasp-release

2.01.09.02   *Recognize differing patterns of manipulative skills among persons with disabilities*

2.01.09.02.01   Modify activities to accommodate differing patterns of manipulative skills

2.01.09.02.02   Implement activities for reach-grasp-release through use of supportive assistive aids to enhance voluntary controls and means-end behaviors

---

2.01

Understand Motor Development

2.01.10   Understand the development of fundamental motor skills and patterns

---

2.01.10.01   *Understand variance in the progression of fundamental motor skill performance among individuals with disabilities*

2.01.10.01.01 Task analyze the progression of fundamental motor skill acquisition according to area of the body (head, trunk, stance) or phase (preparation, action, and follow through) of skill

2.01.10.01.02 Select and design activities to help stimulate the development of fundamental motor skills

2.01.10.01.03 Modify activities to accommodate differing patterns of fundamental skills exhibited in individuals with disabilities

---

2.01

Understand Motor Development

2.01.11

Understand how fundamental motor skills are refined and combined to produce sport skills

---

2.01.11.01 *Understand how to adapt activities to promote development from the fundamental movement stage through the sport skill stage for individuals with disabilities*

2.01.11.01.01 Task analyze the sport related movement according to the level of fundamental motor skill exhibited

2.01.11.01.02 Select and design activities to help stimulate the development of fundamental motor skills within sport related movement

---

2.01

Understand Motor Development

2.01.12

Understand the relationship between mature fundamental motor skill development and performance in the sport related skill development

---

2.01.12.01 *Understand how appropriate modifications of the physical environment enable individuals with disabilities to perform sport skills*

2.01.12.01.01 Modify sport related activities to accommodate differing patterns of fundamental skills exhibited in individuals with disabilities

2.01.12.01.02 Change the structure and organization of sports and games to include diverse skill levels and performance indicators

---

2.01

Understand Motor Development

2.01.13

Understand how motor development impacts on the ability to engage in lifetime recreation and sport activities

---

2.01.13.01 *Understand the influence of sport and leisure on overall development of individuals with disabilities*

2.01.13.01.01 Employ a functional model of skill development

2.01.13.01.02 Utilize equipment that has been specifically designed to enhance participation by individuals with disabilities

2.01.13.02 *Know when to adapt rules to accommodate participation by an individual with a disability in a sport or leisure activity of their choice*

2.01.13.02.01 Provide competitive sport opportunities for individuals with disabilities who are not currently served by established organizations

2.01.13.02.02 Create leisure activities that meet the needs of individuals with disabilities who are not accommodated by existing sport offerings

2.01.13.03   *Know how to modify activities and programs to enhance the cognitive, affective, and psychomotor development of individuals with disabilities (see Standard 10.0)*

2.01.13.03.01   Use knowledge of an individual's cognitive development to select tasks and activities which can be acquired, retained, and transferred to other related tasks and activities

2.01.13.03.02   Use knowledge of an individual's social development to determine which tasks and activities will provide for maximum social integration and acceptance

2.01.13.03.03   Use knowledge of an individual's psychomotor development to establish an integrated approach to program planning which includes enhancement of their cognitive and social development

2.02   **Understand Motor Learning**

2.02.01   Understand factors that contribute to positive and negative transfer such as nature of the task, goal of training, or amount and type of practice

2.02.01.01   *Understand the concepts of transfer and specificity when programming for individuals with disabilities*

2.02.01.01.01   Plan practice and learning tasks that are congruent with the task's application

2.02.01.01.02   Plan practice and learning tasks that will positively transfer to next level of skill acquisition and transfer

2.02.01.01.03   Use transfer to measure attainment of selected criterion skills

2.02.01.01.04   Apply the concept of task specificity with the understanding that it presents certain problems for persons with disabilities

2.02   **Understand Motor Learning**

2.02.02   Understand stages of learning as found in theories and models such as Fitts and Posner's, Adam's, and Gentile's models for learning

2.02.02.01   *Understand the implications of the stages of learning during skill acquisition among individuals with disabilities*

2.02.02.01.01   Plan and give feedback consistent with knowledge needed at each stage of skill acquisition

2.02.02.01.02   Structure practice and learning tasks to support individualizing within class to match different rates of skill acquisition

2.02.02.01.03   Plan for an increase in task complexity commensurate with ability of individuals with disabilities

2.02.02.01.04   Structure practice and learning tasks to move from a closed to an open skill such as from a batting tee to a pitched ball

2.02.02.01.05   Make adjustments in teaching methods and instructions

2.02.02.01.06   Use a variety of instructions, modeling, and demonstrations to facilitate learning during the verbal-cognitive stage

| 2.02 | **Understand Motor Learning** |
| 2.02.03 | Understand factors that positively and negatively affect retention such as practice schedules and failure to provide feedback |

2.02.03.01 *Understand the implications of overlearning on the retention of motor skills by individuals with disabilities*

2.02.03.01.01 Plan how practice variability may influence both positively and negatively individuals with mental retardation and certain types of learning disabilities

2.02.03.01.02 Analyze complex movements to determine which could benefit from structuring randomly ordered practice

2.02.03.01.03 Structure the duration of units to facilitate retention of content by individuals with disabilities

| 2.02 | **Understand Motor Learning** |
| 2.02.04 | Understand pre-practice considerations (e.g., motivation and goal setting) |

2.02.04.01 *Know techniques and procedures that can facilitate motivation and preparation for individuals with disabilities*

2.02.04.01.01 Plan practice and long tasks with appropriate levels of novelty and complexity

2.02.04.01.02 Set and present goals that are challenging but attainable with student input when possible

2.02.04.01.03 Use performance standards to help individuals with disabilities set goals

2.02.04.01.04 Modify activities as a means of achieving success

| 2.02 | **Understand Motor Learning** |
| 2.02.05 | Understand principles of practice including how and when to use guidance techniques, mental practice, and whole versus part practice |

2.02.05.01 *Understand how practice principles can be used for individuals with disabilities*

2.02.05.01.01 Analyze skills to determine the most appropriate type of practice such as whole, whole-part and part

2.02.05.01.02 Use physical and verbal guidance to avoid errors early in learning

2.02.05.01.03 Emphasize the use of mental practice

2.02.05.01.04 Encourage the use of a combination of mental and physical practice to increase learning efficiency

| 2.02 | **Understand Motor Learning** |
| 2.02.06 | Understand how massed and distributed practice are used for continuous and discrete tasks |

2.02.06.01 *Understand the concept of practice variability when promoting skill acquisition for individuals with disabilities*

2.02.06.01.01   Structure across and within practices so time spent on activities is divided into appropriate segments

2.02.06.01.02   Recognize and classify tasks according to their energy cost (see Standard 3.09.04)

2.02.06.01.03   Design practice sessions that include appropriate rest periods for discrete and continuous skills

2.02 2.02.07	**Understand Motor Learning** Understand how to organize and schedule practice with emphasis on instructional efficiency

2.02.07.01   *Understand how task variation complements skill acquisition in individuals with disabilities*

2.02.07.01.01   Vary practice schedules along dimensions such as distance, speed, and time

2.02.07.01.02   Employ random practice selectively depending on the nature of the disability such as with individuals with severe mental retardation

2.02 2.02.08	**Understand Motor Learning** Understand how random practice impacts on learning and retention of motor skills

2.02.08.01   *Know how random practice effects may vary for individuals with disabilities*

2.02.08.01.01   Use random practice to aid retention of a task by individuals with disabilities

2.02.08.01.02   Construct variable practice sessions to incorporate a wide range of movement variations

2.02 2.02.09	**Understand Motor Learning** Understand the factors that affect both transfer of training and the relationship between generalizability and specificity of learning such as automaticity, error detection, and transfer and generalization of learning

2.02.09.01   *Know how these factors relate to the way different disabilities influence error detection and generalizability of learning*

2.02.09.01.01   Develop the ability to detect and correct errors among learners

2.02.09.01.02   Analyze skills to determine which type of feedback is most useful in detecting errors and then direct learners' attention to it

2.02.09.02   *Recognize characteristics of performance that accompany increased automaticity and error detection in individuals with disabilities*

2.02.09.02.01   Use a given stimulus pattern when practicing because it increases the probability of producing the same response

2.02.09.02.02   Design practice sessions to develop high level physical performance in both closed and open skills

| 2.02 | **_Understand Motor Learning_** |
| 2.02.10 | Understand the importance of feedback to learning |

2.02.10.01	_Know how different types of feedback such as KR, KP, intrinsic, and augmented may be used to enhance performance of individuals with disabilities (see Standard 10.02.09)_
2.02.10.01.01	Use feedback to motivate learners
2.02.10.01.02	Use feedback to reinforce appropriate movement patterns
2.02.10.01.03	Use feedback to help learners detect and correct their own errors
2.02.10.02	_Know how to vary methods of feedback delivery to enhance performance of individuals with disabilities_
2.02.10.02.01	Select the types of feedback which enhance learning
2.02.10.02.02	Determine which movement features are most critical for success
2.02.10.02.03	Give feedback that is appropriate
2.02.10.02.04	Use faded feedback and adjust schedules of fading to accommodate individual errors

| 2.02 | **_Understand Motor Learning_** |
| 2.02.11 | Understand the relationship between altering the scheduling of feedback and guidance, reward, and motivation |

2.02.11.01	_Know how to employ a system of least prompts including when it is best to use verbal, visual, environmental, and physical prompts_
2.02.11.01.01	Use kinesthetic prompting to assist individuals with visual impairment
2.02.11.01.02	Employ visual, verbal, and physical prompts in a least prompts instructional hierarchy
2.02.11.01.03	Structure the physical environment to provide extrinsic feedback to learners

| 2.02 | **_Understand Motor Learning_** |
| 2.02.12 | Understand how delays in KR during the intertrial interval and post KR delays affect skill acquisition |

2.02.12.01	_Understand how to manipulate the intertrial interval to enhance skill acquisition among individuals with disabilities_
2.02.12.01.01	Structure the intertrial interval to reduce the effects of delayed knowledge of results for individuals with visual disabilities
2.02.12.01.02	Provide sufficient time after giving feedback for the learner to think about and understand errors
2.02.12.01.03	Provide adequate post-feedback intervals for effective planning of next movement

2.03	**Understand Motor Control**
2.03.01	Understand the stages of information processing (i.e., stimulus identification, response selection, and response programming)

2.03.01.01   *Understand how the stages of information processing are affected by certain types of disabilities*

2.03.01.01.01   Modify tasks and instructions so that they are congruent with students' processing abilities

2.03.01.01.02   Adjust strategies in game-like situations to take into account delayed response processing in individuals with disabilities

2.03	**Understand Motor Control**
2.03.02	Understand the importance of attention and arousal in motor performance

2.03.02.01   *Understand the concept of stimulus overselectivity and its effect on motor performance in individuals with disabilities*

2.03.02.01.01   Manipulate the environment or one's position in the environment for minimum infringement on student attention

2.03.02.01.02   When appropriate, structure and present tasks to elicit optimal arousal levels in individuals with disabilities

2.03.02.01.03   Structure activities involving the tracking of objects to account for certain types of disabilities

2.03	**Understand Motor Control**
2.03.03	Understand the parts of the central nervous system responsible for motor control processes and their function and interaction with other systems

2.03.03.01   *Understand how damage to various neurological structures affects motor performance in individuals with disabilities (see Standard 3.0)*

2.03.03.01.01   Structure tasks and activities to account for damage to the basal ganglion which will influence coordinated movements such as throwing an object by an individual with cerebral palsy

2.03.03.01.02   Structure tasks and activities to account for cerebellar problems such as certain gymnastic activities for individuals with disabilities

2.03	**Understand Motor Control**
2.03.04	Distinguish between simple, choice, and discrimination reaction time

2.03.04.01   *Understand how certain types of disabilities may affect reaction time*

2.03.04.01.01   Modify activities so that they allow more or less processing time, as needed

2.03.04.01.02   Structure tasks and activities to account for greater difficulty responding to multiple choice situations such in team activities

| 2.03 | **_Understand Motor Control_** |
| 2.03.05 | Distinguish among short term sensory memory, short term memory, and long term memory |

2.03.05.01   *Understand how memory types may be influenced by an individual's disability*

2.03.05.01.01   Repeat previously experienced instructions or activities without negative affect

2.03.05.01.02   Evaluate the effects of different types of kinesthetic and proprioceptive deficits on the ability to retain skills such as the way a bat is held

| 2.03 | **_Understand Motor Control_** |
| 2.03.06 | Understand how anticipation affects skill acquisition |

2.03.06.01   *Understand how spatial and temporal uncertainty can exacerbate movement difficulties in individuals with disabilities*

2.03.06.01.01   Structure tasks and activities to account for difficulty in anticipation such as individuals with figure-ground problems involved in ball activities

2.03.06.01.02   Structure tasks and activities involving appearance or flight of objects to control for problems in timing that are evident in certain types of disabilities

| 2.03 | **_Understand Motor Control_** |
| 2.03.07 | Differentiate between controlled and automatic processes with emphasis on the response selection stage |

2.03.07.01   *Understand controlled and automatic processes in open and closed skills with individuals with disabilities*

2.03.07.01.01   Analyze skills in relation to interference resulting from the presence of primitive reflex behavior such as an individual with cerebral palsy executing a forehand in tennis

2.03.07.01.02   Structure tasks and activities to account for reflex action which may interfere with performance in a closed skill such as an individual with cerebral palsy swimming the front crawl stroke

| 2.03 | **_Understand Motor Control_** |
| 2.03.08 | Understand how feedback error and servomechanisms affect a closed loop system |

2.03.08.01   *Understand how positive and negative feedback systems may affect the motor performance of individuals with disabilities*

2.03.08.01.01   Structure activities for success to maximize the positive feedback associated with successful execution

2.03.08.01.02   Reduce the frequency of highlighting errors in skill execution which may adversely affect individuals with disabilities

2.03	**Understand Motor Control**
2.03.09	Understand the elements in a closed loop system that may not be generated with rapid discrete actions (e.g., stages of information processing)

2.03.09.01 *Understand how the stages of information processing impact the execution of a motor skill by individuals with disabilities*

2.03.09.01.01 Program activities that facilitate the use of proprioceptive feedback which in certain types of disabilities may not be utilized effectively

2.03.09.01.02 Develop short term memory for the salient features of the task and activity to be executed

2.03	**Understand Motor Control**
2.03.10	Understand the mechanisms of commonality and difference found both in open and closed loop models

2.03.10.01 *Understand the concepts of the open loop system for programming activities for individuals with disabilities*

2.03.10.01.01 Use an open loop approach for certain types of disabilities such as autism

2.03.10.01.02 Demonstrate care when preprogramming a series of actions for individuals with certain disabilities since the instructor may be limiting certain types of adjustments or improvements

2.03.10.02 *Understand the concepts of the closed loop system for programming activities for individuals with disabilities*

2.03.10.02.01 Instruct and give augmented feedback so as to encourage learners to process intrinsic feedback

2.03.10.02.02 Encourage the use of verbal rehearsal strategies to facilitate appropriate response selection

2.03	**Understand Motor Control**
2.03.11	Understand the speed-accuracy trade-off (e.g., substituting accuracy for speed)

2.03.11.01 *Understand how movement amplitude, the distance between two targets in an aiming task, is incorporated into the assessment process*

2.03.11.01.01 Determine the amount of emphasis placed on the velocity of movement such as how fast to stroke a tennis ball and realize that it differs with various types of disabilities

2.03.11.01.02 Teach a skill with the required movement amplitude so as to avoid causing the individual to relearn the skill numerous times

2.03	**Understand Motor Control**
2.03.12	Understand how motor programs influence the execution of skilled movements

2.03.12.01 *Understand variance in the ability to develop motor programs in individuals with disabilities*

2.03.12.01.01 Structure tasks and activities to account for marked variations between and among disabilities relative to how a person will learn and execute motor skills

2.03.12.01.02   Structure tasks and activities to account for deficits in short term and long term memory in order to combine smaller elements of a skill into longer sequences that are controlled by a single motor program

---

2.03

2.03.13

Understand Motor Control

Understand the mechanisms required to change motor programs (e.g., what defines the essential details of skilled action)

2.03.13.01   *Understand the implications of open and closed loop theories such as Schmidt's Schema Theory, Adam's Closed Loop Theory to skill acquisition for individuals with disabilities*

2.03.13.01.01   Present tasks to learners so that the essential characteristics of the tasks are understandable

2.03.13.01.02   Use knowledge of open and closed loop theory to determine which skills or parts of skills are amenable to correction

---

2.03

2.03.14

Understand Motor Control

Recognize individual differences and capabilities

2.03.14.01   *Relate Henry's specificity hypothesis (tasks are composed of many unrelated abilities) to motor skill execution in individuals with disabilities*

2.03.14.01.01   Realize that the level of proficiency in one skill in a skill class such as underhand throwing may be different in another skill in the same class such as overhand throwing

2.03.14.01.02   Structure activities to consider that the speed of motion of an agonistic muscle group may be faster or slower than the antagonistic muscle group

3.01	**_Exercise Science: Demonstrate knowledge of exercise physiology principles_**
3.01.01	Understand measurement of metabolism and work through formulae, indirect and direct calorimetry

3.01.01.01   *Understand measurement of energy expenditure and work may be affected by alterations in physiology or anatomy for individuals with disabilities*

3.01.01.01.01   Utilize modified protocols for measurement of energy expenditure with individuals with orthopedic disabilities such as spinal cord injury and multiple sclerosis

3.01.01.01.02   Recognize that untrained individuals who utilize upper extremities for exercise demonstrate lower energy expenditure levels than untrained individuals with disabilities

3.01.01.01.03   Recognize trained individuals who utilize upper extremities for exercise demonstrate higher energy expenditure levels than sedentary individuals with or without disabilities

3.01.01.01.04   Recognize individuals with quadriplegia demonstrate lower levels of energy than paraplegia

3.01.01.02   *Understand the effect of body mass on energy expenditure for individuals with disabilities such as obesity*

3.01.01.02.01   Recognize that weight bearing activities such as running require more energy expenditure for those who are overweight

3.01.01.02.02   Utilize non-weight bearing or simplified weight bearing activities initially such as walking

3.01	**_Exercise Science: Demonstrate knowledge of exercise physiology principles_**
3.01.02	Understand metabolic rate, rest, and exercise

3.01.02.01   *Understand metabolic rates may be affected by various syndromes, metabolic and orthopedic disabilities*

3.01.02.01.01   Recognize that individuals with Down's syndrome may have diminished metabolic rates, thus affecting their activity level and ability for weight management

3.01.02.01.02   Recognize that individuals with Prader-Willi syndrome may have diminished metabolic rates, thus affecting their activity level and ability for weight management

3.01	**_Exercise Science: Demonstrate knowledge of exercise physiology principles_**
3.01.03	Understand energy systems and energy sources, storage, mobilization, and roles in different activities (power, speed, endurance)

3.01.03.01   *Understand how various disabilities may affect energy sources*

3.01.03.01.01   Accommodate individuals with McArdle's syndrome who are unable to utilize glycogen as a fuel source, thus limiting their ability to participate in short term activities

3.01.03.01.02   Recognize that individuals with spinal cord injury (SCI) such as quadriplegia, may have a diminished ability to utilize fats as a fuel source, thus limiting their ability to participate in endurance activities

3.01

> ### Exercise Science: Demonstrate knowledge of exercise physiology principles
> 3.01.04 Understand neural and endocrine control of metabolism at rest and during exercise, according to exercise intensity and duration

3.01.04.01 *Understand how various disabilities may affect neural and endocrine control of metabolism*

3.01.04.01.01 Accommodate individuals with uncontrolled diabetes who may have a diminished ability to synthesize fat and glycogen, thus limiting their ability to participate in physical activity

3.01.04.01.02 Recognize that exercise can help an individual with diabetes who is stable by reducing the amount of insulin needed

3.01.04.01.03 Appreciate that exercise can be deadly to an individual with diabetes who is unstable, exacerbating ketosis

3.01.04.01.04 Realize that exercise can be deadly to an individual with diabetes who is unstable by causing excessive release of growth hormone, which may contribute to blood vessel disease

3.02

> ### Neural Control: Demonstrate knowledge of muscular movement
> 3.02.01 Understand the neural and biomechanical control of movement from higher brain centers (anatomy and neural innervation of muscle, nerve transmission)

3.02.01.01 *Understand how various disabilities may alter normal neural control of movement*

3.02.01.01.01 Recognize that multiple sclerosis will have delayed nerve transmissions affecting ability to perform activities, particularly ambulation

3.02.01.01.02 Acknowledge spinal cord injuries have various levels of residual neural activity, affecting ability to perform activities

3.02

> ### Neural Control: Demonstrate knowledge of muscular movement
> 3.02.02 Understand the difference between voluntary and involuntary movement

3.02.02.01 *Understand voluntary control of movement may be altered by various syndromes, metabolic and orthopedic disabilities*

3.02.02.01.01 Recognize that deficiencies in voluntary control of movement due to cerebral palsy affect an individual's ability to perform free-weight lifting

3.02.02.01.02 Acknowledge that use of upper extremities in manual wheelchair propulsion may result in extension of the lower extremities in individuals with cerebral palsy

3.02.02.01.03 Place strapping in front of the legs during manual wheelchair propulsion to prevent knee extension for individuals with extensor pattern disorders

3.02

> ### Neural Control: Demonstrate knowledge of muscular movement
> 3.02.03 Understand the purpose, processes, and how to elicit reflexes (gamma loop, muscle spindles, Golgi tendon organs)

3.02.03.01 *Understand how reflexes can be affected by various disabilities*

3.02.03.01.01   Acknowledge that neuromuscular disorders such as muscular dystrophy will have diminished reflexes that will hinder ability to perform certain activities

3.02.03.01.02   Acknowledge that individuals with spinal abnormalities may have diminished reflexes due to neural impingement

---

3.03   **Muscular Concept: Demonstrate knowledge of various muscular concepts**
3.03.01   Understand skeletal muscle structure and function

3.03.01.01   *Understand how various syndromes, metabolic and orthopedic disabilities may alter skeletal muscle structure and function*

3.03.01.01.01   Emphasize strength training programs for hypotonic individuals

3.03.01.01.02   Emphasize non-weight bearing activities for individuals with degenerative diseases such as muscular dystrophy

3.03.01.01.03   Recognize that individuals with muscular dystrophy such as Duchenne are predisposed to skeletal muscle degeneration

---

3.03   **Muscular Concept: Demonstrate knowledge of various muscular concepts**
3.03.02   Understand the interaction between metabolic and mechanical efficiency

---

3.03.02.01   *Understand how various syndromes, metabolic and orthopedic disabilities may alter metabolic and mechanical efficiency*

3.03.02.01.01   Accommodate individuals who display inefficient motor patterns resulting from mechanical inefficiency

3.03.02.01.02   Accommodate individuals who display inefficient motor patterns resulting from metabolic inefficiency

---

3.03   **Muscular Concept: Demonstrate knowledge of various muscular concepts**
3.03.03   Understand muscular strength and muscular endurance

---

3.03.03.01   *Understand how various syndromes, metabolic and orthopedic disabilities may affect muscular strength and function*

3.03.03.01.01   Acknowledge that individuals with progressive neuromuscular conditions will lose strength

3.03.03.01.02   Acknowledge that individuals with spastic cerebral palsy will have a muscular imbalance between flexor and extensor muscles

---

3.03   **Muscular Concept: Demonstrate knowledge of various muscular concepts**
3.03.04   Understand overload, specificity and muscular adaptations to training and weight training programs

---

3.03.04.01   *Understand how the overload and specificity principles apply to individuals with disabilities*

3.03.04.01.01   Recognize that individuals with disabilities that result in hypotonia such as Down's syndrome may demonstrate responses to muscular training that are slower than those without hypotonia

3.03.04.01.02   Accept that individuals with degenerative muscular diseases may not develop benefits from muscular training

---

3.03   **Muscular Concept: Demonstrate knowledge of various muscular concepts**

3.03.05   Understand aspects of flexibility

3.03.05.01   *Understand how flexibility training applies to individuals with disabilities*

3.03.05.01.01   Recognize that individuals with hypotonic conditions such as Down's syndrome do not need flexibility emphasized in their fitness programs

3.03.05.01.02   Emphasize flexibility exercise for individuals with hypertonic conditions such as cerebral palsy

---

3.04   **Cardiorespiratory Factors: Demonstrate knowledge of various cardiorespiratory factors**

3.04.01   Understand the anatomy and function of the cardiorespiratory system

---

3.04.01.01   *Understand how congenital defects or syndromes such as congenital heart defects, aortic stenosis, atrial septal defects, and Marfan syndrome may alter the anatomy and function of the cardiovascular system*

3.04.01.01.01   Limit duration and intensity of exercise for individuals with impaired cardiac function

3.04.01.01.02   Maintain close contact with the physician for individuals with impaired cardiac function

3.04.01.01.03   Describe the cardiovascular training limitation of individuals with heart disease

---

3.04   **Cardiorespiratory Factors: Demonstrate knowledge of various cardiorespiratory factors**

3.04.02   Understand the electrical and circulatory processes of the cardiac cycle, control of the heart, and basic anatomy of the circulatory system

---

3.04.02.01   *Understand how the variability of the cardiac cycle applies to individuals with congenital defects, syndromes or orthopedic disabilities*

3.04.02.01.01   Recognize that individuals with congenital heart defects may have limited aerobic capacity due to inadequate amount of oxygenated blood or ability to eliminate an adequate amount of carbon dioxide

3.04.02.01.02   Contact physician before engaging individuals with coronary defects prior to defining exercise program

3.04.02.01.03   Define an appropriate level of exercise intensity for individuals with congenital heart defects

3.04	**Cardiorespiratory Factors: Demonstrate knowledge of various cardiorespiratory factors**
3.04.03	Understand oxygen consumption ($\dot{V}O_2$) at rest and during exercise

3.04.03.01   *Understand how oxygen consumption may (or may not) be different between individuals with disabilities and individuals without disabilities*

3.04.03.01.01   Appreciate that individuals with spinal cord injuries including spina bifida will have lower oxygen consumption levels due to use of small muscle mass

3.04.03.01.02   Describe the differences in maximum heart rate (HR) between arm crank and wheelchair ergometry

3.04	**Cardiorespiratory Factors: Demonstrate knowledge of various cardiorespiratory factors**
3.04.04	Understand the determinants and control of circulation at rest and during exercise

3.04.04.01   *Understand how various orthopedic disabilities and metabolic disease such as diabetes result in neural and vascular damage that may affect circulation*

3.04.04.01.01   Recognize that individuals with spinal cord injuries have impaired hemodynamic responses such as reduced blood flow, lowered blood pressure and thermoregulation

3.04.04.01.02   Recognize that individuals with spinal cord injuries have impaired vasoconstriction and vasodilation

3.04	**Cardiorespiratory Factors: Demonstrate knowledge of various cardiorespiratory factors**
3.04.05	Understand cardiorespiratory dynamics (cardiac output, stroke volume, preload, afterload, contractility, heart rate, blood pressure, synergy of contraction, distensibility of ventricles, oxygen transport) at rest and during exercise

3.04.05.01   *Understand how congenital defects, syndromes and orthopedic disabilities may interfere with cardiorespiratory dynamics*

3.04.05.01.01   Recognize that individuals with SCI quadriplegia and Down's syndrome have reduced heart rates

3.04.05.01.02   Acknowledge that the use of standard heart rate values for the determination of exercise intensity is not applicable

3.04	**Cardiorespiratory Factors: Demonstrate knowledge of various cardiorespiratory factors**
3.04.06	Understand the effects and risk factors of coronary heart disease (CHD)

3.04.06.01   *Understand that individuals with disabilities are often at a higher risk for cardiovascular heart disease*

3.04.06.01.01   Appreciate that high blood cholesterol levels are more prevalent in individuals with disabilities

3.04.06.01.02   Review medical records for individuals with disabilities for elevated total cholesterol levels

---

3.05   *Respiratory Factors: Demonstrate knowledge of respiratory system*

3.05.01   Understand the purpose of ventilation and respiration, oxygen exchange and transport, acid-base regulation, and partial pressures of gases

---

3.05.01.01   *Understand how orthopedic or chronic obstructive pulmonary disease (COPD) conditions can interfere with the function of the respiratory system*

3.05.01.01.01   Recognize that exercise may precipitate an asthma attack

3.05.01.01.02   Promote desirable exercise conditions such as allergen free and stress free environments

3.05.01.01.03   Describe techniques to control ventilation and respiration during an asthma attack

3.05.01.01.04   Work with the individual and caregivers on regulating medication

---

3.05   *Respiratory Factors: Demonstrate knowledge of respiratory system*

3.05.02   Understand the anatomy of the pulmonary system, dynamic and static lung volumes, mechanics of ventilation, ventilatory parameters (maximum voluntary ventilation, breathing frequency (BF), tidal volume (TV)) and training adaptations

---

3.05.02.01   *Understand how chronic obstructive pulmonary disease (COPD) and orthopedic disabilities, particularly those that cause ventilatory muscle dysfunction, may interfere with the respiratory system function*

3.05.02.01.01   Be aware that individuals with asthma may panic because they feel they are not receiving enough air

3.05.02.01.02   Practice safety precautions and relaxation techniques so individuals can learn to control their breathing

---

3.05   *Respiratory Factors: Demonstrate knowledge of respiratory system*

3.05.03   Understand the control of ventilation at rest and during exercise

---

3.05.03.01   *Understand how chronic obstructive pulmonary disease (COPD) and orthopedic disabilities may interfere with control of ventilation*

3.05.03.01.01   Recognize that individuals with higher level spinal injuries often lack the muscle control for ventilation thus limiting strenuous activity

3.05.03.01.02   Develop intact accessory muscles through physical activity and respiratory training

---

3.06   *Nutrition: Demonstrate knowledge of nutritional concepts*

3.06.01   Understand nutritional concepts (fats, carbohydrates, proteins), nutritional supplements (vitamins and minerals), and concepts of a balanced diet

---

3.06.01.01   *Understand how individuals with disabilities have specific nutritional needs*

3.06.01.01.01	Provide guidance regarding proper nutrition for individuals with disabilities
3.06.01.01.02	Monitor sugar intake for individuals with diabetes
3.06.01.01.03	Monitor food intake for individuals with Prader-Willi syndrome

3.07	**Body Composition: Demonstrate knowledge of body composition**
3.07.01	Understand the components of body composition

3.07.01.01	*Understand the differences in percent body fat among individuals with disabilities such as mild, moderate, severe, and profound mental retardation*
3.07.01.01.01	Utilize Kelly-Rimmer equation for computing percent body fat for individuals with mental retardation
3.07.01.01.02	Recognize that lean body mass is higher in paraplegics than quadriplegics

3.07	**Body Composition: Demonstrate knowledge of body composition**
3.07.02	Understand the differences between overweight, overfat, underweight, and thin

3.07.02.01	*Describe which individuals with disabilities in general are overweight, overfat, underweight, or thin*
3.07.02.01.01	Demonstrate how to use height and weight tables to classify a person with a disability as overweight using small, medium and large frames
3.07.02.01.02	Refrain from using skinfold calipers over paralyzed muscle groups and scar tissue

3.07	**Body Composition: Demonstrate knowledge of body composition**
3.07.03	Understand the factors associated with treatments for obesity

3.07.03.01	*Understand the factors that are associated with the treatment of obesity in individuals with disabilities such as exercise, nutrition, and behavioral intervention*
3.07.03.01.01	Develop a weight reduction program that emphasizes exercise
3.07.03.01.02	Develop a weight reduction program that emphasizes nutrition
3.07.03.01.03	Develop a weight reduction program that emphasizes behavioral intervention

3.08	**Environmental Effects: Demonstrate knowledge of environmental effects on performance**
3.08.01	Understand the adaptations to thermal stress (hot, cold), what constitutes thermal stress, and symptoms of thermal injury

3.08.01.01	*Understand how individuals with disabilities such as asthma or orthopedic involvement may be susceptible to thermal change conditions*
3.08.01.01.01	Recognize that the body's ability to thermoregulate is increasingly compromised, the higher the spinal cord injury

3.08.01.01.02   Appreciate that individuals with spinal injuries, muscular dystrophy and multiple sclerosis are particularly prone to thermal injuries and must be well hydrated and monitored when performing activity

3.08.01.02   *Understand the impact of high and low pressure environments on individuals with disabilities*

3.08.01.02.01   Monitor respiration rates of individuals with asthma at high altitudes due to reduced oxygen pressure

3.08.01.02.02   Monitor respiration rates of individuals with cystic fibrosis at high altitudes due to reduced oxygen pressure

3.09   **Exercise Prescription and Training: Demonstrate knowledge of exercise prescription and training**

3.09.01   Understand the physiological benefits and adaptations of exercise (decreased blood pressure, decreased submaximal heart rate, improved endurance)

3.09.01.01   *Describe the benefits of exercise training for individuals with exercise-induced asthma*

3.09.01.01.01   Design exercise programs that are safe and effective for individuals with exercise-induced asthma

3.09.01.01.02   Design a conditioning program for individuals utilizing wheelchairs

3.09   **Exercise Prescription and Training: Demonstrate knowledge of exercise prescription and training**

3.09.02   Understand the differences between fitness, physical activity, and rehabilitation

3.09.02.01   *Describe the programmatic differences between a fitness, physical activity and rehabilitation program for individuals with disabilities such as cerebral palsy*

3.09.02.01.01   Assign homework for individuals with disabilities that increase activity levels

3.09.02.01.02   Develop a rehabilitation program for individuals with disabilities, with the assistance of team members from allied medicine

3.09   **Exercise Prescription and Training: Demonstrate knowledge of exercise prescription and training**

3.09.03   Understand the current American College of Sports Medicine (ACSM) recommendations for exercise prescription

3.09.03.01   *Understand that heart rate depends on injury level of individuals with disabilities such as spinal cord injuries*

3.09.03.01.01   Utilize ratings of perceived exertion (RPE) to determine exercise intensity level when heart rate is difficult to obtain

3.09.03.01.02   Emphasize duration of activity rather than activity intensity for individuals with obesity

3.09	**_Exercise Prescription and Training: Demonstrate knowledge of exercise pre-scription and training_**
3.09.04	Understand the concept and use of metabolic equivalent (MET)

3.09.04.01	_Understand the difference in maximum MET levels between persons with and without disabilities_
3.09.04.01.01	Determine MET level for ambulation in a wheelchair
3.09.04.01.02	Determine MET level for ambulation utilizing braces and crutches

3.09	**_Exercise Prescription and Training: Demonstrate knowledge of exercise pre-scription and training_**
3.09.05	Understand the Karvonen formula for estimation of maximal and training heart rate zone

3.09.05.01	_Understand that the Karvonen formula may be ineffective for individuals with disabilities such as Down's syndrome who may have chronotropic incompetence or low motivational levels_
3.09.05.01.01	Estimate training heart rate using the Karvonen formula for individuals with disabilities
3.09.05.01.02	Utilize conservative training heart rates for individuals who are severely deconditioned

3.09	**_Exercise Prescription and Training: Demonstrate knowledge of exercise pre-scription and training_**
3.09.06	Understand the concept and use of ratings of perceived exertion (RPE)

3.09.06.01	_Understand the importance of RPE when gauging exercise intensity in individuals with disabilities such as Type I diabetes mellitus and individuals on beta blockers_
3.09.06.01.01	Utilize ratings for perceived exertion when designing exercise programs for individuals with exercise-induced asthma
3.09.06.01.02	Teach individuals with exercise-induced asthma how to utilize ratings of perceived exertion (RPE)

3.09	**_Exercise Prescription and Training: Demonstrate knowledge of exercise pre-scription and training_**
3.09.07	Understand the different types of maximal and submaximal methods of determining cardiovascular fitness

3.09.07.01	_Understand the different testing protocols for persons with disabilities such as mental retardation and spinal cord injuries (SCI)_
3.09.07.01.01	Utilize the Pacer shuttle run for individuals with disabilities such as mental retardation or partially sighted
3.09.07.01.02	Utilize wheelchair ergometers (rollers) or arm crank ergometers (Monark) to determine sub-maximal test for individuals using manual wheelchairs

3.09	**Exercise Prescription and Training: Demonstrate knowledge of exercise prescription and training**
3.09.08	Understand the different types of direct and indirect determinations of muscular strength and endurance and flexibility

3.09.08.01   *Understand the types of muscular strength and endurance and flexibility tests used for individuals with disabilities*

3.09.08.01.01   Utilize appropriate test of muscular strength and endurance for individuals who use wheelchairs

3.09.08.01.02   Utilize an appropriate flexibility test (goniometer) for individuals who use wheelchairs

3.09	**Exercise Prescription and Training: Demonstrate knowledge of exercise prescription and training**
3.09.09	Understand the principles of the general adaptation system (stress, response, adaptation), alarm reaction, resistance, exhaustion, overload, specificity, reversibility, and individuality and how they relate to exercise prescription

3.09.09.01   *Understand the concept of reversibility, and how it applies to individuals with disabilities such as post-injured SCI*

3.09.09.01.01   Design cardiorespiratory training programs utilizing specificity of exercise such as wheelchair ergometers

3.09.09.01.02   Accommodate the concept of reversibility for an individual with a disability who has been removed from school due to surgery

3.09	**Exercise Prescription and Training: Demonstrate knowledge of exercise prescription and training**
3.09.10	Understand the physiological differences between genders related to exercise performance

3.09.10.01   *Understand the physiological differences in aerobic capacity and body composition between males and females with disabilities such mental retardation*

3.09.10.01.01   Recognize that females with mental retardation have lower $\dot{V}O_2$max than males with mental retardation

3.09.10.01.02   Acknowledge that females with mental retardation have higher obesity levels than males with mental retardation

3.10	**Biomechanics/Kinesiology: Demonstrate knowledge of basic biomechanical and kinesiological concepts and principles**
3.10.01	Understand kinesiology

3.10.01.01   *Understand pathokinesiology and its relationship to altered human movement patterns caused by disabilities*

3.10.01.01.01   Explain basic changes in kinesiological movements or joint positions

3.10.01.01.02   Utilize appropriate activities and equipment that alter movements or accommodate abnormal joint positions

---

3.10

Biomechanics/Kinesiology: Demonstrate knowledge of basic biomechanical and kinesiological concepts and principles

3.10.02
Understand biomechanics

3.10.02.01   *Understand pathobiomechanics and its relationship to kinesiological movement in individuals with disabilities*

3.10.02.01.01   Explain basic changes in biomechanical movements of joint positions

3.10.02.01.02   Utilize appropriate activities and equipment that alter movement patterns

---

3.10

Biomechanics/Kinesiology: Demonstrate knowledge of basic biomechanical and kinesiological concepts and principles

3.10.03
Understand statics

3.10.03.01   *Understand specific biomechanical and kinesiological properties such as static movement, static tension, static stretch, equilibrium and relationships to movement of and activities for individuals with disabilities*

3.10.03.01.01   Recognize that individuals with disabilities such as deafness, developmental delays, some forms of cerebral palsy (ataxia & spasticity) and other neurosomal disorders have impaired static balance skills

3.10.03.01.02   Accommodate individuals exhibiting exaggerated stretch reflexes with abnormally high muscle tone such as spastic cerebral palsy

---

3.10

Biomechanics/Kinesiology: Demonstrate knowledge of basic biomechanical and kinesiological concepts and principles

3.10.04
Understand dynamics

3.10.04.01   *Understand mechanics of dynamic movement, equilibrium, dynamic stretch and dynamic tension and relationships to movement of activities for individuals with disabilities*

3.10.04.01.01   Recognize that individuals with disabilities such as deafness, developmental delays, cerebral palsy, learning disabilities and other neurosomal disorders often have impaired dynamic balance

3.10.04.01.02   Accommodate individuals with disabilities such as athetoid or ataxic cerebral palsy who demonstrate uncoordinated and unintegrated movements

---

3.10

Biomechanics/Kinesiology: Demonstrate knowledge of basic biomechanical and kinesiological concepts and principles

3.10.05
Understand kinematics

3.10.05.01   *Understand effects of time and space upon motion, calculations of mechanical efficiency and their relationship to movement and motor performance for individuals with disabilities*

3.10.05.01.01   Demonstrate patience with individuals with disabilities who take more time to effect a desired motor response

3.10.05.01.02   Recognize that some physical impairments such as amputations change the mechanics of an activity or skill

---

3.10

Biomechanics/Kinesiology: Demonstrate knowledge of basic biomechanical and kinesiological concepts and principles

3.10.06

Understand kinetics

3.10.06.01   *Understand forces that affect movement and motion, and the relationship to movement and motor performance for individuals with disabilities*

3.10.06.01.01   Demonstrate the kinetic open and closed chains and kinetic principles in instructing a variety of activities

3.10.06.01.02   Recognize that individuals with neuromuscular disabilities may take longer to start or stop a movement

---

3.10

Biomechanics/Kinesiology: Demonstrate knowledge of basic biomechanical and kinesiological concepts and principles

3.10.07

Understand anatomical reference position associated with body movement

---

3.10.07.01   *Understand the anatomical positions of the body and how these positions are used for studying movement of individuals with disabilities*

3.10.07.01.01   Describe body and joint positions which are lateral, medial, dorsal, ventral, cephla or caudal to each other

3.10.07.01.02   Describe movements which are lateral, medial, dorsal, ventral, cephal, or caudal to each other

---

3.10

Biomechanics/Kinesiology: Demonstrate knowledge of basic biomechanical and kinesiological concepts and principles

3.10.08

Understand planes associated with body movement

3.10.08.01   *Understand body and segmental planes, axes, frontal/transversal axes, sagittal plane, principle (cardinal) planes, transverse plane, and segmental movements with body movement and their relationship to movement for individuals with disabilities*

3.10.08.01.01   Recognize that shoulder or hip abduction and adduction take place in the frontal plane, rotation occurs in the transverse (or horizontal) plane and flexion and extension occur in the sagittal plane

3.10.08.01.02   Recognize that individuals with orthopedic disabilities may have pathokinesiological joint positions which cause excursion or placement of the joints in other planes such as varum or valgum

---

3.10

Biomechanics/Kinesiology: Demonstrate knowledge of basic biomechanical and kinesiological concepts and principles

3.10.09

Understand axes relationship to corresponding planes of the human body

---

3.10.09.01   *Understand instances where anatomical constraints of certain individuals with disabilities may cause movement to be in different axes of rotation*

3.10.09.01.01   Realize that when individuals with cerebral palsy move, other muscles or joints are called into play due to contractures

3.10.09.01.02   Describe how individuals with joint fusion due to surgery or arthritis may need to initiate movements differently

---

3.10   **Biomechanics/Kinesiology: Demonstrate knowledge of basic biomechanical and kinesiological concepts and principles**

3.10.10   Understand movement analysis

3.10.10.01   *Understand the use of statics, dynamics, kinematics, kinetics, body axes, planes, balance, equilibrium for studying and planning movement activities for individuals with disabilities*

3.10.10.01.01   Demonstrate ability to perform a movement analysis and plan instruction for individuals with disabilities

3.10.10.01.02   Observe abnormal positions of joints or body parts and how these may affect movements

3.10.10.01.03   Demonstrate ability to task analyze a skill into smaller achievable parts

---

3.10   **Biomechanics/Kinesiology: Demonstrate knowledge of basic biomechanical and kinesiological concepts and principles**

3.10.11   Understand fundamental mechanical concepts

3.10.11.01   *Understand Newton's Laws (1, 2, and 3), levers, vectors, force, pulley system, mass/weight, stability, gravity, inertia, momentum, torque, velocity, acceleration and relationship to movement for individuals with disabilities*

3.10.11.01.01   Accommodate individuals who are obese by providing extra time to initiate and cease their motions

3.10.11.01.02   Recognize that individuals who are obese will need more strength to start and stop

3.10.11.01.03   Describe the differences in wheelchair design for sports such as tennis or basketball vs. track or roadracing vs. medical use

---

3.10   **Biomechanics/Kinesiology: Demonstrate knowledge of basic biomechanical and kinesiological concepts and principles**

3.10.12   Understand balance, equilibrium, and stability

3.10.12.01   *Understand the concepts of balance, equilibrium and stability in planning activity programs for individuals with disabilities*

3.10.12.01.01   Demonstrate use of concepts of balance, equilibrium and stability in planning and instructing movement activities such as teaching individuals how they can lower their center of gravity to increase their stability

3.10.12.01.02   Acknowledge that individuals with cerebral palsy, amputations, and neuromuscular disorders may need special instruction in areas of balance and equilibrium

3.10

> ### Biomechanics/Kinesiology: Demonstrate knowledge of basic biomechanical and kinesiological concepts and principles
> 3.10.13   Understand force production and absorption

3.10.13.01   *Understand aerodynamics, lift, drag, inertia, moment of inertia, velocity, spin/rotation, centrifugal, centripetal, lever, force arm, resistance force and speed and their relationship to movement and motor performance for individuals with disabilities*

3.10.13.01.01   Describe effects of primitive reflexes in individuals with disabilities when producing too much force

3.10.13.01.02   Describe the effects of primitive reflexes in individuals with disabilities when absorbing too little force

3.10.13.01.03   Describe effect on anatomical structures in individuals with disabilities when producing too much force

3.10.13.01.04   Describe effect on anatomical structures in individuals with disabilities when absorbing too little force

3.10.13.01.05   Describe mechanical differences between everyday (medical), sport and track/racing wheelchairs

3.10.13.01.06   Describe wheelchair propulsion (torque production) and recovery techniques for sport and track/racing wheelchairs

3.10

> ### Biomechanics/Kinesiology: Demonstrate knowledge of basic biomechanical and kinesiological concepts and principles
> 3.10.14   Understand basic fluid mechanics

3.10.14.01   *Apply fluid mechanics principles of buoyancy to individuals with disabilities*

3.10.14.01.01   Recognize that individuals with paralysis will have some body parts more buoyant due to atrophy of muscle tissue and increased fatty tissue

3.10.14.01.02   Accommodate individuals with paralysis or contractures who cannot demonstrate a horizontal body position resulting in increased drag because lower extremities sink

3.10.14.01.03   Accommodate individuals with muscular dystrophy who demonstrate increased buoyancy due to atrophy of muscle tissue and increased fatty tissue

3.11

> ### Bone Growth and Development: Demonstrate knowledge of the biomechanics of bone growth and development
> 3.11.01   Understand Wolff's Law implies that bones develop and change according to mechanical loads such as compression, tension, shear, torsion, and bending

3.11.01.01   *Understand that individuals with disabilities such as scoliosis demonstrate abnormal orthopedic development*

3.11.01.01.01   Recognize that unequal muscular development will result in abnormal bone growth such as limb deformities

3.11.01.01.02   Recognize that individuals who remain sedentary will undergo bone demineralization and may develop osteoporosis

---

3.11

3.11.02

Bone Growth and Development: Demonstrate knowledge of the biomechanics of bone growth and development

Understand processes such as cartilaginous hyperplasia, hypertrophy and calcification, involved in the normal growth and maturation of bone

---

3.11.02.01   *Understand that certain characteristics of disabilities associated with abnormal bone growth and conditions make individuals prone to bone injury*

3.11.02.01.01   Recognize contraindications such as high impact activities and high resistance weight training may be associated with abnormal bone growth and conditions

3.11.02.01.02   Prescribe exercises and activities that are indicated and encourage healthy bone growth

---

3.11

3.11.03

Bone Growth and Development: Demonstrate knowledge of the biomechanics of bone growth and development

Understand the effects of decreased activity or lack of exercise on bone mineralization

---

3.11.03.01   *Describe the effects of decreased activity or lack of exercise on bone mineralization of individuals with disabilities associated with bone growth problems and/or deformities*

3.11.03.01.01   Realize time spent while bedridden or immobilized results in weakened bone anatomy

3.11.03.01.02   Increase systematically an individual's physical activity time

---

3.11

3.11.04

Bone Growth and Development: Demonstrate knowledge of the biomechanics of bone growth and development

Understand types of bone fractures

3.11.04.01   *Understand common causes of various types of bone fractures such as greenstick, avulsion, longitudinal, and transverse in individuals with disabilities*

3.11.04.01.01   Avoid contact sport and high impact activities for individuals who are at risk for fractures

3.11.04.01.02   Develop a referral policy for individuals who are suspected of being at risk of a fracture

---

3.12

3.12.01

Neuromuscular Function: Demonstrate knowledge of the biomechanical aspects of neuromuscular function

Understand the basic behavioral properties of muscle tissues such as irritability, extensibility, elasticity, and contractility

---

3.12.01.01   *Understand general deviations in basic behavioral properties of muscle tissue found among individuals with disabilities such as hypotonicity*

3.12.01.01.01   Recognize specific deviations in basic behavioral properties of muscle tissue found with disabilities such as spasticity or contractures

3.12.01.01.02 — Describe specific deviations in basic behavioral properties of muscle tissue found with disabilities such as individuals with muscular dystrophy

3.12

> **Neuromuscular Function: Demonstrate knowledge of the biomechanical aspects of neuromuscular function**
>
> 3.12.02 — Understand force-velocity relationships with muscle tissue

3.12.02.01 — *Understand the relationships between force and muscle tissue as they relate to individuals with disabilities such as cerebral palsy, degenerative muscle conditions and spina bifida*

3.12.02.01.01 — Describe that it takes more time to generate muscular forces for a given movement in individuals with disabilities

3.12.02.01.02 — Describe that it takes more time to generate the desired motor action in individuals with disabilities such as cerebral palsy

3.12.02.01.03 — Describe that it is more difficult for individuals with disabilities such as cerebral palsy to generate faster purposeful movements

3.12.02.01.04 — Describe that individuals with degenerative muscle conditions cannot move quickly

3.12

> **Neuromuscular Function: Demonstrate knowledge of the biomechanical aspects of neuromuscular function**
>
> 3.12.03 — Understand force-length relationships with muscle tissue

3.12.03.01 — *Understand force-length relationship (isometric) with individuals with disabilities such as cerebral palsy, degenerative muscle conditions and spina bifida*

3.12.03.01.01 — Recognize the optimal muscle length to generate the most force in an individual with cerebral palsy

3.12.03.01.02 — Recognize the optimal muscle length to generate the most force in an individual with degenerative muscle disease

3.12

> **Neuromuscular Function: Demonstrate knowledge of the biomechanical aspects of neuromuscular function**
>
> 3.12.04 — Understand force-time relationships with muscle tissue

3.12.04.01 — *Understand force-time relationship with individuals with disabilities such as cerebral palsy, degenerative muscle conditions, spina bifida, and mental retardation*

3.12.04.01.01 — Recognize powerful and forceful movements will be more difficult for individuals with disabilities such as degenerative muscle conditions

3.12.04.01.02 — Identify how power can be improved in these individuals

3.12

> **Neuromuscular Function: Demonstrate knowledge of the biomechanical aspects of neuromuscular function**
>
> 3.12.05 — Understand the concept of strength from a biomechanical perspective

3.12.05.01 — *Understand that faulty biomechanics adversely impacts the strength of some individuals with disabilities*

3.12.05.01.01   Recognize that the body's system of levels may be influenced by posture and spinal deformities

3.12.05.01.02   Recognize that decreased range of motion affects force production

---

3.12   **Neuromuscular Function: Demonstrate knowledge of the biomechanical aspects of neuromuscular function**

3.12.06   Understand the concept of power from a biomechanical perspective

---

3.12.06.01   *Understand that the ability of some individuals with disabilities to generate power is compromised due to faulty mechanics*

3.12.06.01.01   Adapt activities for some individuals with disabilities to allow for additional time to effectively generate power

3.12.06.01.02   Utilize lightweight equipment to compensate for deficits in strength to increase power output

---

3.12   **Neuromuscular Function: Demonstrate knowledge of the biomechanical aspects of neuromuscular function**

3.12.07   Understand the concept of endurance from a biomechanical perspective

---

3.12.07.01   *Understand that faulty biomechanics adversely impacts the endurance of some individuals with disabilities*

3.12.07.01.01   Recognize that alterations in movement such as gait and range of motion may interfere with the ability of some individuals with disabilities to sustain activity

3.12.07.01.02   Modify activity to recognize the endurance needs of some individuals with disabilities such as hand ergometry

---

3.12   **Neuromuscular Function: Demonstrate knowledge of the biomechanical aspects of neuromuscular function**

3.12.08   Understand how sensory receptors in muscles (muscle spindles) contribute to neuromuscular control of human movement

---

3.12.08.01   *Understand sensory receptors in muscles (muscle spindles) for individuals with disabilities such as cerebral palsy, Down's syndrome, and muscular dystrophy*

3.12.08.01.01   Describe contraindicated movements for individuals with cerebral palsy which would stimulate the stretch reflex and result in increased hypertonicity (spasticity)

3.12.08.01.02   Describe exercise which stimulates the stretch reflex which helps enhance power in individuals with Down's syndrome

---

3.12   **Neuromuscular Function: Demonstrate knowledge of the biomechanical aspects of neuromuscular function**

3.12.09   Understand how sensory receptors in tendons (Golgi tendon organs) contribute to neuromuscular control of human movement

---

3.12.09.01   *Understand differences for sensory receptors in tendons among individuals with disabilities such as cerebral palsy and muscular dystrophy*

| 3.12.09.01.01 | Utilize proprioceptive neuromuscular facilitation (PNF) exercises to enhance range of motion |
| 3.12.09.01.02 | Utilize proprioceptive neuromuscular facilitation exercises to enhance strength |

| 3.12 | **Neuromuscular Function: Demonstrate knowledge of the biomechanical aspects of neuromuscular function** |
| 3.12.10 | Understand how sensory receptors in other body tissues contribute to neuromuscular control of human movement |

3.12.10.01	*Understand structure and functions of vestibular, cutaneous, visual, and auditory receptors in individuals with disabilities*
3.12.10.01.01	Recognize individuals with sensorineural hearing impairments may demonstrate balance problems or vestibular dysfunction
3.12.10.01.02	Recognize individuals with visual impairments may demonstrate diminished balance skills due to a lack of visual feedback
3.12.10.01.03	Recognize individuals with sensory losses demonstrate impaired kinesthetic awareness

| 3.13 | **Human Skeletal Articulations: Demonstrate knowledge of biomechanics of human skeletal articulations** |
| 3.13.01 | Understand the characteristics of joints based on structure and movement |

3.13.01.01	*Understand joint anomalies in individuals with disabilities such as arthritis and cerebral palsy*
3.13.01.01.01	Utilize aquatics as a mode for physical activity
3.13.01.01.02	Schedule physical education later in the day for individuals with rheumatoid arthritis
3.13.01.01.03	Schedule physical education earlier in the day for individuals with osteoporosis

| 3.13 | **Human Skeletal Articulations: Demonstrate knowledge of biomechanics of human skeletal articulations** |
| 3.13.02 | Understand three sources of joint stability are structure of bony, ligamentous and muscular arrangements |

3.13.02.01	*Understand specific disabilities associated with too much or too little of joint mobility, such as cerebral palsy, juvenile arthritis, osteoarthritis, rheumatoid arthritis, osteogenesis imperfecta, lax ligaments, and neuromuscular control*
3.13.02.01.01	Describe strength and muscular endurance exercises that enhance specific motor control and movement functions
3.13.02.01.02	Design an activity program to insure safe strength development

| 3.13 | **Human Skeletal Articulations: Demonstrate knowledge of biomechanics of human skeletal articulations** |
| 3.13.03 | Understand the concept of joint flexibility or range of motion (ROM) |

| 3.13.03.01 | *Understand specific disabilities associated with hyper joint flexibility such as cerebral palsy and Down's syndrome* |

3.13.03.01.01	Describe programming needs of individuals with hypo and hyper joint flexibility such as cerebral palsy and Down's syndrome
3.13.03.01.02	Describe specific proprioceptive neuromuscular facilitation (PNF) exercises utilizing the stretch reflex to enhance the range of motion (ROM) of individuals with cerebral palsy and arthritis
3.13.03.02	*Understand that specific disabilities may develop varying degrees of contractures and antagonistic stretching resulting in loss of flexibility*
3.13.03.02.01	Restore joint flexibility and balance by stretching contracted muscle and strengthening stretched muscle
3.13.03.02.02	Utilize a warm-up that stretches agonists and strengthens antagonists in involved muscles
3.13.03.02.03	Incorporate assistive stretching activities of affected musculature indicated for individuals with flaccid paralysis
3.13.03.02.04	Prevent contractures using a balanced training program within the tolerance of the individual
3.13.03.02.05	Utilize multidisciplinary approach with the physical therapist and the occupational therapist (see Standard 15.0)

3.13	**Human Skeletal Articulations: Demonstrate knowledge of biomechanics of human skeletal articulations**
3.13.04	Understand the advantages of the different approaches such as sustained and Proprioceptive Neuromuscular Facilitation (PNF) to increasing flexibility

3.13.04.01	*Understand various approaches such as passive stretching, active static stretching and proprioceptive neuromuscular facilitation to increasing flexibility of individuals with disabilities*
3.13.04.01.01	Apply various approaches to increasing flexibility of individuals with specific disabilities known to have low flexibility levels such as cerebral palsy
3.13.04.01.02	Utilize rhythms as a mode for performing flexibility exercises for individuals with disabilities

3.13	**Human Skeletal Articulations: Demonstrate knowledge of biomechanics of human skeletal articulations**
3.13.05	Understand the disadvantages of different approaches such as ballistic stretching to increasing flexibility

3.13.05.01	*Understand how individuals with contractures, such as cerebral palsy, benefit from both active and passive stretching techniques*
3.13.05.01.01	Acknowledge that after warm-up, therapeutic stretching aids in injury prevention and relaxes joints and muscles
3.13.05.01.02	Utilize a balanced program of activities that allow stretching of contracted muscles and strengthening of weakened (stretched) muscles
3.13.05.01.03	Realize that dynamic (ballistic) stretching exercises for stretching contracted muscles are contraindicated for all individuals
3.13.05.01.04	Adapt flexibility exercise program based on therapeutic assessment performed by multidisciplinary team

3.14

> ### Neck and Upper Extremity Movement: Demonstrate knowledge of the biomechanics of neck and upper extremity movement
>
> 3.14.01   Understand the anatomical structure of neck and upper extremity articulations

3.14.01.01   *Understand how deviations such as atlantoaxial instability, scoliosis, lordosis, kyphosis, and growth plate irregularities such as Scheurmann disease affect anatomical structure and movement capabilities of the neck and upper extremities*

3.14.01.01.01   Avoid activities that compress or hyperflex the neck such as back rolls and headstands for individuals with atlantoaxial instability

3.14.01.01.02   Employ exercises which mobilize the spine in extension for individuals with spinal curvatures

3.14

> ### Neck and Upper Extremity Movement: Demonstrate knowledge of the biomechanics of neck and upper extremity movement
>
> 3.14.02   Understand the functions of the neck and upper extremities

3.14.02.01   *Understand restrictions such as limited range of motion can affect basic functions of the neck and upper extremities*

3.14.02.01.01   Avoid contraindicated exercises such as neck bridges

3.14.02.01.02   Seek medical advice when working with individuals with neck pain or motor limitations

3.14

> ### Neck and Upper Extremity Movement: Demonstrate knowledge of the biomechanics of neck and upper extremity movement
>
> 3.14.03   Understand ways in which the spine and pelvic girdle are adapted to carry out functions such as shock absorption and ambulation

3.14.03.01   *Recognize neck and upper extremity function in terms of disc size, disc arrangement, compression/tensile/shear forces, structure in relationship to neck and upper extremity movements in individuals with disabilities*

3.14.03.01.01   Recognize individuals with fused spines will lack the mobility and shock absorption characteristic of those without fusions

3.14.03.01.02   Refer individuals with herniated disc to physician for exercises that can help relieve the pain and swelling

3.14.03.01.03   Prohibit activity that places stress on the neck for individuals with atlantoaxial instability

3.14

> ### Neck and Upper Extremity Movement: Demonstrate knowledge of the biomechanics of neck and upper extremity movement
>
> 3.14.04   Understand the muscle groups that are active during specific neck and upper extremity movement

3.14.04.01   *Understand problems such as hypertonic muscles associated with muscles that are active during neck and upper extremity movement*

3.14.04.01.01   Utilize therapeutic stretching of internal rotators and strengthening of external rotators at shoulder joint such as spastic cerebral palsy

3.14.04.01.02   Encourage individuals to utilize remaining functional capacity such as flaccid paralysis resulting from spinal cord injuries

---

3.14   **Neck and Upper Extremity Movement: Demonstrate knowledge of the biomechanics of neck and upper extremity movement**

3.14.05   Understand the biomechanical factors contributing to injuries of the neck and upper extremities

---

3.14.05.01   *Understand causes and characteristics of neck and upper extremity injuries such as soft tissue injuries, ruptured/herniated disc, fractures, dislocations, and tendinitis*

3.14.05.01.01   Discuss structural and functional deviations with members of the multidisciplinary assessment team

3.14.05.01.02   Describe the mechanical deviations of the various neuromuscular and orthopedic conditions, and their affect on movement and program considerations

3.14.05.01.03   Apply mechanical principles such as strength or cardiorespiratory endurance to solutions and/or modifications of movement problems

3.14.05.01.04   Utilize orthotics such as wheelchairs, canes, braces to improve functional movement for skill and physical fitness acquisition

3.14.05.01.05   Recognize adaptations and modifications of movement patterns via mechanical principles to ambulatory individuals to increase physical fitness and skill acquisition

3.14.05.01.06   Utilize basic mechanical principles such as low center of gravity, laws of levers, and motion, to minimize injury

3.14.05.01.07   Utilize proper transfer techniques

3.15   **Spine and Pelvis Movement: Demonstrate knowledge of the biomechanics of spine and pelvis movement**

3.15.01   Understand how anatomical structure affects movement capabilities of the spine

---

3.15.01.01   *Understand how deviations such as scoliosis, lordosis, anterior pelvic tilt, kyphosis, growth plate irregularities such as Scheurmann disease affect load-bearing and movement capabilities of the spine and pelvic girdle*

3.15.01.01.01   Assess movement capacity based on type and degree of deformity

3.15.01.01.02   Utilize treatment and indicated activities for the deviations of the spine and pelvic girdle such as scoliosis and lordosis

3.15.01.01.03   Assess movement capacity based on type and degree of condition, and prescribe activities, including adaptations and modifications based on evaluation

3.15.01.01.04   Incorporate prescribed orthotic devices into activities based on type and degree of condition

3.15
Spine and Pelvis Movement: Demonstrate knowledge of the biomechanics of spine and pelvis movement

3.15.02
Understand functions of the spine and pelvic girdle

3.15.02.01
Understand restrictions that can affect basic functions such as compression, flexion, extension, hyperextension, lateral flexion, and rotation of the spine and pelvic girdle for individuals with disabilities

3.15.02.01.01
Recognize that individuals with upper and lower level spinal paresis lose functional support, stability and mobility below level of lesion

3.15.02.01.02
Recognize that functional and skillful movement of the trunk, pelvis and lower extremity will be considerably diminished relative to type, degree and actual spinal level of lesion

3.15.02.01.03
Recognize limitations to functional maintenance of posture and consequent trunk and pelvic stability, balance and symmetry

3.15.02.01.04
Use flexibility training for the lower body

3.15
Spine and Pelvis Movement: Demonstrate knowledge of the biomechanics of spine and pelvis movement

3.15.03
Understand ways the spine and pelvic girdle are adapted to carry out functions such as vertical posture and ambulation

3.15.03.01
Understand vertebral structure in terms of size, disc, compression, shear forces and pelvic girdle structure in relationship to spinal and lower extremity movements for individuals with disabilities

3.15.03.01.01
Identify problems that can affect basic functions of the spine and pelvic girdle

3.15.03.01.02
Discuss contraindications which can lead to or exacerbate disc problems

3.15
Spine and Pelvis Movement: Demonstrate knowledge of the biomechanics of spine and pelvis movement

3.15.04
Understand the relationship between muscle location and the nature and the effectiveness of muscle action in the trunk

3.15.04.01
Understand actions of muscles of upper and lower extremities, spine and abdomen in trunk action for individuals with disabilities

3.15.04.01.01
Describe problems in action of upper and lower extremity muscles

3.15.04.01.02
Recognize that muscle size and strength are relative to the degree of spasticity and that contracture, flaccidity, paralysis, or general paresis will cause limitations in trunk movement

3.15.04.01.03
Conduct postural screening early to identify spinal curvatures to prevent further deformity

3.15
Spine and Pelvis Movement: Demonstrate knowledge of the biomechanics of spine and pelvis movement

3.15.05
Understand the biomechanical contributors to injuries of the spine

3.15.05.01
Understand causes and characteristics of spinal injuries such as soft tissue injuries, herniated disc and fractures

3.15.05.01.01   Describe treatment for spinal injuries such as soft tissue injuries, herniated disc and fractures

3.15.05.01.02   Describe contraindicated activities for spinal injuries such as soft tissue injuries, herniated disc and fractures

---

3.16   **Lower Extremity Movement: Demonstrate knowledge of the biomechanics of lower extremity movement**

3.16.01   Understand how anatomical structure affects the movement capabilities of lower extremity articulations

---

3.16.01.01   *Understand deviations in anatomical structure affect movement capabilities of the pelvis, hip joint, and ankle joint for individuals with disabilities*

3.16.01.01.01   Recognize that deviations such as coxa valga and coxa vara in anatomical structure affect the movement capabilities of the hip joint

3.16.01.01.02   Recognize that deviations in anatomical structure such as genu valgum, varum, and recurvatum affect the movement capabilities of the knee joint

3.16.01.01.03   Utilize strength and flexibility training for muscle contracture in hip and pelvic region

3.16.01.01.04   Institute flexibility training and compensatory strength and endurance training (upper extremity) for muscle flaccidity of hip and pelvic muscle attachments

3.16.01.01.05   Utilize strength and flexibility training for muscle contractures around the knee joint

3.16.01.01.06   Implement flexibility training (for flaccidity of muscles around knee) and compensatory strength and endurance training (for involved muscles)

3.16.01.01.07   Implement strength and flexibility training for muscle contracture around the ankle and foot

---

3.16   **Lower Extremity Movement: Demonstrate knowledge of the biomechanics of lower extremity movement**

3.16.02   Understand how the lower extremity is adapted to weight bearing functions

---

3.16.02.01   *Understand how deviations in alignment of the lower extremity can affect both lower and upper extremities for individuals with disabilities*

3.16.02.01.01   Describe stance and gait of individuals with coxa valga and vara

3.16.02.01.02   Describe stance and gait of individuals with genu valgum, varum and recurvatum

3.16.02.01.03   Describe stance and gait of individuals with foot pronation and supination

3.16.02.01.04   Utilize various methods of measurement and appraisal of postural deviation, such as plumb line, posture grids, and goniometers

3.16.02.01.05   Recognize structural and functional mechanics of various postural deviations and their implications for exercise and sport

3.16.02.01.06   Utilize assessment of gait (see Standard 8.0)

3.16.02.01.07   Accommodate structural and functional mechanics as they affect gait

3.16.02.01.08   Design programs, use equipment and modify activities for individuals with postural deviations

3.16.02.01.09   Utilize physical fitness activities in conjunction with therapists for functional postural deviations

3.16.02.01.10   Use orthotic devices for individuals with severe postural deformity

---

3.16

> ## *Lower Extremity Movement: Demonstrate knowledge of the biomechanics of lower extremity movement*
>
> **3.16.03**   Understand muscle groups that are active during specific lower extremity movements

3.16.03.01   *Understand how weight bearing stance and gait are affected when some muscle groups are too active for individuals with disabilities*

3.16.03.01.01   Describe muscle groups and possible stretching exercises for hip abnormalities such as coxa valga and vara

3.16.03.01.02   Describe muscle groups and possible stretching exercises for knee abnormalities such as genu valgum, varum, and recurvatum

3.16.03.01.03   Describe muscle groups and stretching exercises for ankle and foot abnormalities such as pronation and supination

3.16.03.01.04   Use orthotic devices for individuals with severe foot deformities

---

3.16

> ## *Lower Extremity Movement: Demonstrate knowledge of the biomechanics of lower extremity movement*
>
> **3.16.04**   Understand the biomechanical factors contributing to injuries of the lower extremity

3.16.04.01   *Understand causes and characteristics of lower extremity injuries such as soft tissue injuries, fractures, dislocations, and tendinitis for individuals with disabilities*

3.16.04.01.01   Describe treatment for lower extremity injuries such as soft tissue injuries, fractures, dislocations, and tendinitis

3.16.04.01.02   Describe contraindicated activities, including inappropriate footwear, for lower extremity injuries, such as soft tissue injuries, fractures, dislocations, and tendinitis

Standard 4 MEASUREMENT AND EVALUATION

4.01

> ### *Standardized Procedures: A set of conditions, equipment, and instructions to which data collection must conform in order for the data to be valid*
>
> 4.01.01   Knowledge of standardized instruments and procedures for use in determining current level of motor performance such as fitness tests, motor development profiles, motor skills tests, reflex and perceptual motor inventories as well as direct measures

4.01.01.01   *Understand instruments and procedures for measuring physical and motor fitness of individuals with disabilities*

4.01.01.01.01   Utilize standardized instruments and procedures for measuring and evaluating physical fitness such as AAHPERD Health Related Fitness Test, Prudential Fitnessgram, Project UNIQUE

4.01.01.01.02   Measure physical fitness using methods such as skin fold calipers for body composition and goniometers for range of motion with individuals with disabilities

4.01.01.02   *Understand instruments and procedures for measuring motor skills of individuals with disabilities*

4.01.01.02.01   Utilize standardized instruments or procedures for measuring and evaluating motor skill acquisition such as Ohio State University Scale of Intra-Gross Motor Assessement (SIGMA), Project ACTIVE, Test of Gross Motor Development (TGMD)

4.01.01.02.02   Measure the acquisition of motor skills among individuals with disabilities using curriculum based procedures such as I-CAN, Data-Based Gymnasium, and ABC

4.01.01.03   *Understand instruments and procedures for measuring motor development in individuals with disabilities*

4.01.01.03.01   Utilize instruments such as the Brigance Diagnostic Inventory of Early Development, Denver Developmental Screening Test, Peabody Developmental Motor Scales with individuals with disabilities

4.01.01.03.02   Measure motor development using direct measures such as reflex testing, results of caloric tests, or Apgar scores

4.01.01.04   *Understand the use of instruments and procedures that have implications for other aspects of motor performance such as motor components of language tests and perceptual motor tests*

4.01.01.04.01   Interpret the motor demands of standardized instruments measuring language and cognitive function

4.01.01.04.02   Observe procedures used by other professionals to evaluate movement including reflex testing, mobility, flexibility, sensory motor strengths & weaknesses, gross & fine motor skills, positioning/handling techniques, leisure skills, and postural analysis

4.01.01.04.03   Interpret the effects of culture on the motor demands made by motor performance instruments

4.01.01.05   *Knowledge of the use of instruments in determining eligibility for adapted physical education and individualized program planning*

4.01.01.05.01   Utilize measurement and evaluation procedures prescribed by the LEA

4.01.01.05.02   Ability to use specific standardized instruments or procedures for determining needs in related services such as checklists or observation techniques suggested by other professionals

4.01

4.01.02

> **Standardized Procedures: A set of conditions, equipment, and instructions to which data collection must conform in order for the data to be valid**
>
> Knowledge of how to locate and obtain standardized instruments and procedures for use

4.01.02.01   *Understand how to access resources for measuring motor performance of individuals with disabilities in the local educational agency*

4.01.02.01.01   Identify resource centers within the LEA where test instruments can be obtained

4.01.02.01.02   Locate a library that has Buros Mental Measurement Yearbook for use in identifying tests available

4.01.02.02   *Know other teachers/staff who could assist in locating resources*

4.01.02.02.01   Meet the resource specialists available in the LEA

4.01.02.02.02   Communicate with other adapted physical educators in the LEA regarding the availability of resources for measurement

4.01

4.01.03

> **Standardized Procedures: A set of conditions, equipment, and instructions to which data collection must conform in order for the data to be valid**
>
> Evaluate the quality of available standardized instruments

4.01.03.01   *Understand the test characteristics such as measures of central tendency and variability that describe the nature of the instrument/procedure as it pertains to individuals with disabilities*

4.01.03.01.01   Explain the difference between the mean and median on standardized instruments

4.01.03.01.02   Explain the standard deviation and what it means in the interpretation of test scores

4.01.03.02   *Familiarity with information sources for evaluating tests for individuals with disabilities*

4.01.03.02.01   Use information published on standardized instruments to make judgements on their use with individuals with disabilities

4.01.03.02.02   Describe test characteristics used in the selection of standardized instruments and procedures such as validity and reliability

4.01

4.01.04

> **Standardized Procedures: A set of conditions, equipment, and instructions to which data collection must conform in order for the data to be valid**
>
> Recognize potential limitations and problems related to the use of standardized instruments and procedures

4.01.04.01   *Understand the limitations of using standardized test instruments with different disabilities*

4.01.04.01.01   Determine appropriate tests for specific types of disabilities such as Project UNIQUE for individuals with physical and sensory impairments

4.01.04.01.02   Recognize when the use of standardized instruments is inappropriate for use with individuals with disabilities

4.01.04.02   *Understand the problems of using standardized instruments with individuals with different disabilities*

4.01.04.02.01   Modify standardized test instructions to accommodate language problems as needed

4.01.04.02.02   Select appropriate alternative test items as needed

---

4.01

Standardized Procedures: A set of conditions, equipment, and instructions to which data collection must conform in order for the data to be valid

4.01.05   Recognize the necessity to construct instruments and/or modify procedures to measure the current level of motor performance of individuals

---

4.01.05.01   *Understand the effect of modifying a standardized test on the reliability and validity of the test and test results*

4.01.05.01.01   Modify testing procedures and/or instruments to accommodate individuals with disabilities

4.01.05.01.02   Identify and utilize appropriate alternative test items for measuring parameters of interest

---

4.01

Standardized Procedures: A set of conditions, equipment, and instructions to which data collection must conform in order for the data to be valid

4.01.06   Understand the process of developing a teacher-made test

---

4.01.06.01   *Determine the basis for identifying and selecting performances to be measured that are appropriate to the needs, capacities and limitations of individuals with disabilities*

4.01.06.01.01   Select test items reflecting the major instructional areas identified in federal law

4.01.06.01.02   Select test items reflecting school, LEA or state curriculum guidelines

---

4.02

Types of Scores: The nature of scores which determines their use (e.g., interpretation, improvement, comparison with standards, achievement, manipulation)

4.02.01   Knowledge of continuous, discrete, dichotomous, interval, ordinal and nominal scores

---

4.02.01.01   *Knowledge of the types of scores generated by standardized instruments/procedures commonly used to measure individuals with disabilities*

4.02.01.01.01   Use dichotomous, ordinal and nominal scores when explaining student progress or class standing

4.02.01.01.02   Use continuous, discrete and interval scores when determining eligibility of special class placement

4.02.01.02   *Understand the use of various types of scores for use in determining current levels of performance of individuals with disabilities*

4.02.01.02.01   Explain the characteristics of the different types of scores for determining the current level of performance of individuals with disabilities

4.02.01.02.02   Utilize different types of scores for determining the current level of performance of individuals with disabilities

4.02.01.02.03   Compare the relative values of the different types of scores for determining the current level of performance of individuals with disabilities

4.02.01.02.04   Explain the limitations of the different types of scores for determining the current level of performance of individuals with disabilities

4.03   **Standard Scores: Scores on a scale that have been generated by transforming a set of raw scores to a common unit of measure using the mean and standard deviation**

4.03.01   Understand the concept of conversion from raw scores to standard scores such as T & z scores

4.03.01.01   *Recognize the use of standard scores in reporting current level of performance of individuals with disabilities*

4.03.01.01.01   Interpret T and z scores in terms of the mean of each scale on tests for individuals with disabilities

4.03.01.01.02   Interpret T and z scores in terms of the standard deviation of each scale on tests for individuals with disabilities

4.03   **Standard Scores: Scores on a scale that have been generated by transforming a set of raw scores to a common unit of measure using the mean and standard deviation**

4.03.02   Understand the value of standard scores in communicating test results

4.03.02.01   *Understand how to communicate test results to parents or guardians of individuals with disabilities and to other professionals*

4.03.02.01.01   Convert class raw scores on other performances to standard scores to enhance comparison and communication

4.03.02.01.02   Explain standard scores used in expressing motor performance to parents and guardians of individuals with disabilities and other professionals

4.03.02.02   *Understand how to communicate test results expressed in age equivalencies or motor quotients for individuals with disabilities*

4.03.02.02.01   Explain developmental motor quotient and age equivalent scores to parents and guardians of individuals with disabilities and other professionals

4.03.02.02.02   Correlate developmental motor quotients and age equivalent scores to standard scores or scores expressing position in a group such as percentile ranks

4.03   **Standard Scores: Scores on a scale that have been generated by transforming a set of raw scores to a common unit of measure using the mean and standard deviation**

4.03.03   Understand established standards for referring students for special services such as adapted physical education and related services

4.03.03.01   *Understand eligibility criteria for adapted physical education in terms of standard scores*

4.03.03.01.01   Explain eligibility criteria for adapted physical education

4.03.03.01.02   Determine eligibility for adapted physical education (see Standard 8.0)

4.04	**Indicators of the Relationship Between Performances: Relationships of measurements gathered on varied performances by one individual**
4.04.01	Understand how performance on one test or test item may relate to performance on another test or test item

4.04.01.01   *Recognize that relationships may exist among scores gathered on individuals with disabilities*

4.04.01.01.01   Draw conclusions on the present level of performance of individuals with disabilities using test scores expressed in different units of measure, standard score or position in a group

4.04.01.01.02   Draw conclusions on the present level of performance of individuals with disabilities utilizing scores made on one performance to explain scores made on another performance

4.05	**The Normal Curve: A symmetrical curve centered around a point that is the mean score; also called a bell-shaped curve**
4.05.01	Understand the concept of a normal distribution of scores

4.05.01.01   *Understand that students with disabilities will usually obtain scores at the low end of a normal distribution of scores*

4.05.01.01.01   Compare a raw score on a distribution of scores obtained on individuals without disabilities with a distribution of scores obtained on individuals with disabilities

4.05.01.01.02   Explain the relationship between percentile rank and the normal curve

4.05.01.02   *Recognize that tests normed on a general population usually exclude individuals with disabilities from their norming sample*

4.05.01.02.01   Qualify statements when reporting the performance of individuals with disabilities who are compared with norms on individuals without disabilities

4.05.01.02.02   Explain that scores compared with individuals without disabilities appear lower than when compared with individuals with disabilities

4.05	**The Normal Curve: A symmetrical curve centered around a point that is the mean score; also called a bell-shaped curve**
4.05.02	Understand that while many scores in a normal distribution cluster near the mean, some disperse away from the mean

4.05.02.01   *Understand the meaning of obtained test scores that range two or more standard deviations below the mean as related to individuals with disabilities*

4.05.02.01.01   Explain that scores two or more standard deviations below the mean are significantly outside the normal range

4.05.02.01.02   Prioritize needs of individuals with disabilities based on their deviation from the mean

4.05.02.02   *Understand that a normal distribution is not always obtained unless a large number of scores are plotted including high scores obtained by individuals who are gifted as well as low scores obtained by individuals with disabilities*

4.05.02.02.01	Interpret the distribution of scores obtained in a single class in terms of heterogeneity of performance
4.05.02.02.02	Interpret the distribution of scores obtained in a single class in terms of homogeneity of performance

4.06	**Descriptive Values: Results of score analysis that bring meaning to a set of scores**
4.06.01	Understand the concepts involved in measures of central tendency such as the influence of extreme scores, use of mean and median, small number of scores

4.06.01.01	*Understand when to use the median as a reference for comparing a raw score with group performance of individuals with disabilities*
4.06.01.01.01	Explain a student's score relative to the median when a few scores skew the distribution of a single class
4.06.01.01.02	Explain how the number of scores affects the differential between the median and the mean
4.06.01.02	*Understand when to use the mean as a reference for comparing a raw score with group performance of individuals with disabilities*
4.06.01.02.01	Explain a student's score relative to the mean when a few scores skew the distribution of a single class
4.06.01.02.02	Explain how the number of scores affects the differential between the mean and the median

4.06	**Descriptive Values: Results of score analysis that bring meaning to a set of scores**
4.06.02	Understand the concepts involved in measures of variability such as the reflection of the homogeneity or heterogeneity of a group of scores

4.06.02.01	*Understand when to use standard deviation for comparing a raw score with group performance of individuals with disabilities*
4.06.02.01.01	Explain a student's score in terms of standard deviations
4.06.02.01.02	Explain how the number of scores affects the standard deviation of a set of scores from a single class
4.06.02.02	*Understand when to use variance for comparing a raw score with group performance of individuals with disabilities*
4.06.02.02.01	Explain the variance of a set of scores when reporting the median
4.06.02.02.02	Determine the variance of a set of scores for use in determining eligibility for special services
4.06.02.03	*Understand the use of measures of central tendency and variability to gain a perspective of obtained scores for individuals with disabilities*
4.06.02.03.01	Explain a student's score relative to the mean and standard deviation of a set of scores
4.06.02.03.02	Explain a student's score relative to the mean and standard deviation of a standardized instrument

4.07	***Measures of Position: A score that has a specified proportion of the population below it in a distribution thereby defining its position in the distribution***
4.07.01	Understand the concept of conversion from raw scores to measures of group position such as percentile ranks, quartiles, and stanines

4.07.01.01	*Recognize the use of percentiles, quartiles, or stanines when reporting current level of performance of individuals with disabilities*
4.07.01.01.01	Express student's scores in terms of percentiles and explain their meaning to parents
4.07.01.01.02	Express student's scores in terms of quartiles and explain their meaning to parents
4.07.01.01.03	Express student's scores in terms of stanines and explain their meaning to parents

4.07	***Measures of Position: A score that has a specified proportion of the population below it in a distribution thereby defining its position in the distribution***
4.07.02	Recognize the relative value of percentiles, percentile ranks, quartiles and stanines for communicating test results

4.07.02.01	*Understand how measures of position compare the raw score of an individual with a disability with its position in a larger distribution*
4.07.02.01.01	Explain the position of a student's raw score that converts to a given percentile
4.07.02.01.02	Explain the position of a student's raw score that converts to a given quartile
4.07.02.01.03	Explain the position of a student's raw score that converts to a given stanine
4.07.02.02	*Recognize that percentiles and quartiles work from a base of ten and therefore may be easier to interpret to parents of individuals with disabilities*
4.07.02.02.01	Explain to parents that the percentile or quartile reflects the point below which that percentage of others who took the test have scored
4.07.02.02.02	Explain to parents of individuals with disabilities that a percentile or quartile score is not the percentage correct on the test

4.08	***Test Characteristics: The qualities about a test such as reliability, validity & objectivity that make it functional for a given purpose such as placement, diagnosis, evaluation of achievement, prediction, program evaluation or motivation***
4.08.01	Understand the relationship between the purpose for testing and characteristics of the test

4.08.01.01	*Understand the desirable characteristics of tests used for screening individuals with disabilities*
4.08.01.01.01	Explain the administrative feasibility of a selected screening device
4.08.01.01.02	Explain the economy of a screening instrument for individuals with disabilities
4.08.01.02	*Understand the desirable characteristics of tests used for placement decisions for individuals with disabilities*

4.08.01.02.01   Describe the discrimination ability of tests used for placement

4.08.01.02.02   Explain how norm-referenced standards assist with placement decisions

4.08.01.03   *Understand the desirable characteristics of tests used for developing individualized educational, family or transitional plans for individuals with disabilities*

4.08.01.03.01   Explain the value of test validity

4.08.01.03.02   Utilize norm-referenced standards for establishing performance criteria when writing goals for individualized education programs

4.08

> **Test Characteristics: The qualities about a test such as reliability, validity & objectivity that make it functional for a given purpose such as placement, diagnosis, evaluation of achievement, prediction, program evaluation or motivation**
>
> 4.08.02   Understand the most important characteristics of motor performance tests such as reliability, validity, objectivity and utility

4.08.02.01   *Understand standard error of measurement and its common sources especially with individuals with disabilities*

4.08.02.01.01   Understand standard error of measurement and how it affects the reliability and validity of a test score

4.08.02.01.02   Understand what standard error of measurement means relative to a single test score

4.08.02.02   *Understand the multicultural and linguistic issues affecting the valid and reliable measurement of motor performance among individuals with disabilities*

4.08.02.02.01   Encourage dress codes that maximize motor performance while being sensitive to cultural practices of dress

4.08.02.02.02   Limit the amount of competition during measurement of individuals with disabilities whose cultural mores preclude competition

4.08.02.03   *Understand additional desirable characteristics of tests used in adapted physical education (e.g., administrative feasibility, economy of time, order effect, utility, etc.)*

4.08.02.03.01   Recognize the characteristics of various disabilities that can adversely affect the reliability (test-retest) of assessment results

4.08.02.03.02   Recognize the characteristics of various disabilities that can adversely affect the content, concurrent and face validity of an assessment instrument

4.08.02.03.03   Recognize the attributes of various disabilities that can adversely affect the objectivity (inter-rater reliability) of the test results

4.08.02.03.04   Evaluate a measurement instrument or procedure for its appropriateness for individuals with disabilities

4.08	***Test Characteristics: The qualities about a test such as reliability, validity & objectivity that make it functional for a given purpose such as placement, diagnosis, evaluation of achievement, prediction, program evaluation or motivation***
4.08.03	Select appropriate test instruments and procedures based on intended purpose, test characteristics, attributes and characteristics of the population to be tested

4.08.03.01   *Understand that instruments selected must be validated for use with individuals having disabilities recognized by federal law (IDEA)*

4.08.03.01.01   Determine the cost, ease of administration, training time and type of scores of selected tests

4.08.03.01.02   Assure that selected instruments meet all mandated criteria for individuals with disabilities

4.08.03.02   *Understand measurement terminology such as reliability, validity, administrative feasibility and objectivity when selecting measurement instruments for testing individuals with disabilities*

4.08.03.02.01   Select administratively feasible tests for placement, reporting progress and measuring achievement of individuals with disabilities

4.08.03.02.02   Select instruments that are objective, reliable, and valid for various purposes

4.09	***Pretest Planning: All of the preparation that occurs before test administration***
4.09.01	Understand the purposes for testing in physical education

4.09.01.01   *Understand the difference between screening, diagnostic testing, assessment and evaluation relative to individuals with disabilities*

4.09.01.01.01   Coordinate the testing of motor performance from screening to program evaluation

4.09.01.01.02   Establish criteria for screening that can be implemented consistently

4.09.01.02   *Recognize the unique roles of instructional assessment, diagnostic testing and monitoring progress in programs for individuals with disabilities*

4.09.01.02.01   Describe the purposes for testing to parents at each stage of the assessment process

4.09.01.02.02   Explain the purpose of different types of instruments used at each stage of the assessment process

4.09	***Pretest Planning: All of the preparation that occurs before test administration***
4.09.02	Understand what planning must be done prior to testing

4.09.02.01   *Understand the importance of planning a testing program for individuals with disabilities*

4.09.02.01.01   Establish a plan for testing individuals with disabilities on a regular basis

4.09.02.01.02   Select appropriate times, facilities, and instruments or procedures for testing a variety of individuals with disabilities

4.09.02.01.03   Identify and utilize appropriate communication techniques required by some individuals with disabilities

4.09.02.02 *Understand what equipment is needed for administering the selected instruments or procedures to individuals with disabilities*

4.09.02.02.01 Obtain equipment necessary for testing apart from the test itself

4.09.02.02.02 Maintain consistency in testing conditions such as same equipment, facility, and instructions

---

4.10 **Standards: Levels of achievement that reflect a desirable level of performance based on health or other movement-related benefits**

4.10.01 Compare and contrast norm-referenced, criterion-referenced and content-referenced standards

---

4.10.01.01 *Understand that content-referenced standards have criteria embedded in a domain, community program or curriculum for individuals with disabilities*

4.10.01.01.01 Utilize content-referenced, domain-referenced, community-based and curriculum-based instruments such as I-CAN, ABC or Data-Based Gymnasium

4.10.01.01.02 Utilize content-referenced, domain-referenced, community-based and curriculum-based instruments for specific disabilities

4.10.01.02 *Understand the relative value of norm-referenced, content-referenced and criterion-referenced instruments for testing individuals with disabilities*

4.10.01.02.01 Utilize norm-referenced standards in making placement decisions

4.10.01.02.02 Utilize content-referenced standards in planning IEPs

4.10.01.02.03 Utilize criterion-referenced standards in establishing annual goals

---

4.10 **Standards: Levels of achievement that reflect a desirable level of performance based on health or other movement-related benefits**

4.10.02 Demonstrate an understanding of the construction of norm-referenced and criterion-referenced instruments

---

4.10.02.01 *Understand the differences between norm-referenced and criterion-referenced standards for individuals with disabilities*

4.10.02.01.01 Explain the comparison of individuals with a given population when using norm-referenced standards

4.10.02.01.02 Explain the comparison of a performance with a target performance when using criterion-referenced standards

4.10.02.02 *Understand the similarities between norm-referenced and criterion-referenced standards for individuals with disabilities*

4.10.02.02.01 Describe the segment of the population on whom the criterion-referenced standards are based in terms of percentage

4.10.02.02.02 Utilize criterion-referenced tests when clear criteria can be set

4.11

> **_Data Gathering: The process of gathering information on students for the purpose of assessment; may take the form of formal or informal testing, objective or subjective testing and may use criterion-, content- or norm-referenced standards_**
>
> 4.11.01   Ability to utilize informal procedures such as checklists, task analysis, curriculum-embedded measures and behavioral observation (see Standards 10.03.02 and 12.0)

4.11.01.01   *Understand the use of unobtrusive measures such as rating scales, case studies and anecdotal records with individuals with disabilities*

4.11.01.01.01   Maintain anecdotal records related to students' IEPs

4.11.01.01.02   Observe student's motor behavior during unstructured and unplanned play

4.11.01.02   *Understand the use of systematic observational techniques such as academic learning time (ALT) and opportunity to respond (OTR) for individuals with disabilities*

4.11.01.02.01   Utilize event recording techniques to observe behavior

4.11.01.02.02   Utilize duration recording techniques to observe behavior

4.11.01.02.03   Utilize interval recording techniques to observe behavior

4.11.01.03   *Understand the use of student reports in the process of gathering data on individuals with disabilities*

4.11.01.03.01   Utilize student self-report evaluation when appropriate

4.11.01.03.02   Utilize peer evaluation when appropriate

4.11

> **_Data Gathering: The process of gathering information on students for the purpose of assessment; may take the form of formal or informal testing, objective or subjective testing and may use criterion-, content- or norm-referenced standards_**
>
> 4.11.02   Understand various protocols used in administration of tests such as performance testing, direct measures, formal standardized procedures, informal unstructured activity, etc.

4.11.02.01   *Understand various testing protocols, forms of data gathering, environmental settings and organizational structures used in physical education and the effects of these on performance of individuals with disabilities*

4.11.02.01.01   Describe various testing protocols for measuring motor development, physical fitness, motor skill acquisition and sensory motor function

4.11.02.01.02   Describe various forms of data gathering for individuals with disabilities such as parent report, standardized testing, self-report, observation, task analysis and direct measures

4.11.02.02   *Understand the difference between coaching and encouraging a student while administering a test to individuals with disabilities*

4.11.02.02.01   Determine the amount of time needed to administer selected tests

4.11.02.02.02   Understand the effect of knowledge of results on the performance of individuals with disabilities

4.11.02.03	*Understand the effects of medication on attention, coordination and responsiveness when administering tests to individuals with disabilities*
4.11.02.03.01	Note the presence of psychotropic drugs in individuals with disabilities during testing
4.11.02.03.02	Observe the motor behavior of students taking medication at various times during the day
4.11.02.04	*Recognize the value of establishing rapport with individuals with disabilities prior to testing*
4.11.02.04.01	Demonstrate the ability to establish rapport with individuals with disabilities
4.11.02.04.02	Validate the comfort level of individuals with disabilities with the examiner by observing their interaction with other teachers

4.11	**Data Gathering: The process of gathering information on students for the purpose of assessment; may take the form of formal or informal testing, objective or subjective testing and may use criterion-, content- or norm-referenced standards**
4.11.03	Understand the basic principles of subjective data gathering in contrast to objective testing protocols

4.11.03.01	*Understand the essential functional motor performances (gross and fine) marking significant motor milestones throughout the lifespan (infancy-adult)*
4.11.03.01.01	Make further adaptations of test items to accommodate limited motor development as needed
4.11.03.01.02	Observe infants engaged in motor activity and report observations
4.11.03.02	*Understand the biomechanical elements expected in fundamental motor patterns and skills for individuals without disabilities before testing individuals with disabilities*
4.11.03.02.01	Describe when biomechanical elements of movement are absent, substituted or changed by individuals with disabilities
4.11.03.02.02	Explain the differences between observed biomechanical elements of movement and expected biomechanical elements
4.11.03.03	*Understand data gathering through curriculum-embedded features of movement for individuals with disabilities*
4.11.03.03.01	Explain the curricular elements (features) describing the student's current level of performance
4.11.03.03.02	Select curricular activities based on current level of performance
4.11.03.04	*Understand the value of conducting play-based assessment with individuals with disabilities*
4.11.03.04.01	Create a play-based environment for observing play behaviors and motor performances of individuals with disabilities
4.11.03.04.02	Utilize a variety of environments or settings in which to observe play behaviors and motor performances of individuals with disabilities
4.11.03.04.03	Gather data from the significant other interview regarding play behaviors, individual and/or family preferences and practices relative to physical activity
4.11.03.04.04	Gather data from the multidisciplinary team members regarding play behaviors, individual and/or family preferences and practices relative to physical activity
4.11.03.04.05	Obtain measurements through video recording

4.11.03.04.06	Obtain measurements using ecological inventories
4.11.03.05	*Understand the value of a task analysis of motor skills for gathering data on individuals with disabilities*
4.11.03.05.01	Utilize task analysis to develop criterion-referenced tests for measuring instructional content
4.11.03.05.02	Utilize task analysis for defining instructional sequences
4.11.03.06	*Understand how to gather data through review of written reports and medical records of individuals with disabilities*
4.11.03.06.01	Read written reports from other professionals and correlate with findings in motor performance testing
4.11.03.06.02	Read medical records and correlate with findings in motor performance testing

4.11	**Data Gathering: The process of gathering information on students for the purpose of assessment; may take the form of formal or informal testing, objective or subjective testing and may use criterion-, content- or norm-referenced standards**
4.11.04	Understand direct measures for gathering data other than through motor performance such as dynamometry, telemetry, and goniometry

4.11.04.01	*Recognize the need to use direct measures instead of performance measures of individuals with disabilities*
4.11.04.01.01	Utilize skin fold calipers for measuring body composition of individuals with disabilities
4.11.04.01.02	Utilize dynamometry for measuring strength of individuals with disabilities
4.11.04.01.03	Utilize goniometry for measuring range of motion among individuals with disabilities

4.11	**Data Gathering: The process of gathering information on students for the purpose of assessment; may take the form of formal or informal testing, objective or subjective testing and may use criterion-, content- or norm-referenced standards**
4.11.05	Understand the use of screening methods

4.11.05.01	*Appreciate the legislative restrictions on the use of screening individuals with disabilities*
4.11.05.01.01	Utilize screening methods as an informal procedure to gather initial data on individuals with disabilities
4.11.05.01.02	Limit screening to the requirements of legislation and the guidelines of the local educational agency
4.11.05.02	*Understand how screening methods can be used as an informal procedure to validate other data on individuals with disabilities or when other procedures are untenable*
4.11.05.02.01	Utilize a checklist of behaviors that validates formally obtained data
4.11.05.02.02	Write a descriptive narrative of the motor behaviors of individuals considered untestable

4.11

> **Data Gathering: The process of gathering information on students for the purpose of assessment; may take the form of formal or informal testing, objective or subjective testing and may use criterion-, content- or norm-referenced standards**

4.11.06   Understand the advantages of individual vs. mass organizational testing of classes such as reliability and validity of scores, consistency of motivation, precision of performance

4.11.06.01   *Recognize the types of testing environments appropriate to the characteristics of individuals with disabilities*

4.11.06.01.01   Arrange the testing environment appropriate to the characteristics of individuals with disabilities

4.11.06.01.02   Provide a distraction-free testing environment for individuals with attention disorders

4.11.06.02   *Understand the effects of mass vs. individual testing on individuals with specific disabilities*

4.11.06.02.01   Determine when individual testing is appropriate based on individual's characteristics

4.11.06.02.02   Provide opportunities for practice trials in a mass testing environment when appropriate

4.11.06.03   *Understand the limitations of individual vs. mass organizational testing of classes of individuals with disabilities*

4.11.06.03.01   Describe the competencies needed by students in a mass testing environment

4.11.06.03.02   Verify the validity of test results obtained in an individual vs. mass testing environment

4.12

> **Performance Sampling: The practice of measuring representative factors of motor performance as a means of obtaining an overview of an individual's true ability**

4.12.01   Understand the concept of performance sampling using objective and subjective testing

4.12.01.01   *Understand the use of performance sampling in determining a student's eligibility for adapted physical education*

4.12.01.01.01   Identify motor parameters to be sampled when considering eligibility for adapted physical education

4.12.01.01.02   Determine an efficient and effective sampling procedure for adapted physical education

4.12.01.02   *Understand the use of baseline data collection of individuals with disabilities*

4.12.01.02.01   Utilize multiple trials to establish baseline performance

4.12.01.02.02   Pre-establish baseline performance at each annual review

4.12.01.02.03   Utilize baseline data to write annual goals and objectives

4.12.01.03   *Understand the concept of performance generalization across contexts for individuals with disabilities*

4.12.01.03.01   Provide opportunities for motor performance of a given skill in a variety of contexts

4.12.01.03.02   Utilize the student's ability to generalize to community-based activities

5.01 **Trends in Education: Knowledge of trends in education of individuals with disabilities**

5.01.01 Understand evolution of educational reform in relation to individuals with disabilities

5.01.01.01 *Understand era of no education and no treatment of individuals with disabilities*

5.01.01.01.01 Explain persecution of individuals with disabilities in society before the 1800's

5.01.01.01.02 Explain neglect of individuals with disabilities in regard to education prior to the 1800's

5.01.01.02 *Understand segregated educational placements for individuals with disabilities*

5.01.01.02.01 Explain strengths of segregated educational placements

5.01.01.02.02 Explain weaknesses of segregated educational placements

5.01.01.03 *Understand least restrictive environment*

5.01.01.03.01 Discuss continuum of placement alternatives

5.01.01.03.02 Identify the characteristics of each placement as it relates to individual needs

5.01.01.04 *Understand Regular Education Initiative/Total Inclusion*

5.01.01.04.01 Explain Regular Education Initiative/Total Inclusion from a "pro" standpoint

5.01.01.04.02 Explain Regular Education Initiative/Total Inclusion from a "con" standpoint

5.01 **Trends in Education: Knowledge of trends in education of individuals with disabilities**

5.01.02 Understand evolution of physical education for individuals with disabilities

5.01.02.01 *Understand trend of physical education in separate schools and classes*

5.01.02.01.01 Explain the "pros" of separate physical education

5.01.02.01.02 Explain the "cons" of separate physical education

5.01.02.02 *Understand trend of least restrictive environment for individuals with disabilities in the physical education setting*

5.01.02.02.01 Explain least restrictive environment

5.01.02.02.02 Explain continuum of placement alternatives in relation to least restrictive environment in physical education

5.01 **Trends in Education: Knowledge of trends in education of individuals with disabilities**

5.01.03 Understand evolution of multidisciplinary concepts in education

5.01.03.01 *Understand multidisciplinary approach with regard to adapted physical education (see Standard 15.04.01.01)*

5.01.03.01.01	Explain role of the adapted physical educator in the multidisciplinary team
5.01.03.01.02	Explain cooperation of the adapted physical educator within the multidisciplinary team
5.01.03.02	*Understand interdisciplinary approach with regard to adapted physical education*
5.01.03.02.01	Explain role of the adapted physical educator in the interdisciplinary team
5.01.03.02.02	Explain cooperation of the adapted physical educator within the interdisciplinary team
5.01.03.03	*Understand crossdisciplinary/transdisciplinary approach with regard to adapted physical education*
5.01.03.03.01	Explain role of the adapted physical educator in the crossdisciplinary/transdisciplinary team
5.01.03.03.02	Explain cooperation of the adapted physical educator within the crossdisciplinary/transdisciplinary team
5.01.03.03.03	Contrast multidisciplinary, interdisciplinary, and crossdisciplinary/transdisciplinary

5.01	**Trends in Education: Knowledge of trends in education of individuals with disabilities**
5.01.04	Understand evolution of funding education for individuals with disabilities

5.01.04.01	*Understand funding terminology with relation to individuals with disabilities legislation*
5.01.04.01.01	Explain authorization of funds with relation to legislation about individuals with disabilities
5.01.04.01.02	Explain appropriation of funds with relation to legislation about individuals with disabilities
5.01.04.01.03	Explain discretionary funds with relation to legislation about individuals with disabilities

5.02	**Law: Knowledge of Public Law 93-112 (The Rehabilitation Act of 1973)**
5.02.01	Understand major components of this law in relation to education and physical activity

5.02.01.01	*Understand nondiscrimination clause (Section 504)*
5.02.01.01.01	Advocate for qualified students with disabilities to participate in interscholastic athletics and extraclass activities
5.02.01.01.02	Advocate for activities to be conducted in architecturally accessible structures
5.02.01.01.03	Advocate for program accessibility

5.03	**Law: Knowledge of Public Law 94-142 (The Education for All Handicapped Children Act of 1975)**
5.03.01	Understand major components in relation to education and physical activity

5.03.01.01	*Understand free, appropriate education in the least restrictive environment for individuals with disabilities*
5.03.01.01.01	Explain individualized education program (IEP)
5.03.01.01.02	Explain least restrictive environment

5.03.01.02	*Understand direct services with regard to Education for All Handicapped Children Act*
5.03.01.02.01	Explain the legal definition of special education
5.03.01.02.02	Explain the legal definition of physical education
5.03.01.03	*Understand related services for individuals with disabilities*
5.03.01.03.01	Suggest related services, such as physical and occupational therapy, when needed to succeed in physical education
5.03.01.03.02	Explain the scope and content of related services
5.03.01.04	*Understand categories of disabilities listed in the law*
5.03.01.04.01	List examples of who is qualified by law to receive adapted physical education based on federal qualifications
5.03.01.04.02	Explain definition of disabilities
5.03.01.05	*Understand parental involvement in the education of all children with disabilities*
5.03.01.05.01	Discuss parent and guardian role in the IEP process
5.03.01.05.02	Discuss parent and guardian input in the adapted physical education process
5.03.01.05.03	Explain due process in relation to parent and guardian involvement

5.04	**Law: Knowledge of Public Law 95-606 (The Amateur Sports Act of 1978)**
5.04.01	Understand major components in relation to physical activity

5.04.01.01	*Understand clause describing the inclusion of athletes with disabilities*
5.04.01.01.01	Advocate for individuals with disabilities in integrated and segregated sports programs
5.04.01.01.02	Read current literature related to the committee on disability sport

5.05	**Law: Knowledge of Public Law 99-457 (1986 Revision to Education for All Handicapped Children Act)**
5.05.01	Understand implications for education and physical activity

5.05.01.01	*Understand change in age for services for individuals with disabilities*
5.05.01.01.01	Advocate for infant and toddler motor activities
5.05.01.01.02	Explain state age requirements
5.05.01.02	*Understand individual family service plan in relation to families and children with disabilities (see Standard 9.03.02)*
5.05.01.02.01	Explain components of individualized family service plan such as family needs and resources
5.05.01.02.02	Explain how physical activities fit into the individualized family service plan
5.05.01.03	*Understand what types of individuals with disabilities are served by PL 99-457*
5.05.01.03.01	Explain developmentally delayed

5.05.01.03.02	Explain at risk for developmental delay
5.05.01.03.03	Explain identified disabilities

5.06	**Law: Knowledge of Public Law 101-336 (Americans with Disabilities Act of 1990)**
5.06.01	Understand implications for physical activity

5.06.01.01	*Understand public accommodation and access*
5.06.01.01.01	Advocate for physical activity sites to become accessible
5.06.01.01.02	Describe program accommodation

5.07	**Law: Knowledge of Public Law 101-476 of 1990 (Individuals with Disabilities Education Act)**
5.07.01	Understand implications for education and physical activity

5.07.01.01	*Understand age change for individuals with disabilities*
5.07.01.01.01	Advocate for physical activities for individuals birth through 21
5.07.01.01.02	Advocate for community resources for physical activities for infants, toddlers, and their parents and guardians
5.07.01.02	*Understand transition services*
5.07.01.02.01	Describe adapted physical educator's role in the transition from home to school
5.07.01.02.02	Describe adapted physical educator's role in transition from school to vocation and community
5.07.01.03	*Understand addition of disability categories*
5.07.01.03.01	Explain autism as a separate category
5.07.01.03.02	Explain traumatic brain injury as a separate category

5.08	**History: Knowledge of history of physical education for individuals with disabilities**
5.08.01	Understand medical model

5.08.01.01	*Understand medical gymnastics and its early role in the adapted physical education movement*
5.08.01.01.01	Identify individuals associated with the medical gymnastics movement
5.08.01.01.02	Explain components of medical gymnastics that have had an impact on current adapted physical activity practices such as individually prescribed exercises

5.08	**History: Knowledge of history of physical education for individuals with disabilities**
5.08.02	Understand corrective/remedial physical education

5.08.02.01	*Understand corrective/remedial physical education and its impact on early adapted physical education*

| 5.08.02.01.01 | Explain components of corrective/remedial physical education such as orthopedic and structural remediation that have had an impact on current practices in adapted physical education |
| 5.08.02.01.02 | Identify individuals associated with corrective/remedial physical education |

| 5.08 | **History: Knowledge of history of physical education for individuals with disabilities** |
| 5.08.03 | Understand movement from adapted physical education as a separate service to the broader concept of continuum of service delivery in the mainstream |

5.08.03.01	*Understand adapted physical education as a program*
5.08.03.01.01	Identify components of adapted physical education as a program such as assessment, placement, evaluation
5.08.03.01.02	Explain the adapted physical education process
5.08.03.02	*Understand adapted physical education as a continuum of service delivery system*
5.08.03.02.01	Explain continuum of placements in adapted physical education
5.08.03.02.02	Advocate for most appropriate placement

| 5.09 | **Philosophy: Knowledge of philosophy of physical education, recreation, sport** |
| 5.09.01 | Understand the role of physical education in the curriculum |

5.09.01.01	*Understand how physical education contributes to the total development of individuals with disabilities*
5.09.01.01.01	Advocate for physical education in the total curriculum of individuals with disabilities
5.09.01.01.02	Advocate for physical education in the IEP and the IFSP (see Standard 9.03)

| 5.09 | **Philosophy: Knowledge of philosophy of physical education, recreation, sport** |
| 5.09.02 | Understand the philosophy of physical education as education "of the physical" |

5.09.02.01	*Understand the importance of physical and motor fitness such as flexibility, agility, and strength as it relates to individuals with disabilities*
5.09.02.01.01	Explain the importance of physical fitness in the life of an individual with disabilities
5.09.02.01.02	Explain the importance of motor skills in the life of an individual with disabilities

| 5.09 | **Philosophy: Knowledge of philosophy of physical education, recreation, sport** |
| 5.09.03 | Understand the philosophy of physical education as education "through the physical" |

| 5.09.03.01 | *Understand physical, cognitive, and affective outcomes in adapted physical education* |
| 5.09.03.01.01 | Explain physical outcomes of physical education with individuals who have a disability to allied educators and parents and guardians |

5.09.03.01.02   Explain cognitive outcomes of physical education with individuals who have a disability to allied educators and parents and guardians

5.09.03.01.03   Explain affective outcomes of physical education with individuals who have a disability to allied educators and parents and guardians

5.09 5.09.04	*Philosophy: Knowledge of philosophy of physical education, recreation, sport* Understand the role of sport in the total curriculum

5.09.04.01   *Understand sport opportunities for individuals with disabilities*

5.09.04.01.01   Advocate for adapted (segregated) sport opportunities within the physical education curriculum

5.09.04.01.02   Advocate for inclusive sport opportunities within the physical education curriculum

5.09 5.09.05	*Philosophy: Knowledge of philosophy of physical education, recreation, sport* Understand the role of recreation in the life of an individual with a disability

5.09.05.01   *Understand physical recreation opportunities for individuals with disabilities (see Standard 15.03.03)*

5.09.05.01.01   Advocate for physical recreation activities within the physical education curriculum

5.09.05.01.02   Advocate for appropriate physical recreation activities in transition planning

5.09.05.02   *Understand therapeutic recreation and relationship to adapted physical education*

5.09.05.02.01   Explain leisure counseling and its application to adapted physical education

5.09.05.02.02   Explain therapeutic recreation as a related service

5.10 5.10.01	*Philosophy: Knowledge of philosophy of special education* Understand multidisciplinary functioning

5.10.01.01   *Understand coordination of resources for individuals with disabilities*

5.10.01.01.01   Utilize philosophy that supports cooperation

5.10.01.01.02   Share resources to optimize educational goals

5.10.01.01.03   Create partnerships to maximize the use of resources for individuals with disabilities

5.10 5.10.02	*Philosophy: Knowledge of philosophy of special education* Understand philosophy of transition process

5.10.02.01   *Understand transition services*

5.10.02.01.01   Explain adapted physical educator's role in the transition process

5.10.02.01.02   Advocate for adapted physical educator's role in the transition process

5.10	**_Philosophy: Knowledge of philosophy of special education_**
5.10.03	Understand least restrictive environment from a philosophical standpoint

5.10.03.01   *Understand least restrictive and most restrictive environments in physical education for individuals with disabilities*

5.10.03.01.01   Explain the least restrictive environment for an individual with a disability

5.10.03.01.02   Advocate for a variety of placements in physical education for individuals with disabilities

5.10.03.01.03   Advocate for a variety of support in the regular physical education setting

5.10	**_Philosophy: Knowledge of philosophy of special education_**
5.10.04	Understand inclusion from a philosophical standpoint

5.10.04.01   *Understand inclusion as it relates to physical education for individuals with disabilities*

5.10.04.01.01   Explain criteria for exclusion from regular physical education

5.10.04.01.02   Explain split placement (part regular physical education/part adapted physical education)

5.10	**_Philosophy: Knowledge of philosophy of special education_**
5.10.05	Understand rationale for educating children birth to three years old

5.10.05.01   *Understand rationale for providing physical activity to young children with disabilities*

5.10.05.01.01   Advocate for physical activity for young children with disabilities

5.10.05.01.02   Advocate for an adapted physical education specialist to consult and assist in providing physical activity for young children with disabilities

Standard 6 — UNIQUE ATTRIBUTES OF LEARNERS: CONSIDERATIONS FOR PROFESSIONAL PRACTICE

6.01	***Mental Retardation: Understand unique attributes of individuals with mental retardation***
6.01.01	Understand motor attributes such as low levels of health related physical fitness and motor ability

6.01.01.01 *Describe problems achieving health related physical fitness such as medical conditions*

6.01.01.01.01   Establish appropriate expectations and goals

6.01.01.01.02   Adapt fitness activities to individuals with low motor skills

6.01.01.01.03   Adapt physical activities to medical limitations

6.01.01.02 *Awareness of trends in motor skills such as difficulty acquiring locomotor and object control skills*

6.01.01.02.01   Repeat fundamental motor skills and patterns in a variety of activities

6.01.01.02.02   Incorporate individual into regular physical education with developmentally appropriate peers

6.01.01.02.03   Modify activities only as needed to allow for maximum participation

6.01.01.02.04   Adapt activities for individuals with specific motor deficits such as poor fine motor skills and balance

6.01	***Mental Retardation: Understand unique attributes of individuals with mental retardation***
6.01.02	Understand cognitive attributes such as low cognitive ability

6.01.02.01 *Recognize various levels of cognitive ability*

6.01.02.01.01   Adapt activities for individuals with mild level of mental retardation

6.01.02.01.02   Adapt activities for individuals with severe level of mental retardation

6.01.02.02 *Understand the implications of low cognitive ability to the understanding of directions*

6.01.02.02.01   Use various modalities for instruction

6.01.02.02.02   Use continuum of prompts and cues

6.01.02.02.03   Use alternate methods of communication (see Standard 9.04.02)

6.01.02.02.04   Adapt directions to appropriate mental age/ability

6.01.02.02.05   Task analyze motor skills

6.01.02.03 *Understand the implications of low cognitive ability for motivation*

6.01.02.03.01   Motivate with age appropriate, relevant reinforcers

6.01.02.03.02   Make purpose of activity known

6.01.02.03.03   Help set realistic goals

6.01.02.03.04	Provide ongoing, immediate feedback
6.01.02.04	*Understand the implications of low cognitive ability on attention span*
6.01.02.04.01	Plan multitude of activities
6.01.02.04.02	Repeat directions
6.01.02.04.03	Structure environment for maximal attention
6.01.02.04.04	Provide reinforcement for staying on task
6.01.02.04.05	Utilize other teachers and paraprofessionals to provide low student to teacher ratio (see Standard 10.01.02.02 and Standard 9.02)
6.01.02.05	*Understand implications of low cognitive ability on social behavior such as poor group cooperation or behavioral outbursts*
6.01.02.05.01	Identify inappropriate social behavior
6.01.02.05.02	Identify antecedent to poor social behavior
6.01.02.05.03	Use behavior management techniques (See Standard 10.03)
6.01.02.05.04	Collaborate with psychologist and/or behavior specialist

6.01	**Mental Retardation: Understand unique attributes of individuals with mental retardation**
6.01.03	Understand health and medical attributes of individuals with mental retardation such as secondary or multiple disabilities

6.01.03.01	*Recognize incidence of atlantoaxial instability syndrome (AAIS) among individuals with Down's syndrome*
6.01.03.01.01	Check medical records for results of cervical x-rays before starting program
6.01.03.01.02	Avoid activities that place the neck in extreme flexion, such as tumbling, in individuals who test positive for atlantoaxial instability syndrome
6.01.03.02	*Recognize incidence of susceptibility to respiratory infections in individuals with Down's syndrome and other conditions such as secondary disabilities*
6.01.03.02.01	Avoid activities that may reduce resistance
6.01.03.02.02	Coordinate with medical community to prevent contraindications
6.01.03.03	*Recognize incidence of heart conditions among individuals with mental retardation such as those with Down's syndrome*
6.01.03.03.01	Check medical release prior to beginning program
6.01.03.03.02	Adapt cardiovascular activities
6.01.03.04	*Recognize incidence of hypotonus among individuals with mental retardation such as Down's syndrome*
6.01.03.04.01	Discourage hyperflexible postures
6.01.03.04.02	Encourage muscular strengthening especially around the joints

6.01.03.04.03	Adapt activities involving movement on uneven surfaces
6.01.03.04.04	Adapt activities involving agility and changing directions
6.01.03.05	*Recognize propensity toward being overweight in individuals with mental retardation*
6.01.03.05.01	Determine cause of problem with other health professionals
6.01.03.05.02	Incorporate family into solution
6.01.03.05.03	Provide calorie burning activity
6.01.03.05.04	Utilize nutrition lessons
6.01.03.06	*Recognize incidence of poor eyesight in individuals with Down's syndrome*
6.01.03.06.01	Adapt targets
6.01.03.06.02	Adapt receptive objects
6.01.03.07	*Recognize incidence of poor hearing in individuals with Down's syndrome*
6.01.03.07.01	Utilize visual demonstrations
6.01.03.07.02	Utilize tactile demonstrations

6.02 — **Deafness and Hard of Hearing: Understand unique attributes of individuals who are deaf or hard of hearing**

6.02.01 Understand motor attributes such as vestibular considerations

---

6.02.01.01	*Awareness of implications of impaired vestibular system in some individuals who are deaf or hard of hearing*
6.02.01.01.01	Use appropriate tests for balance
6.02.01.01.02	Teach compensation such as using vision and proprioception
6.02.01.01.03	Emphasize principles of equilibrium such as wide base of support and low center of gravity

---

6.02 — **Deafness and Hard of Hearing: Understand unique attributes of individuals who are deaf or hard of hearing**

6.02.02 Understand cognitive attributes (strategies) such as use of vision as primary input for learning

---

6.02.02.01	*Awareness of methods of presenting information besides auditory (see Standard 9.04.02)*
6.02.02.01.01	Use visual demonstration
6.02.02.01.02	Use tactile demonstration
6.02.02.01.03	Use task cards

6.02	**_Deafness and Hard of Hearing: Understand unique attributes of individuals who are deaf or hard of hearing_**
6.02.03	Understand communication attributes such as nonverbal communication and use of hearing aids

6.02.03.01   _Awareness of tips to enhance communication (see Standard 9.04.02)_

6.02.03.01.01   Use sign language

6.02.03.01.02   Provide safe place for hearing aids in aquatics and contact sports

6.02.03.01.03   Use handouts and chalkboard for learning enhancement

6.02.03.01.04   Talk to individual, not to interpreter

6.02.03.01.05   Use enhancements for speech reading such as placing student in good visual positioning and stand in well lit area

6.02.03.02   _Recognize various levels of hearing ability_

6.02.03.02.01   Adapt teaching methods to individuals who are deaf

6.02.03.02.02   Adapt teaching methods to individuals who are hard of hearing

6.02.03.02.03   Use assistive devices such as auditory trainers, wearing a microphone, etc.

6.02.03.03   _Understand implications of unique methods of communication on safety in physical activity_

6.02.03.03.01   Use visual cues for attention, stop, start, etc.

6.02.03.03.02   Use buddy system

6.02.03.03.03   Use handouts for key rules and strategies

6.02.03.03.04   Meet with students before class to discuss additional concerns

6.02.03.03.05   Check with individual for understanding of rules and concepts

6.02.03.03.06   Use sign language

6.02.03.03.07   Make sure student can see signs, lips, visual cues

6.02.03.03.08   Use tactile cues such as floor vibrations

6.02.03.04   _Recognize the philosophy of the individual's family for communication, such as totally oral, total communication_

6.02.03.04.01   Respect philosophy of communication mode

6.02.03.04.02   Use student/family preferred communication mode

6.03	**_Speech and Language Disorders: Understand unique attributes of individuals with speech and language disorders_**
6.03.01	Understand receptive language disorders such as receptive aphasia

6.03.01.01   _Understand implications of various methods of receiving messages in physical activity_

6.03.01.01.01	Use sign or pantomime
6.03.01.01.02	Use pictures or symbols
6.03.01.01.03	Use nonverbal games
6.03.01.01.04	Encourage classmates to adapt communication
6.03.01.01.05	Use consistent language
6.03.01.01.06	Consult with speech and language therapist for additional strategies for optimal communication

6.03	**Speech and Language Disorders: Understand unique attributes of individuals with speech and language disorders**
6.03.02	Understand expressive language disorders such as mechanical disorders and expressive aphasia

6.03.02.01	*Understand the implications of various methods of expressive communication in physical activity*
6.03.02.01.01	Encourage use of communication devices
6.03.02.01.02	Adapt communication devices to various physical activity settings such as aquatics
6.03.02.01.03	Allow time for individual's responses
6.03.02.01.04	Ask open ended questions as well as yes-no questions
6.03.02.01.05	Protect communication devices from damage
6.03.02.01.06	Cooperate with interpreter
6.03.02.01.07	Provide student with signal to alert teacher to emergency
6.03.02.01.08	Validate person's frustration when message is hard to get across
6.03.02.01.09	Show student appropriate ways to show frustration
6.03.02.01.10	Persist in finding out what is said when it is difficult to understand
6.03.02.01.11	Consult with speech and language therapist for additional strategies for optimal communication

6.04	**Blindness and Visual Disabilities: Understand the unique attributes of individuals with blindness and visual disabilities**
6.04.01	Understand the implications of blindness and visual disability for motor skill acquisition

6.04.01.01	*Awareness of problems with body image and awareness*
6.04.01.01.01	Conduct assessment of body part identification and body part movements
6.04.01.01.02	Conduct posture assessment
6.04.01.01.03	Use variety of tactile cues to elicit proper body mechanics
6.04.01.01.04	Use imagery and non-visual cues
6.04.01.01.05	Teach self-monitoring of movement
6.04.01.01.06	Provide stretching activities for tight muscle groups

6.04.01.01.07	Provide strengthening activities for weak muscles
6.04.01.01.08	Coordinate with physical therapists
6.04.01.02	*Awareness of poor movement potential in individuals who are blind or visually disabled*
6.04.01.02.01	Provide opportunity to explore movement potential
6.04.01.02.02	Utilize a variety of movement experiences
6.04.01.02.03	Use sound to enhance desire to try new experiences
6.04.01.02.04	Use hands-on assistance
6.04.01.02.05	Use success tasks to gain the trust of individual
6.04.01.02.06	Consider safety in planning activities (see Standard 9.02.03)
6.04.01.02.07	Provide spatial awareness activities
6.04.01.03	*Awareness of low levels of fitness in skills that are movement oriented in individuals who are blind or visually disabled*
6.04.01.03.01	Focus on orientation and mobility during fitness activities
6.04.01.03.02	Give individual orientation to the activity environment
6.04.01.03.03	Provide individuals with feedback about their own performance and others'
6.04.01.03.04	Use different textures or ropes for guides and boundaries
6.04.01.03.05	Use auditory devices for directional orientation
6.04.01.03.06	Teach other students to aid in orientation and mobility
6.04.01.03.07	Develop landmarks in instructional areas
6.04.01.03.08	Work with Orientation and Mobility specialist to determine proper use of canes and dogs as well as proper mobility when participating in games and activities
6.04.01.03.09	Teach activities that can be done without dependence on others such as riding a stationary bike or using a treadmill

6.04	**Blindness and Visual Disabilities: Understand the unique attributes of individuals with blindness and visual disabilities**
6.04.02	Understand implications of blindness and visual disability for cognitive skills

6.04.02.01	*Awareness that learning is not primarily through the visual sense*
6.04.02.01.01	Provide braille, or large print tests and handouts, or oral tests when necessary
6.04.02.01.02	Teach individual the types of things that other individuals learn by sight and by watching others such as strategies, innovative moves and rules
6.04.02.01.03	Teach using verbal and tactile demonstrations

6.04

Blindness and Visual Disabilities: Understand the unique attributes of individuals with blindness and visual disabilities

6.04.03

Understand medical and health considerations of various types and causes of blindness and visual disability

6.04.03.01   *Awareness that retinal detachment has implications for contact activities and jarring*

6.04.03.01.01   Adapt activities to reduce/eliminate head bumping

6.04.03.01.02   Report signs of acute detachment

6.04.03.02   *Awareness that glaucoma may have implications on physical activity choices*

6.04.03.02.01   Plan activities that do not cause increased eye pressure

6.04.03.02.02   Consult physician when providing underwater activities

6.04.03.03   *Awareness of the various types of visual disabilities and blindness*

6.04.03.03.01   Adapt activities for individuals with total blindness

6.04.03.03.02   Adapt activities for individuals with tunnel vision

6.04.03.03.03   Adapt activities for individuals with various levels of partial sight

6.04.03.04   *Awareness of various conditions that include blindness such as retinitis pigmentosa*

6.04.03.04.01   Collaborate with medical community when individual has condition that includes blindness

6.04.03.04.02   Adapt activities for accompanying conditions such as mental retardation, deafness, and neurological impairment

6.05

Behavioral Conditions: Understand the unique attributes of individuals with behavioral conditions

6.05.01

Understand impact of behavioral conditions on learning motor skills

6.05.01.01   *Awareness of multitude of behaviors that an individual may exhibit when diagnosed as having a behavioral condition such as seriously emotionally disturbed and the impact of each on learning motor skills*

6.05.01.01.01   Adapt environment and teaching strategies for individuals with hypoactivity

6.05.01.01.02   Adapt environment and teaching strategies for individuals with hyperactivity

6.05.01.01.03   Adapt environment and teaching strategies for individuals with attention deficit

6.05.01.01.04   Adapt environment and teaching strategies for individuals who are withdrawn

6.05.01.01.05   Adapt environment and teaching strategies for individuals who exhibit anxiety

6.05.01.01.06   Adapt environment and teaching strategies for individuals who are non-compliant

6.05.01.01.07   Adapt environment and teaching strategies for individuals who are socially maladjusted

6.05.01.01.08   Adapt environment and teaching strategies for individuals with poor self-concept

6.05.01.01.09   Adapt environment and teaching strategies for individuals who exhibit disruptive behavior

6.05.01.01.10	Adapt environment and teaching strategies for individuals who exhibit self-injurious behaviors
6.05.01.01.11	Adapt environment and teaching strategies for individuals who exhibit self-stimulatory behaviors
6.05.01.01.12	Adapt environment and teaching strategies for individuals who have phobias
6.05.01.01.13	Adapt environment and teaching strategies for individuals who exhibit obsessions
6.05.01.01.14	Adapt environment and teaching strategies for individuals who exhibit compulsion
6.05.01.01.15	Adapt environment and teaching strategies for individuals who are schizophrenic
6.05.01.01.16	Adapt environment and teaching strategies for individuals who are at risk

6.05	**Behavioral Conditions: Understand the unique attributes of individuals with behavioral conditions**
6.05.02	Understand the impact of behavioral conditions on medical/health issues

6.05.02.01	*Awareness of the implications of medication (drug therapy) used for various behavior disorders on motor performance and learning*
6.05.02.01.01	Use the Physician's Desk Reference for medication information
6.05.02.01.02	Consult with medical community on individual side effects and contraindications

6.05	**Behavioral Conditions: Understand the unique attributes of individuals with behavioral conditions**
6.05.03	Understand the impact of behavioral conditions on safety in physical activities

6.05.03.01	*Awareness of behavior problems that may lead to safety problems such as impulsivity and non-compliance*
6.05.03.01.01	Provide a definite routine to be followed
6.05.03.01.02	Provide clear limits
6.05.03.01.03	Provide rules student can achieve
6.05.03.01.04	Use applied behavior analysis principles (See Standard 10.03 - 10.07)
6.05.03.01.05	Display appropriate authority
6.05.03.01.06	Develop consistent rules with consequences
6.05.03.01.07	Provide heavily structured environments when necessary

6.06	**Learning Disabilities: Understand the unique attributes of individuals with learning disabilities**
6.06.01	Understand aspects of motor dysfunction

6.06.01.01	*Understand the implication of general body coordination dysfunction*
6.06.01.01.01	Assess individual to determine the severity of awkwardness (see Standard 8.0)

6.06.01.01.02	Use different size and weight balls
6.06.01.01.03	Use simple to complex skills
6.06.01.01.04	Provide for extra practice
6.06.01.01.05	Adapt rules for success
6.06.01.02	*Understand the implications of visual motor dysfunction*
6.06.01.02.01	Adapt equipment
6.06.01.02.02	Provide for extra practice
6.06.01.02.03	Consult with eye specialist about visual dysfunction
6.06.01.03	*Understand the implications of balance dysfunction*
6.06.01.03.01	Use a gradual balance progression from static to dynamic
6.06.01.03.02	Teach wide base support and low center of gravity
6.06.01.03.03	Use caution with risky balance tasks such as high balance beam
6.06.01.04	*Understand the implications of spatial awareness dysfunction*
6.06.01.04.01	Use floor spots for "home base"
6.06.01.04.02	Provide high color contrast of boundary lines
6.06.01.04.03	Use multisensory approach such as providing tactile, kinesthetic and vestibular input at the same time
6.06.01.05	*Understand implications of laterality dysfunction*
6.06.01.05.01	Use mirroring techniques for increased visual feedback
6.06.01.05.02	Use foot prints on floor
6.06.01.05.03	Constantly reinforce left and right in games, motor patterns, and exercises
6.06.01.05.04	Use cuing techniques such as colored bracelets, ankle bands, and uneven wrist weights
6.06.01.06	*Understand the implications of body image dysfunction*
6.06.01.06.01	Use mirroring for increased visual feedback
6.06.01.06.02	Use activities where maximal tactile input is achieved such as aquatics, wrestling, and log rolls
6.06.01.07	*Understand the implications of sensory system dysfunction*
6.06.01.07.01	Adapt environment to individuals who are tactile defensive
6.06.01.07.02	Provide a variety of equipment in various shapes, textures, and weights
6.06.01.08	*Understand implications of kinesthetic awareness problems*
6.06.01.08.01	Provide activities that increase pressure on body surfaces, joints, and muscles such as pushing and pulling
6.06.01.08.02	Provide activities that use quick change of direction and uneven surfaces to stimulate proprioceptors
6.06.01.08.03	Use visual feedback such as mirrors during movement activities

6.06.01.08.04	Provide games that involve body shape imitation
6.06.01.09	*Understand implications of a continuum of responsivity such as hyperresponsivity or hyporesponsivity*
6.06.01.09.01	Adapt environment and teaching strategies to individuals with hyperresponsivity
6.06.01.09.02	Adapt environment and teaching strategies to individuals with hyporesponsivity
6.06.01.09.03	Adapt environment and teaching strategies to individuals with vacillating responsivity (varying activity levels)

6.06	**Learning Disabilities: Understand the unique attributes of individuals with learning disabilities**
6.06.02	Understand cognitive difficulties

6.06.02.01	*Describe implications of attention span problems*
6.06.02.01.01	Provide for smooth and timely transitions from one activity to another
6.06.02.01.02	Plan several different activities for each session
6.06.02.01.03	Minimize distractions
6.06.02.01.04	Gradually increase time in an activity
6.06.02.02	*Describe implications of disorders of written language*
6.06.02.02.01	Use alternate means to give tests
6.06.02.02.02	Read written material aloud
6.06.02.03	*Describe disorder of auditory processing*
6.06.02.03.01	Simplify language
6.06.02.03.02	Reinforce auditory directions with visual cues
6.06.02.03.03	Use consistent language

6.06	**Learning Disabilities: Understand the unique attributes of individuals with learning disabilities**
6.06.03	Understand social difficulties

6.06.03.01	*Describe the implications of social imperception*
6.06.03.01.01	Create activities that encourage peer interaction in a small group basis
6.06.03.01.02	Identify nonverbal communication to individual
6.06.03.02	*Understand the implications of perseveration*
6.06.03.02.01	Avoid activities that cause perseveration
6.06.03.02.02	Provide high contrast between activities

6.07	**Cerebral Palsy: Understand the unique attributes of individuals with cerebral palsy**
6.07.01	Understand motor attributes of individuals with cerebral palsy

6.07.01.01   *Awareness of the "types" of cerebral palsy*

6.07.01.01.01   Adapt activities for individuals with ataxia

6.07.01.01.02   Adapt activities for individuals with spasticity

6.07.01.01.03   Adapt activities for individuals with athetosis

6.07.01.01.04   Adapt activities for individuals with rigidity

6.07.01.01.05   Adapt activities for individuals with tremors

6.07.01.01.06   Adapt activities for individuals with mixed cerebral palsy

6.07.01.02   *Awareness of the implications of hypertonus on motor performance*

6.07.01.02.01   Adapt activities for limited range of motion

6.07.01.02.02   Discuss strength training with therapists and physicians

6.07.01.02.03   Avoid activities that will increase tone substantially such as quick, jumping movements

6.07.01.02.04   Teach relaxation activities

6.07.01.03   *Awareness of the implications of hyperactive stretch reflex on motor performance*

6.07.01.03.01   Adapt activity for movement limitations

6.07.01.03.02   Use slow, static stretches

6.07.01.03.03   Position individual for maximal movement

6.07.01.04   *Awareness of the implications of primitive reflex patterns on motor performance*

6.07.01.04.01   Adapt activities to avoid unwanted reflexes

6.07.01.04.02   Position students to avoid unwanted reflex patterns

6.07.01.04.03   Avoid sudden noises and touches

6.07.01.05   *Awareness of the implications of disordered motor development*

6.07.01.05.01   Adapt for problems working against gravity

6.07.01.05.02   Adapt activities to account for splinter skills

6.07.01.06   *Awareness of mobility aids used to improve function in motor activity (see Standard 9.05-06)*

6.07.01.06.01   Adapt activities for users of orthotics

6.07.01.06.02   Adapt activities for users of wheelchairs

6.07.01.06.03   Adapt activities for users of walkers

6.07.01.06.04   Adapt activities for users of crutches

6.07.01.06.05   Provide safety for non-user individuals when mobility aids are used in group situations

6.07.01.06.06   Consult with physical and occupational therapist for adaptations to physical education equipment

---

6.07   ***Cerebral Palsy: Understand the unique attributes of individuals with cerebral palsy***

6.07.02   Understand cognitive attributes of individuals with cerebral palsy

---

6.07.02.01   *Awareness of incidence of secondary disabilities in individuals with cerebral palsy such as mental retardation, learning disabilities, and visual perceptual problems*

6.07.02.01.01   Adapt activities to meet the needs of secondary disabilities

6.07.02.01.02   Collaborate with special education teacher for academic reinforcement

---

6.07   ***Cerebral Palsy: Understand the unique attributes of individuals with cerebral palsy***

6.07.03   Understand health and medical attributes of individuals with cerebral palsy

---

6.07.03.01   *Awareness of types of medical conditions found in individuals with cerebral palsy*

6.07.03.01.01   Collaborate with medical community about post-surgical activity programs

6.07.03.01.02   Communicate with medical community about individuals with seizure disorders

---

6.07   ***Cerebral Palsy: Understand the unique attributes of individuals with cerebral palsy***

6.07.04   Understand communication attributes of individuals with cerebral palsy

---

6.07.04.01   *Awareness of incidence of communication disorders in individuals with cerebral palsy*

6.07.04.01.01   Consult with speech and language pathologist

6.07.04.01.02   Reinforce language and speech during physical activity

6.07.04.01.03   Adapt activity to encourage use of communication devices

---

6.08   ***Muscular Dystrophy: Understand the unique attributes of individuals with muscular dystrophy***

6.08.01   Understand motor attributes of individuals with muscular dystrophy

---

6.08.01.01   *Describe various types of muscular dystrophy such as Duchenne*

6.08.01.01.01   Adapt activity to the specific type of muscular dystrophy

6.08.01.01.02   Communicate with parents and guardians and multidisciplinary team members about condition of the individual during physical activity (see Standard 15.01)

6.08.01.02   *Describe the implications of gait problems for physical activity*

6.08.01.02.01   Adapt activities involving locomotor skills such as running, jumping, climbing stairs

6.08.01.02.02   Use proper assistance in recovery from falls

6.08.01.03   *Describe implications of muscle atrophy for motor skills*

6.08.01.03.01   Adapt activity for posture problems due to muscle imbalance from atrophy

6.08.01.03.02   Avoid activities that may cause dislocations due to poor muscle tone

6.08.01.03.03   Provide activities that maintain current level of muscular strength and endurance

6.08

> **Muscular Dystrophy: Understand the unique attributes of individuals with muscular dystrophy**

6.08.02

> Understand health and medical considerations of individuals with muscular dystrophy such as respiratory involvement

6.08.02.01   *Describe the implications of respiratory fatigue on motor skills*

6.08.02.01.01   Limit length and intensity of activity

6.08.02.01.02   Provide interval work with rest periods

6.08.02.01.03   Emphasize maintenance of fitness

6.08.02.01.04   Use breath control activities such as aquatics

6.08.02.01.05   Avoid areas where air quality is poor such as damp areas

6.08

> **Muscular Dystrophy: Understand the unique attributes of individuals with muscular dystrophy**

6.08.03

> Understand emotional effects of muscular dystrophy on the individual

6.08.03.01   *Describe emotional effect of a progressive disability on the learning of motor skills*

6.08.03.01.01   Focus on individuals enjoyment and fun

6.08.03.01.02   Use out of wheelchair activities

6.08.03.01.03   Encourage participation in regular physical education as long as possible

6.09

> **Spina Bifida: Understand the unique attributes of individuals with spina bifida**

6.09.01

> Understand motor attributes of individuals with spina bifida

6.09.01.01   *Understand the implications of the various levels of motor involvement*

6.09.01.01.01   Adapt activities for motor involvement due to myelomeningocele

6.09.01.01.02   Adapt activities for motor involvement due to meningocele

6.09.01.01.03   Adapt activities for motor involvement due to occulta

6.09.01.02   *Understand the implications of mobility impairment and limitations in individuals with spina bifida*

6.09.01.02.01   Incorporate mobility aids into activities

6.09.01.02.02   Utilize upper body activities

6.09.01.02.03   Provide introduction to wheelchair sports

6.09.01.03	*Understand the implications of orthopedic dysfunction common in spina bifida*
6.09.01.03.01	Adapt activities for increased incidence of fractures
6.09.01.03.02	Adapt activities for increased incidence of paraplegia
6.09.01.03.03	Adapt activities for increased incidence of orthotic use
6.09.01.03.04	Adapt activities for increased incidence of club foot and other foot deformities

6.09	***Spina Bifida: Understand the unique attributes of individuals with spina bifida***
6.09.02	Understand health and medical considerations

6.09.02.01	*Understand the implications of hydrocephalus*
6.09.02.01.01	Avoid contraindications for shunt wearers
6.09.02.01.02	Avoid upside-down positions for long periods of time
6.09.02.01.03	Avoid deep pressure on the shunt or head
6.09.02.01.04	Discuss diving with physician before incorporating into aquatics
6.09.02.01.05	Discuss risky activities such as headstands, soccer heading and forward rolls with physician before incorporating it into program
6.09.02.02	*Understand the implications of limited skin sensation*
6.09.02.02.01	Adapt activities to encourage change of positions
6.09.02.02.02	Encourage self-monitoring of bruises and cuts
6.09.02.02.03	Use care in transferring and physical assistance
6.09.02.03	*Understand the implications of obesity as a complication*
6.09.02.03.01	Provide activities for calorie burning
6.09.02.03.02	Provide nutrition information
6.09.02.04	*Understand implications of bowel and bladder dysfunction*
6.09.02.04.01	Remind individual to empty bag before physical activities
6.09.02.04.02	Provide for privacy in dressing

6.10	***Amputations: Understand the unique attributes of individuals with amputations***
6.10.01	Understand various levels of amputations

6.10.01.01	*Understand the implications of lower body amputation on motor function*
6.10.01.01.01	Adapt activity to increased energy requirements due to upper body being solely used
6.10.01.01.02	Plan strengthening activities for atrophy in surrounding muscles to stump
6.10.01.01.03	Provide stationary activities such as arm ergometry for individuals with mobility restrictions

6.10.01.02   *Understand implications of upper body amputations on motor functions*

6.10.01.02.01   Provide adapted equipment

6.10.01.02.02   Teach safe falling techniques due to inability to catch oneself

---

6.10   **Amputations: Understand the unique attributes of individuals with amputations**

6.10.02   Understand health and medical considerations that may be present in individuals with amputations

---

6.10.02.01   *Understand implications of increased perspiration due to reduced cooling surfaces*

6.10.02.01.01   Advise individuals on appropriate exercise clothing

6.10.02.01.02   Keep water available for hydration

6.10.02.01.03   Monitor individual for heat related illness

6.10.02.02   *Understand the incidence of obesity due to inactivity*

6.10.02.02.01   Advocate for physical activity opportunities

6.10.02.02.02   Use effective motivators for participation (see Standard 10.03 - 10.05)

6.10.02.02.03   Provide adaptations to calorie burning activities

6.10.02.03   *Understand implications of skin irritations and skin breakdown on stump*

6.10.02.03.01   Encourage stump care

6.10.02.03.02   Adapt activities when skin breakdown occurs

6.11   **Spinal Cord Injury: Understand the unique attributes of individuals with spinal cord injuries**

6.11.01   Understand motor attributes at various levels of spinal injury

---

6.11.01.01   *Understand the implications of paraplegia*

6.11.01.01.01   Teach upper body activities

6.11.01.01.02   Adapt activities for use with mobility aids (see Standard 9.05 - 9.06)

6.11.01.01.03   Plan activities to avoid overuse injuries to arms and hands

6.11.01.02   *Understand the implications of quadriplegia*

6.11.01.02.01   Plan activities for limited mobility such as quad rugby

6.11.01.02.02   Plan activities with wheelchair use in mind

6.11   **Spinal Cord Injury: Understand the unique attributes of individuals with spinal cord injuries**

6.11.02   Understand medical and health attributes

6.11.02.01   *Understand the implications of bowel and bladder dysfunction*

6.11.02.01.01	Provide area for privacy in toileting and dressing
6.11.02.01.02	Remind individual to empty external collection bag
6.11.02.02	*Understand the implications of skin abrasions and ulcers*
6.11.02.02.01	Check skin frequently
6.11.02.02.02	Encourage weight shifting and position changes
6.11.02.02.03	Educate about proper hygiene such as showering after physical activity and proper workout clothing
6.11.02.03	*Understand the implications of body regulation dysfunction*
6.11.02.03.01	Make appropriate heart rate modifications to calculate target heart rate based on lesion level
6.11.02.03.02	Monitor blood pressure during initial exercise sessions
6.11.02.03.03	Monitor individual for temperature related illnesses
6.11.02.03.04	Check extremities during temperature extremes
6.11.02.03.05	Keep individual hydrated

6.12	**Posture Disorders: Understand the unique attributes of individuals with posture problems**
6.12.01	Understand various forms of posture disorders found in individuals with disabilities

6.12.01.01	*Understand the implications of scoliosis*
6.12.01.01.01	Secure medical clearance for activities
6.12.01.01.02	Provide symmetrical activities
6.12.01.01.03	Remove jackets or braces for swimming
6.12.01.01.04	Monitor skin for breakdowns
6.12.01.02	*Understand the implications of lordosis*
6.12.01.02.01	Teach correct postural alignment
6.12.01.02.02	Teach lower back stretches such as sit and reach
6.12.01.02.03	Teach abdominal strengthening exercises such as crunches
6.12.01.03	*Understand the implications of kyphosis*
6.12.01.03.01	Incorporate chest muscle stretches
6.12.01.03.02	Incorporate upper back extension exercises
6.12.01.04	*Understand the implications of foot deformities*
6.12.01.04.01	Refer individuals with suspected foot problems to physician
6.12.01.04.02	Collaborate with therapist and physician for activities to promote proper foot alignment

6.13	**Juvenile Rheumatoid Arthritis: Understand the unique attributes of individuals with juvenile rheumatoid arthritis (JRA)**
6.13.01	Understand physical attributes of juvenile rheumatoid arthritis

6.13.01.01   *Understand the implications of limited range of motion (ROM)*

6.13.01.01.01   Provide daily ROM exercises

6.13.01.01.02   Use warm water aquatic exercises

6.13.01.01.03   Adapt activities for limited ROM

6.13.01.02   *Understand the implications of chronic pain*

6.13.01.02.01   Provide other less strenuous activities during flare ups of the condition

6.13.01.02.02   Monitor post-activity condition to plan for next class

6.13.01.02.03   Use isometric activities

6.13	**Juvenile Rheumatoid Arthritis: Understand the unique attributes of individuals with juvenile rheumatoid arthritis (JRA)**
6.13.02	Understand psychological attributes of juvenile rheumatoid arthritis

6.13.02.01   *Understand the implications of changing symptoms on physical activity participation*

6.13.02.01.01   Communicate with individual daily

6.13.02.01.02   Communicate with medical personnel

6.13.02.01.03   Communicate with parent or caretaker

6.13.02.01.04   Adapt attitude to meet the changing needs of the individual with JRA

6.13.02.02   *Understand the implications of sedentary lifestyle*

6.13.02.02.01   Emotionally support the individual who is afraid to do physical activity due to anticipation of pain

6.13.02.02.02   Advocate for aquatics in the IEP

6.13	**Juvenile Rheumatoid Arthritis: Understand the unique attributes of individuals with juvenile rheumatoid arthritis (JRA)**
6.13.03	Understand medical and health considerations of juvenile rheumatoid arthritis

6.13.03.01   *Understand the implications of joint instability*

6.13.03.01.01   Use knowledge of individual symptoms in providing weight bearing activities

6.13.03.01.02   Use caution in contact activities

6.13.03.01.03   Use caution in activities where falls are common such as skating

6.13.03.01.04   Consult with medical personnel as to contraindications

| 6.14 | **Dwarfism: Understand the unique attributes of individuals with short stature** |
| 6.14.01 | Understand physical attributes of achondroplasia |

6.14.01.01 · *Understand the implications of spinal anomalies*

6.14.01.01.01 · Provide posture screening

6.14.01.01.02 · Check medical records for activity contraindications

6.14.01.01.03 · Use caution in contact sports and high impact aerobics

6.14.01.02 · *Understand the implications of lower body limitations such as bowed legs and decreased length of legs*

6.14.01.02.01 · Adapt activities involving locomotor efficiency

6.14.01.02.02 · Adapt distances to travel

6.14.01.03 · *Understand the implications of upper body limitations such as restricted elbow range of motion and decreased length of arms*

6.14.01.03.01 · Adapt equipment size

6.14.01.03.02 · Adapt distance to target

6.14.01.03.03 · Adapt activities that use weight bearing on arms

| 6.14 | **Dwarfism: Understand the unique attributes of individuals with short stature** |
| 6.14.02 | Understand medical and health considerations of dwarfism |

6.14.02.01 · *Understand the implications of small chest size and narrow nasal passages*

6.14.02.01.01 · Adapt cardiorespiratory endurance activities

6.14.02.01.02 · Check with physician for contraindicated activities

6.14.02.02 · *Understand the implications of frequent hip and knee dislocations*

6.14.02.02.01 · Adapt activity to post surgical limitations

6.14.02.02.02 · Adapt activities for individuals who need to avoid contact sports and lateral movements

| 6.15 | **Osteogenesis Imperfecta: Understand the unique attributes of individuals with osteogenesis imperfecta** |
| 6.15.01 | Understand physical attributes of osteogenesis imperfecta |

6.15.01.01 · *Understand the implications of brittle bones*

6.15.01.01.01 · Adapt activities for those who use wheelchairs

6.15.01.01.02 · Use soft equipment such as yarn balls

6.15.01.01.03 · Adapt risky activities such as jumping, high impact activities, contact sports, twisting and turning

6.15.01.01.04 · Encourage opportunities for aquatic participation

6.15.01.01.05	Use continuous, smooth moving activities vs. quick, start and stop movements
6.15.01.02	*Understand the implications of chest deformaties such as funnel chest*
6.15.01.02.01	Adapt cardiorespiratory fitness activities
6.15.01.02.02	Adapt activities for limited trunk range of motion
6.15.01.03	*Understand the implications of spinal anamolies*
6.15.01.03.01	Obtain medical clearance for activity contraindications
6.15.01.03.02	Provide posture screening

6.16	**Autism: Understand the unique attributes of individuals with autism**
6.16.01	Understand unique cognitive attributes

6.16.01.01	*Understand the implications of perseveration*
6.16.01.01.01	Provide closure of lessons and activities
6.16.01.01.02	Redirect inappropriate behavior
6.16.01.02	*Understand the implications of poor eye contact*
6.16.01.02.01	Use verbal cues to direct attention
6.16.01.02.02	Perform demonstrations several times

6.16	**Autism: Understand the unique attributes of individuals with autism**
6.16.02	Understand unique communication attributes

6.16.02.01	*Understand implications of speech and language disorders*
6.16.02.01.01	Use sign language when appropriate
6.16.02.01.02	Interpret gestures used by the individual such as pointing and leading you to an area
6.16.02.01.03	Encourage speech and speech sounds when appropriate

6.16	**Autism: Understand the unique attributes of individuals with autism**
6.16.03	Understand unique social interaction attributes

6.16.03.01	*Understand implications of poor interaction in groups*
6.16.03.01.01	Use one to one instruction
6.16.03.01.02	Use peer tutors
6.16.03.01.03	Use small group interaction at first

| 6.16 | **_Autism: Understand the unique attributes of individuals with autism_** |
| 6.16.04 | Understand health and medical issues |

6.16.04.01	*Understand implications of lack of danger awareness*
6.16.04.01.01	Monitor for safety
6.16.04.01.02	Work in areas that are secure and free from potential hazards
6.16.04.01.03	Provide small student to teacher ratio
6.16.04.01.04	Provide adequate supervision
6.16.04.02	*Understand the implications of self-stimulatory and self-injurious behavior*
6.16.04.02.01	Provide careful supervision
6.16.04.02.02	Provide small student/teacher ratio
6.16.04.02.03	Cooperate with multidisciplinary team recommendations for behavior management program (see Standard 10.03 - 10.07)
6.16.04.02.04	Provide feedback to multidisciplinary team about behavior in physical education class (see Standard 15.02.01)
6.16.04.02.05	Provide opportunity for regular, vigorous activity

| 6.17 | **_Traumatic Brain Injury: Understand unique attributes of individuals with traumatic brain injury_** |
| 6.17.01 | Understand motor attributes |

6.17.01.01	*Understand implications of excessive muscle tone*
6.17.01.01.01	Emphasize stretching
6.17.01.01.02	Coordinate strength training program with therapists and physicians
6.17.01.01.03	Avoid activities that will increase tone substantially such as quick, jumping movements
6.17.01.01.04	Teach relaxation activities
6.17.01.01.05	Adapt activities
6.17.01.01.06	Plan for extra time on agility activities
6.17.01.02	*Understand implications of hemiplegia*
6.17.01.02.01	Adapt activities for balance problems
6.17.01.02.02	Adapt activities for one hand usage
6.17.01.02.03	Adapt equipment
6.17.01.03	*Understand implications of ataxia*
6.17.01.03.01	Use a wider area for activities such as agility run
6.17.01.03.02	Use caution with activities involving balance

6.17.01.03.03	Modify activities that depend on agility
6.17.01.03.04	Provide area for safe landing and stopping points such as a finish line
6.17.01.03.05	Provide protective equipment such as elbow pads and helmets for those who are prone to falls
6.17.01.04	*Understand implications of visual motor dysfunction*
6.17.01.04.01	Adapt activities using high speed projectiles
6.17.01.04.02	Adapt activities where depth perception is needed
6.17.01.04.03	Plan activities using bright and contrasting objects and targets
6.17.01.05	*Understand implications of poor body awareness*
6.17.01.05.01	Use visual demonstrations
6.17.01.05.02	Use verbal cues for body movement desired
6.17.01.05.03	Use physical prompts
6.17.01.05.04	Plan for specific body awareness activities

6.17	**Traumatic Brain Injury: Understand unique attributes of individuals with traumatic brain injury**
6.17.02	Understand cognitive attributes

6.17.02.01	*Understand implications of cognitive deficits in new learning*
6.17.02.01.01	Use repetition
6.17.02.01.02	Use task analysis
6.17.02.02	*Understand implications of problems with short term memory*
6.17.02.02.01	Link verbal explanation with physical "walk through"
6.17.02.02.02	Use repetition
6.17.02.02.03	Use cue words and key terms
6.17.02.02.04	Use handouts for studying rules

6.17	**Traumatic Brain Injury: Understand unique attributes of individuals with traumatic brain injury**
6.17.03	Understand social attributes

6.17.03.01	*Understand implications of poor social skills*
6.17.03.01.01	Use success oriented activities to decrease fear of failure
6.17.03.01.02	Use small group or dual activities
6.17.03.01.03	Use proper reinforcement of correct social behavior
6.17.03.01.04	Point out inappropriate social skills

6.17	**Traumatic Brain Injury: Understand unique attributes of individuals with traumatic brain injury**
6.17.04	Understand speech and language disorders

6.17.04.01   *Understand the implications of receptive language disorders*

6.17.04.01.01   Consult with speech and language specialist

6.17.04.01.02   Use sign and pantomime

6.17.04.01.03   Use pictures or symbols

6.17.04.01.04   Use nonverbal games

6.17.04.01.05   Encourage classmates to be patient and helpful

6.17.04.01.06   Use consistent language

6.17.04.02   *Understand implications of expressive language disorders (see Standard 9.04.02)*

6.17.04.02.01   Encourage use of communication boards

6.17.04.02.02   Adapt communication boards to various settings such as aquatics

6.17.04.02.03   Allow time for responses

6.17.04.02.04   Ask open-ended questions as well as yes-no questions

6.17.04.02.05   Protect communication devices from damage

6.17.04.02.06   Cooperate with interpreter

6.17.04.02.07   Provide student with signal to alert teacher to emergency

6.17.04.02.08   Validate person's frustration when message is difficult to get across

6.17.04.02.09   Show student appropriate ways to show frustration

6.17.04.02.10   Persist in finding out what is said when it is difficult to understand

6.17	**Traumatic Brain Injury: Understand unique attributes of individuals with traumatic brain injury**
6.17.05	Understand behavioral attributes

6.17.05.01   *Understand implications of lack of initiation*

6.17.05.01.01   Plan for movement exploration to discover potential

6.17.05.01.02   Plan success oriented activities

6.17.05.01.03   Use hierarchy of cues that allow for increasing self-direction

6.17.05.02   *Understand implications of impulsivity*

6.17.05.02.01   Provide structured environment

6.17.05.02.02   Anticipate impulsive behavior

6.17.05.02.03   Set behavior limits

6.17.05.02.04   Teach self-monitoring techniques

6.17.05.03   *Understand implications of lack of judgement*

6.17.05.03.01   Provide contained choices

6.17.05.03.02   Monitor for safety

6.17.05.03.03   Use questioning for review of rules

6.17   **Traumatic Brain Injury: Understand unique attributes of individuals with traumatic brain injury**

6.17.06   Understand health and safety attributes

6.17.06.01   *Understand implication of thermoregulation disorders*

6.17.06.01.01   Plan for time needed to go slowly from one temperature extreme to another

6.17.06.01.02   Avoid contraindicated activities if advised such as sauna and hot tub

6.17.06.01.03   Monitor individual for illnesses resulting from excessive heat and cold

6.17.06.02   *Understand implications of seizure disorders*

6.17.06.02.01   Devise emergency plan in the event of a seizure

6.17.06.02.02   Collaborate with parents and medical personnel to determine individual contraindications

---

6.18   **Heart Conditions: Understand unique attributes of individuals with heart conditions**

6.18.01   Understand physical attributes

6.18.01.01   *Understand implication of acquired and congenital heart conditions*

6.18.01.01.01   Adapt activities for individuals with low exercise tolerance

6.18.01.01.02   Obtain medical clearance

6.18.01.01.03   Teach self-monitoring of level of exertion

6.18.01.01.04   Monitor individual's heart rate

6.18.01.01.05   Recognize warning signs such as blue tinge to lips and nail beds

6.18.01.01.06   Use results of stress testing to plan individual program

6.18.01.02   *Understand implications of heart conditions as secondary disorders*

6.18.01.02.01   Read medical records of individuals with syndromes that have a high incidence of heart conditions as secondary disorders

6.18.01.02.02   Adapt activities to exercise tolerance

6.19

6.19.01

Tuberculosis: Understand unique attributes of tuberculosis (TB)
Understand physical attributes of tuberculosis of the spine (Pott's disease)

6.19.01.01   *Understand implications of tuberculosis spondylitis*

6.19.01.01.01   Adapt activities for low fitness level

6.19.01.01.02   Adapt activities to pain level

6.19.01.01.03   Encourage individual to work up to potential

6.20

6.20.01

Nephritis: Understand unique attributes of individuals with nephritis
Understand elevated blood pressure

6.20.01.01   *Describe precautions to fitness activities*

6.20.01.01.01   Avoid fitness activities when infection is present

6.20.01.01.02   Monitor blood pressure

6.20

6.20.02

Nephritis: Understand unique attributes of individuals with nephritis
Understand anemia

6.20.02.01   *Describe limited amount of oxygen available to cells*

6.20.02.01.01   Plan for rest periods

6.20.02.01.02   Use caution/avoid cardiovascular tests and activities according to medical feedback

6.20

6.20.03

Nephritis: Understand unique attributes of individuals with nephritis
Understand problems with poor fitness

6.20.03.01   *Describe increased heart rate and breathing rate*

6.20.03.01.01   Adapt aerobic exercise to work in lower target heart rate zones

6.20.03.01.02   Plan for rest periods

6.21

6.21.01

Asthma: Understand unique attributes of individuals with asthma
Understand physical attributes

6.21.01.01   *Understand implications of intrinsic asthma*

6.21.01.01.01   Provide slow, long warm up

6.21.01.01.02   Provide information for individual to self-monitor

6.21.01.01.03   Adapt cardiorespiratory fitness activities

6.21.01.02   *Understand implications of extrinsic asthma*

6.21.01.02.01	Provide alternate to aerobic exercise on hot and humid days
6.21.01.02.02	Avoid placing individual near allergens such as dust, fresh cut grass, and smog
6.21.01.02.03	Use individual medical history when providing outside activities on windy and polluted days
6.21.01.02.04	Avoid exposing student to sudden temperature changes
6.21.01.02.05	Encourage aquatics as activity of choice
6.21.01.03	*Understand implications of signs and symptoms*
6.21.01.03.01	Respond to individual with rounded shoulders (as an indicator to an asthma problem)
6.21.01.03.02	Provide exercises for stretching of pectorals due to hunched shoulder syndrome
6.21.01.03.03	Begin emergency procedures in response to wheezing
6.21.01.03.04	Encourage individual to drink plenty of water in response to increased mucus production
6.21.01.03.05	Allow inhalers to be available before, during and after exercise

6.21	**Asthma: Understand unique attributes of individuals with asthma**
6.21.02	Understand health and medical attributes

6.21.02.01	*Understand implications of an asthma episode*
6.21.02.01.01	Identify early signs and symptoms
6.21.02.01.02	Provide quiet area for breathing exercise routine
6.21.02.01.03	Provide area for inhaler use
6.21.02.01.04	Follow preestablished emergency procedures
6.21.02.02	*Understand implications of medication*
6.21.02.02.01	Refer to the Physician's Desk Reference for side effects
6.21.02.02.02	Communicate concerns to parents and medical staff

6.22	**Sickle Cell Anemia: Understand unique attributes of individuals with sickle cell anemia**
6.22.01	Understand physical attributes

6.22.01.01	*Understand the implications of anemia*
6.22.01.01.01	Use caution/avoid cardiovascular tests and activities according to medical feedback
6.22.01.01.02	Provide rest intervals

6.22	**Sickle Cell Anemia: Understand unique attributes of individuals with sickle cell anemia**
6.22.02	Understand medical and health attributes

6.22.02.01	*Understand implications of heat intolerance*

6.22.02.01.01   Recognize symptoms such as heat headaches, listlessness and exhaustion

6.22.02.01.02   Avoid overheating

6.22   **Sickle Cell Anemia: Understand unique attributes of individuals with sickle cell anemia**

6.22.03   Understand emotional attributes

6.22.03.01   *Understand the implications of erratic nature of symptoms*

6.22.03.01.01   Communicate with individual prior to each session to ascertain condition

6.22.03.01.02   Communicate with caretakers and medical personnel

---

6.23   **Lead Poisoning: Understand unique attributes of individuals who have lead poisoning**

6.23.01   Understand physical attributes

6.23.01.01   *Understand the implications of clumsiness*

6.23.01.01.01   Adapt activities for appropriate level of motor ability

6.23.01.01.02   Provide activities that are achievable and challenging

6.23.01.01.03   Provide activities that increase quality of movement

---

6.23   **Lead Poisoning: Understand unique attributes of individuals who have lead poisoning**

6.23.02   Understand health and medical attributes

6.23.02.01   *Understand the implication of seizure involvement*

6.23.02.01.01   Consult with physician and parents for contraindications

6.23.02.01.02   Avoid activities that may be contraindicated for specific individuals

6.23.02.02   *Understand the implications of limited amount of oxygen available to cells*

6.23.02.02.01   Plan for rest periods

6.23.02.02.02   Adhere to contraindications in medical records

---

6.23   **Lead Poisoning: Understand unique attributes of individuals who have lead poisoning**

6.23.03   Understand emotional attributes

6.23.03.01   *Understand implications of irritability*

6.23.03.01.01   Respond to the irritable nature of individual

6.23.03.01.02   Adjust disciplinary measures appropriately to level of irritability

6.24

6.24.01

> ### Hemophilia: Understand unique attributes of individuals with hemophilia
> Understand physical attributes

6.24.01.01   *Understand hemarthrosis*

6.24.01.01.01   Avoid activities involving contact/bumping

6.24.01.01.02   Use caution in activities involving high impact such as jumping, and catching fast, hard projectiles

6.24.01.01.03   Teach individual how to self-monitor to know physical limits

6.24.01.01.04   Incorporate strength training for muscles around joint with physician's permission

6.24.01.01.05   Use caution in quick start and stop activities

6.24

6.24.02

> ### Hemophilia: Understand unique attributes of individuals with hemophilia
> Understand health and medical attributes

6.24.02.01   *Understand implications of a bleed*

6.24.02.01.01   Identify early signs of internal bleeding such as swelling and heat in a joint

6.24.02.01.02   Follow preestablished emergency procedures

6.24.02.01.03   Apply cold compress to affected joint

6.24.02.01.04   Ask individual to elevate affected part

6.24.02.01.05   Avoid giving aspirin

6.24

6.24.03

> ### Hemophilia: Understand unique attributes of individuals with hemophilia
> Understand emotional issues

6.24.03.01   *Understand the implications of having a life threatening disability*

6.24.03.01.01   Offer support

6.24.03.01.02   Avoid emotional manipulation

6.24.03.01.03   Integrate as much as possible into regular physical education

6.25

6.25.01

> ### Seizure Disorders: Understand unique attributes of individuals with seizure disorders
> Understand health and medical attributes

6.25.01.01   *Understand implications of partial seizures*

6.25.01.01.01   Report sudden behavior change to medical staff

6.25.01.01.02   Adapt activities that may be risky due to sudden partial seizure activity

6.25.01.02   *Understand implications of generalized seizures*

6.25.01.02.01   Provide plan of action for other students during care of the individual with a generalized seizure

6.25.01.02.02   Protect from injury by placing soft materials under/near any moving body parts

6.25.01.02.03   Do not place anything in mouth

6.25.01.02.04   Check for breathing following seizure

6.25.01.02.05   Provide place for rest following seizure

6.25.01.02.06   Fill out appropriate incident/accident forms

6.25.01.03   *Understand implication of factors that may precipitate seizures*

6.25.01.03.01   Avoid situations such as stress that may trigger a seizure

6.25.01.03.02   Know individual precautions

6.25.01.04   *Understand the implications of identified high risk activities*

6.25.01.04.01   Provide additional staff during high risk activities

6.25.01.04.02   Use caution in activities such as scuba diving

6.25.01.04.03   Use caution in activities with heights due to possibility of falls during seizure

6.25.01.04.04   Consult with physician before doing contact and collision sports

6.25.01.05   *Understand the implications of medication*

6.25.01.05.01   Be aware of common side effects of anti-convulsant medication

6.25.01.05.02   Refer individual for medical care for atypical behavior such as irritability, drowsiness, increase in clumsiness, blurred vision, etc.

6.26   **Leukemia: Understand unique attributes of individuals with leukemia**
6.26.01   Understand health and medical attributes of individuals with leukemia

6.26.01.01   *Understand the implications of chemotherapy*

6.26.01.01.01   Adapt activities for individuals with anemia

6.26.01.01.02   Adapt activities for decreased resistance to infections

6.27   **Diabetes: Understand unique attributes of individuals with Type I diabetes**
6.27.01   Understand health and medical attributes of individuals with diabetes

6.27.01.01   *Understand the implications of varying sugar/insulin levels*

6.27.01.01.01   Supervise blood sugar test before and after class, if indicated

6.27.01.01.02   Communicate with parents and medical staff

6.27.01.01.03   Keep sugar drinks or glucose gel in office

6.27.01.01.04   Avoid conducting all components of fitness test in one session if individual is unaccustomed to such activities

6.27.01.01.05	Follow predetermined emergency plan
6.27.01.01.06	Monitor adjustments to diet/insulin administration with respect to physical activity as per physician's instructions
6.27.01.01.07	Identify signs of hypoglycemia and hyperglycemia
6.27.01.02	*Understand implications of brittle diabetes*
6.27.01.02.01	Help student care for skin abrasions
6.27.01.02.02	Encourage proper foot care
6.27.01.02.03	Encourage peripheral skin checks
6.27.01.02.04	Report any change in vision

6.28	***Multiple Disabilities: Understand unique attributes of individuals with multiple disabilities***
6.28.01	Understand physical and motor attributes

6.28.01.01	*Understand implications of gross motor deficits*
6.28.01.01.01	Adapt activities for movement limitations
6.28.01.01.02	Adapt activities for various assistive devices such as wheelchairs, walkers
6.28.01.02	*Understand implications of fine motor deficits*
6.28.01.02.01	Adapt activities involving grasping
6.28.01.02.02	Adapt activities involving releasing objects

6.28	***Multiple Disabilities: Understand unique attributes of individuals with multiple disabilities***
6.28.02	Understand cognitive attributes

6.28.02.01	*Appreciate range of cognitive levels in individuals with multiple disabilities*
6.28.02.01.01	Inquire about mental age
6.28.02.01.02	Present information according to mental age
6.28.02.01.03	Use age-appropriate activities
6.28.02.02	*Appreciate multidisciplinary approach to education of individuals with multiple disabilities*
6.28.02.02.01	Cooperate with multidisciplinary team
6.28.02.02.02	Reinforce goals of classroom teacher, special education and related services

6.28	***Multiple Disabilities: Understand unique attributes of individuals with multiple disabilities***
6.28.03	Understand speech and language attributes

6.28.03.01	*Understand implications of alternate communication modes (see Standard 9.02.04)*

6.28.03.01.01   Use any means to encourage communication such as communication boards, signing and pointing

6.28.03.01.02   Collaborate with classroom teacher and speech and language specialist

6.28   **Multiple Disabilities: Understand unique attributes of individuals with multiple disabilities**

6.28.04   Understand health and medical issues

6.28.04.01   *Awareness of incidence of body secretion dysfunction such as drooling and incontinence*

6.28.04.01.01   Follow preestablished routine for handling body secretions when changing diapers and caring for injuries involving body fluids

6.28.04.01.02   Reinforce independent behaviors such as wiping mouth

6.28.04.02   *Awareness of incidence of appliance use such as gastrointestinal tubes*

6.28.04.02.01   Use caution with trunk exercises for those who are tube fed as indicated

6.28.04.02.02   Consult physician about contraindications for ventilator-dependent individuals

6.28.04.02.03   Adapt activities for those with a tracheotomy

6.29   **Deaf/Blind: Understand unique attributes of individuals who are deaf/blind**

6.29.01   Understand physical and motor attributes

6.29.01.01   *Understand implications of mobility impairment*

6.29.01.01.01   Incorporate activities to enhance orientation and mobility

6.29.01.01.02   Allow individual to explore surroundings

6.29.01.01.03   Encourage individual to feel position and movement of your body whenever possible

6.29   **Deaf/Blind: Understand unique attributes of individuals who are deaf/blind**

6.29.02   Understand cognitive attributes

6.29.02.01   *Understand implications of tactile and kinesthetic sense as the modes of learning*

6.29.02.01.01   Use physical guidance and prompts

6.29.02.01.02   Use tactile markers for boundaries

6.29.02.01.03   Provide a variety of movement experiences

6.29.02.01.04   Use consistent organization of space and equipment

6.29   **Deaf/Blind: Understand unique attributes of individuals who are deaf/blind**

6.29.03   Understand communication attributes

6.29.03.01   *Understand implications of auditory and visual communication impairment*

6.29.03.01.01   Use tactile signing and finger spelling in hand

6.29.03.01.02   Utilize residual hearing and sight

6.29.03.01.03   Use multiple cues

6.29.03.01.04   Minimize extraneous visual and auditory stimuli

6.29.03.01.05   Use tactile cues to indicate upcoming events

6.29   ***Deaf/Blind: Understand unique attributes of individuals who are deaf/blind***

6.29.04   Understand health and medical attributes

6.29.04.01   *Understand incidence of secondary disabilities*

6.29.04.01.01   Adhere to individual contraindications in medical records

6.29.04.01.02   Adapt activities to individual medical profile

---

6.30   ***Attention Deficit Disorder (ADD) and Attention Deficit Disorder with Hyper-activity (ADD-H)***

6.30.01   Understand the difference between ADD and ADD-H

6.30.01.01   *Recognize the characteristics of individuals with ADD*

6.30.01.01.01   Adapt environment and teaching strategies for inattention (see Standard 6.06.02.01)

6.30.01.01.02   Adapt environment and teaching strategies for impulsive behaviors (see Standard 6.17.05.02)

6.30.01.02   *Recognize the characteristics of individuals with ADD-H*

6.30.01.02.01   Adapt environment and teaching strategies for inattention (see Standard 6.06.02.01)

6.30.01.02.02   Adapt environment and teaching strategies for impulsive behaviors (see Standard 6.17.05.02)

6.30.01.02.03   Adapt environment and teaching strategies for hyperactive individuals

---

6.31   ***Acquired Immune Deficiency Syndrome (AIDS): Understand unique attributes of individuals with AIDS***

6.31.01   Understand health and medical attributes

6.31.01.01   *Understand implications of fatigue*

6.31.01.01.01   Plan rest periods

6.31.01.01.02   Provide adequate but not overtaxing physical activities

6.31.01.02   *Awareness of susceptibility to infections*

6.31.01.02.01   Avoid close contact with child who has cold or communicable disease

6.31.01.02.02   Consult with physician for contraindicated activities

6.31.01.03   *Awareness of modes of transmission*

| 6.31.01.03.01 | Use latex gloves when handling blood and body fluids |
| 6.31.01.03.02 | Follow preestablished plan for handling body fluid waste and clean up on mats and gym floors |

| 6.31 | **Acquired Immune Deficiency Syndrome (AIDS): Understand unique attributes of individuals with AIDS** |
| 6.31.02 | Understand psychosocial issues |

6.31.02.01	*Awareness of prejudice and stigmatization of the individual*
6.31.02.01.01	Prepare others in class with facts about AIDS
6.31.02.01.02	Use information about current status of confidentiality laws to guide behavior
6.31.02.01.03	Model an attitude of acceptance

| 6.32 | **Congenital Effects of Drug Dependency: Understand unique attributes of individuals who were born to individuals addicted to drugs or alcohol** |
| 6.32.01 | Understand physical attributes |

6.32.01.01	*Understand implications of abnormal movement patterns*
6.32.01.01.01	Adapt activities for individuals with tremors
6.32.01.01.02	Adapt activities for individuals with muscle spasms
6.32.01.02	*Understand implications of developmental delays*
6.32.01.02.01	Plan activities that are developmentally appropriate
6.32.01.02.02	Include into regular physical education with developmental appropriate peers
6.32.01.03	*Understand implications of abnormal muscle tone*
6.32.01.03.01	Consult with physical therapist
6.32.01.03.02	Adapt activities to poor muscle control

| 6.32 | **Congenital Effects of Drug Dependency: Understand unique attributes of individuals who were born to individuals addicted to drugs or alcohol** |
| 6.32.02 | Understand cognitive attributes |

6.32.02.01	*Understand implications of abnormalities in alertness*
6.32.02.01.01	Plan activities that command attention
6.32.02.01.02	Use students' names to gain attention
6.32.02.01.03	Provide incentives to maintain attention

6.32

Congenital Effects of Drug Dependency: Understand unique attributes of individuals who were born to individuals addicted to drugs or alcohol

6.32.03

Understand health and medical attributes

6.32.03.01

Understand implications of congenital heart defects

6.32.03.01.01

Consult with physician for limitations

6.32.03.01.02

Adapt activities for exercise tolerance limitations

Standard 7 CURRICULUM THEORY AND DEVELOPMENT

7.01

> ### Understand that organizing centers (i.e., frames of reference, themes, or emphases) are the focus for curriculum design

7.01.01

> Understand the influence of educational trends such as culturally responsive pedagogy, inclusive education, knowledge based approaches, and outcome based education on physical education curriculum

7.01.01.01 *Understand the adapted physical educator's role in an inclusive physical education curriculum*

7.01.01.01.01 Collaborate with the regular physical education teacher about the progress and participation of the individuals with disabilities

7.01.01.01.02 Teach fundamental motor and play skills to enable individuals with and without disabilities to participate together in an inclusive physical education program

7.01.01.01.03 Develop and assist in implementing a plan to enable individuals' successful and maximum participation

7.01.01.01.04 Develop curricula that are accessible and that build on the concept of the least restrictive environment (LRE)

7.01

> ### Understand that organizing centers (i.e., frames of reference, themes, or emphases) are the focus for curriculum design

7.01.02

> Recognize the existence of curricular models in physical education such as movement education, fitness, developmental, activity based, humanistic/social development, and personal meaning

7.01.02.01 *Discuss the pros and cons of various curricular models designed specifically for adapted physical education such as I-CAN and Data-Based Gymnasium*

7.01.02.01.01 Write IEP and lesson plan objectives compatible with curricular models such as I-CAN and Data-Based Gymnasium

7.01.02.01.02 Implement curricular objectives consistent with individuals' current levels of educational performance

7.01

> ### Understand that organizing centers (i.e., frames of reference, themes, or emphases) are the focus for curriculum design

7.01.03

> Understand how information from society, learner needs and interests (including strengths and abilities), and physical education subject matter relate in the identification of organizing centers

7.01.03.01 *Understand how to operationalize the concept of "reasonable accommodation" within the curriculum design process for individuals with disabilities*

7.01.03.01.01 Individualize learning objectives to facilitate inclusion of individuals into the instructional activities of the regular class

7.01.03.01.02 Adapt activities/skills based upon the individual's abilities

7.01

Understand that organizing centers (i.e., frames of reference, themes, or emphases) are the focus for curriculum design

7.01.04
Understand how philosophical and psychological concerns influence selection of organizing centers

7.01.04.01   *Understand the implications of social views and values in selection of organizing centers for individuals with disabilities*

7.01.04.01.01   Plan for and adapt organizing centers that are accessible

7.01.04.01.02   Prepare all individuals without disabilities for inclusion of individuals with a disability in a regular physical education class

7.01.04.02   *Understand the implications of relevant assessment data in identification of organizing centers for individuals with disabilities*

7.01.04.02.01   Account for all individuals' abilities when organizing the curriculum

7.01.04.02.02   Plan for the successful and maximum participation of individuals with disabilities

7.01

Understand that organizing centers (i.e., frames of reference, themes, or emphases) are the focus for curriculum design

7.01.05
Generate alternative organizing centers as the focus for the physical education curriculum

7.01.05.01   *Understand implications of contemporary trends related to individuals with disabilities (e.g., Least Restrictive Environment (LRE), Regular Education Initiative (REI), Full Inclusion)*

7.01.05.01.01   Implement organizing centers that meet the needs of individuals with disabilities

7.01.05.01.02   Collaborate with the IEP team and include the regular physical education teacher, if relevant, to determine program placement

7.01.05.01.03   Defend the selection of organizing centers based on implementation of either LRE or inclusion

7.02

Understand how to select content goals based on relevant and appropriate assessment

7.02.01
Understand how to specify content using approaches such as structure-of-content, objective-taxonomic, and task descriptive

7.02.01.01   *Distinguish between the developmental and functional approaches to curriculum design for individuals with disabilities*

7.02.01.01.01   Devise goals that are individually and age appropriate

7.02.01.01.02   Plan for goals using a task specific or developmental approach depending on learner needs

7.03	**_Understand how to conduct learner analysis_**
7.03.01	Understand the purpose of pretest data for selection of relevant and appropriate assessment tools

7.03.01.01   *Understand the requirement for establishing the present level of performance in individuals with disabilities*

7.03.01.01.01   Assess present level of educational performance in physical education

7.03.01.01.02   Analyze results of tests used to establish individual's present level of performance in physical education

7.03.01.02   *Understand how pretest data are factored into the IEP process*

7.03.01.02.01   Interpret the results of tests used to establish the individual's present level of performance

7.03.01.02.02   Use test results to write objectives that are related to the individual's present level of performance

7.03.01.02.03   Present the results of the assessment process at the IEP meeting

7.03	**_Understand how to conduct learner analysis_**
7.03.02	Interpret pretest data as a basis for instruction

7.03.02.01   *Understand how placement decisions are made as a function of the IEP process*

7.03.02.01.01   Discuss assessment results with the IEP team prior to program placement decisions

7.03.02.01.02   Consider all factors (motor, social, behavioral) when making a placement decision

7.03	**_Understand how to conduct learner analysis_**
7.03.03	Understand how to devise a process for collecting pretest data that reveals entry learning levels related to individual strengths and weaknesses

7.03.03.01   *Understand the requirement for using valid and reliable tests to measure the motor attributes of individuals with disabilities prior to development of the IEP*

7.03.03.01.01   Identify the strengths and weaknesses of the major assessment instruments used in adapted physical education (see Standard 4.0)

7.03.03.01.02   Conduct assessments in accordance with the procedures established for administration of the instrument selected

7.03.03.02   *Understand the distinction between using informal assessment techniques such as rating scales and checklists versus formal techniques such as criterion-referenced tests (see Standard 8.0)*

7.03.03.02.01   Utilize informal assessment procedures to screen for areas of strength and weakness in physical education to determine need for further testing prior to IEP development

7.03.03.02.02   Utilize formal assessment measures to test for areas of strength and weakness in physical education to determine program placement and IEP development

7.04	**Understand how to derive learning objectives based on relevant and appropriate assessment**
7.04.01	Understand how to specify learning objectives that are congruent with the underlying goals of the curriculum

7.04.01.01 — *Derive learning objectives that are congruent with the definition of physical education as it appears in the Individuals with Disabilities Education Act (IDEA) (PL 101-476)*

7.04.01.01.01 — Utilize assessment results to individualize instruction for each individual

7.04.01.01.02 — Devise appropriate objective criteria and evaluative procedures to determine the achievement of instructional objectives

7.04	**Understand how to derive learning objectives based on relevant and appropriate assessment**
7.04.02	Understand how to develop precise learning objectives

7.04.02.01 — *Understand the criteria required for writing measurable objectives as specified for the IEP*

7.04.02.01.01 — Write objectives that are observable, identifiable, and measurable (see Standard 9.03.01.03.01)

7.04.02.01.02 — Write objectives that relate directly to the individual's needs as determined by motor assessment

7.04	**Understand how to derive learning objectives based on relevant and appropriate assessment**
7.04.03	Understand how to conduct a task analysis for the purpose of ordering learning objectives

7.04.03.01 — *Recognize task analysis that illuminates the essential ecological components of skill acquisition for individuals with disabilities*

7.04.03.01.01 — Teach to the levels of the ecological task analysis that are appropriate for each individual

7.04.03.01.02 — Utilize ecological task analysis to establish appropriate skill sequences for each individual

7.04	**Understand how to derive learning objectives based on relevant and appropriate assessment**
7.04.04	Understand how to conduct an activity analysis for the purpose of ordering learning objectives

7.04.04.01 — *Understand the impact of cognitive, affective, and psychomotor development of individuals with a disability on the selection of an activity in which they will participate*

7.04.04.01.01 — Modify activities to meet each individual's needs

7.04.04.01.02 — Adapt activities to complement the individual's strengths

| 7.05 | **Understand how to devise learning experiences** |
| 7.05.01 | Understand how to substantiate the selection of learning experiences |

7.05.01.01   *Understand the cyclical nature of the IEP process and how content can be revised in light of attainment of short term instructional objectives*

7.05.01.01.01   Write short term instructional objectives designed to meet long term goals (see Standard 9.03.01.03.02)

7.05.01.01.02   Use the appropriate developmental sequence of motor skills

7.05.01.01.03   Revise, at least on an annual basis, goals and objectives commensurate with the individual's achievement

| 7.05 | **Understand how to devise learning experiences** |
| 7.05.02 | Understand how to utilize individualization (such as learning style options, pacing, and level of difficulty) as a basis for implementing learning experiences |

7.05.02.01   *Understand how to organize practice in a manner that capitalizes on the learning styles of individuals with disabilities (see Standard 10.01.01-10.01.07)*

7.05.02.01.01   Utilize peer trainers to enable maximum participation of individuals with disabilities

7.05.02.01.02   Teach peers how to interact in a positive manner with individuals with disabilities

Standard **8** ASSESSMENT

8.01	**Legislative Issues: Legislation in regard to assessment of individuals with disabilities throughout the lifespan (see Standard 5.0)**
8.01.01	Awareness of federal and state legislation for assessment of individuals with disabilities

8.01.01.01   *Understand personnel requirements for assessment under federal and state law*

8.01.01.01.01   Demonstrate adequate training for valid test administration

8.01.01.01.02   Explain requirements of federal and state law to parents relative to motor assessment

8.01.01.02   *Understand the criteria that the instrument(s) used must meet to be considered acceptable under the law in terms of validity and reliability*

8.01.01.02.01   Utilize instruments that meet criteria acceptable under the law

8.01.01.02.02   Identify characteristics of instruments used that comply with federal law such as validity

8.01.01.03   *Understand the process of assessment under the law*

8.01.01.03.01   Conduct assessment in a nondiscriminatory manner

8.01.01.03.02   Assess according to the frequency required by law

8.01.01.04   *Understand the difference between instructional services and related services for individuals with disabilities*

8.01.01.04.01   Explain the differences between instructional services and related services for individuals with disabilities to parents and guardians

8.01.01.04.02   Recommend related services to parents and guardians as appropriate

8.01	**Legislative Issues: Legislation in regard to assessment of individuals with disabilities throughout the lifespan (see Standard 5.0)**
8.01.02	Awareness of state and school district regulations/guidelines for assessment of individuals with disabilities

8.01.02.01   *Knowledge of LEA eligibility criteria for adapted physical education*

8.01.02.01.01   Communicate the rationale and use of eligibility criteria for adapted physical education

8.01.02.01.02   Implement eligibility criteria for placing students into adapted physical education

8.01	**Legislative Issues: Legislation in regard to assessment of individuals with disabilities throughout the lifespan (see Standard 5.0)**
8.01.03	Knowledge of the referral process

8.01.03.01   *Understand the processes involved in referring and assessing individuals with disabilities for special education services*

8.01.03.01.01   Comply with the timelines for responsiveness to a referral

118

| 8.01.03.01.02 | Complete assessment process within the specified time under the law |

8.01.03.02   *Recognize the physical educator's domain of motor performance*

| 8.01.03.02.01 | Explain the motor domain related to physical activities for individuals with disabilities |

| 8.01.03.02.02 | Initiate and support referrals to appropriate professionals for assessment |

8.01.03.03   *Select appropriate procedures for data gathering based on referral information and suspected areas of motor disability*

| 8.01.03.03.01 | Conduct appropriate screening for individuals with suspected motor disabilities |

| 8.01.03.03.02 | Relate areas of screening with parameters measured in the assessment process |

8.01.03.04   *Refer individuals with disabilities to other professionals*

| 8.01.03.04.01 | Understand the roles of related services personnel in serving individuals with disabilities such as physical, occupational, and speech therapy |

| 8.01.03.04.02 | Explain to parents and guardians the role and purpose(s) of various related services professionals |

8.01

> ### Legislative Issues: Legislation in regard to assessment of individuals with disabilities throughout the lifespan (see Standard 5.0)

8.01.04
> Understand the ethical issues of assessment such as non-biased assessment, use of individual's native language or commonly used form of communication (see Standard 5.0)

8.01.04.01   *Understand what is meant by informed consent of parents and guardians*

| 8.01.04.01.01 | Obtain informed consent for assessment process |

| 8.01.04.01.02 | Explain a student's need for motor assessment to parents and guardians hesitant to give consent for assessment |

8.01.04.02   *Understand due process and its ethical implications*

| 8.01.04.02.01 | Comply with the due process procedures for all physical education services |

| 8.01.04.02.02 | Explain due process to parents and guardians as needed |

8.01.04.03   *Understand the cultural as well as the language conditions for assessment*

| 8.01.04.03.01 | Apply all necessary modifications for all possible cultural and language conditions |

| 8.01.04.03.02 | Use an interpreter in instances in which students speak English as a second language |

8.01.04.04   *Understand the need for confidentiality of records*

| 8.01.04.04.01 | Read appropriate records on individual prior to gathering assessment data |

| 8.01.04.04.02 | Obtain information discretely from classroom teacher and other professionals prior to gathering data |

8.01

> ***Legislative Issues: Legislation in regard to assessment of individuals with disabilities throughout the lifespan (see Standard 5.0)***
>
> 8.01.05   Acknowledge the rights of parents or guardians to obtain an appropriate and objective evaluation of performance by personnel outside the educational agency

8.01.05.01   *Articulate the relationship between the results of an outside evaluation and the results of motor assessment conducted by appropriately trained professionals under the law*

8.01.05.01.01   Communicate, where appropriate, with outside personnel who conducted the evaluations

8.01.05.01.02   Resolve or validate the results of motor assessment with results of assessment by outside personnel

8.02

> ***Terminology: The nomenclature utilized in the specialized field of motor assessment of individuals with disabilities***
>
> 8.02.01   Awareness of the differences between screening, assessment, measurement and evaluation

8.02.01.01   *Understand the purpose of screening*

8.02.01.01.01   Conduct appropriate screening

8.02.01.01.02   Articulate the findings of the screening process to other professionals, parents and guardians

8.02.01.02   *Understand the purpose of assessment*

8.02.01.02.01   Explain the various purposes for which assessment data are collected

8.02.01.02.02   Describe the primary purposes for which assessment data are used in adapted physical education

8.02.01.03   *Understand the purpose of measurement*

8.02.01.03.01   Distinguish between the purposes of measurement of individuals with disabilities with measurement of individuals without disabilities

8.02.01.03.02   Describe how measurements are used in adapted physical education

8.02.01.04   *Understand the purpose for evaluation*

8.02.01.04.01   Compare and contrast the purposes of program evaluation for individuals with disabilities and individuals without disabilities

8.02.01.04.02   Explain how program evaluation can be used for comparing adapted physical education to regular physical education programs

8.02

> ***Terminology: The nomenclature utilized in the specialized field of motor assessment of individuals with disabilities***
>
> 8.02.02   Knowledge of formal and informal methods for gathering qualitative as well as quantitative data on motor performance

8.02.02.01   *Understand how to use the various forms of data collected as related to individuals with disabilities*

8.02.02.01.01   Utilize diagnostic evaluations, instructional assessment, and program evaluation for monitoring progress

8.02.02.01.02   Relate information obtained from parent and guardian reports and other informal measures to formally obtained performance measures

8.02   **Terminology: The nomenclature utilized in the specialized field of motor assessment of individuals with disabilities**

8.02.03   Awareness of curriculum-embedded methods of gathering data

8.02.03.01   *Understand the process of gathering data on play behavior*

8.02.03.01.01   Administer one or more curriculum-based evaluation procedures such as I-CAN, Data-Based Gymnasium, and ABC

8.02.03.01.02   Utilize data gathered on play behavior in reporting present levels of performance of individuals with disabilities

8.02   **Terminology: The nomenclature utilized in the specialized field of motor assessment of individuals with disabilities**

8.02.04   Awareness of terminology such as eligibility criteria, individualized educational plan and current level of performance

8.02.04.01   *Knowledge of terminology related to motor assessment*

8.02.04.01.01   Communicate utilizing terminology unique to assessment of individual with disabilities

8.02.04.01.02   Teach colleagues appropriate terminology for movement parameters

8.02   **Terminology: The nomenclature utilized in the specialized field of motor assessment of individuals with disabilities**

8.02.05   Understand reasons for discrepancies between performance on standardized tests and curriculum-embedded performance

8.02.05.01   *Knowledge of how performance score discrepancies relate to individuals with disabilities*

8.02.05.01.01   Defend or refute scores on standardized tests against performance-based observations of a pupil's present level of performance

8.02.05.01.02   Use appropriate assessment procedures such as age appropriate evaluation, functional skills assessment, life-skills measurement, developmentally appropriate, bottom-up and top-down approaches

8.02.05.01.03   Integrate motor performance data with behaviors reported by other professionals and caregivers

8.03   **Administration: Knowledge of an assortment of instruments measuring all aspects of human performance**

8.03.01   Awareness of instruments measuring the qualities necessary for physical and motor fitness, fundamental motor skills and patterns, skills in aquatics, dance and individual and group games and sports as well as functional living skills

8.03.01.01   *Knowledge of curriculum-based assessment procedures such as I-CAN, Data-Based Gymnasium, and ABC*

8.03.01.01.01	Utilize at least one curriculum-based assessment procedure
8.03.01.01.02	Describe some of the administrative advantages of curriculum-based assessment procedures
8.03.01.02	*Knowledge of the instruments most commonly used by adapted physical educators*
8.03.01.02.01	Utilize tests measuring physical fitness such as AAHPERD Health Related Fitness Test, AAHPERD Special Fitness Test for Mildly Mentally Retarded Persons, AAHPERD Youth Fitness Test, Fit for Me, Project Unique, and The Prudential Fitnessgram
8.03.01.02.02	Utilize tests measuring the acquisition of motor skills such as: Bruininks-Oseretsky Test of Motor Proficiency, Hughes Basic Gross Motor Assessment, Ohio State University Scale of Intra-Gross Motor Assessment (SIGMA), Motor Ability Test
8.03.01.02.03	Utilize tests measuring motor development such as: Brigance Diagnostic Inventory of Early Development, Denver Developmental Screening Test, Peabody Developmental Motor Scales, Test of Gross Motor Development (TGMD), Project M.O.V.E.
8.03.01.02.04	Utilize tests measuring perceptual motor function such as: Purdue Perceptual Motor Survey
8.03.01.03	*Know other measurement and evaluation procedures prescribed by the LEA*
8.03.01.03.01	Utilize the measurement and evaluation procedures used by the local education agency when appropriate
8.03.01.03.02	Explain advantages of the LEA's prescribed measurement and evaluation procedures to other professionals
8.03.01.04	*Use specific standardized instruments or procedures for determining needs in related services such as checklists or observation techniques suggested by other specialists*
8.03.01.04.01	Explain motor demands made by instruments measuring language and cognitive function
8.03.01.04.02	Explain procedures used by other professionals to evaluate movement including reflex testing, mobility, flexibility, sensory motor, gross motor and fine motor skills, positioning/handling techniques, and leisure skills
8.03.01.05	*Know other measurement and evaluation procedures used by related service personnel*
8.03.01.05.01	Distinguish interrelationship of motor skills with related services such as speech and language, occupational and physical therapy
8.03.01.05.02	Recognize the variety of motor skills and abilities assessed by other professionals on the multidisciplinary team

8.03	**Administration: Knowledge of an assortment of instruments measuring all aspects of human performance**
8.03.02	Recognize the need for staff training, additional administrative support and reallocation of resources in utilizing a diversity of instruments

8.03.02.01	*Determine the level of need for inservices on test administration for individuals with disabilities*
8.03.02.01.01	Inservice regular physical educators on the administration of appropriate data gathering techniques, instruments, or procedures
8.03.02.01.02	Inservice regular physical educators on screening procedures for making appropriate referrals to adapted physical education

8.04

8.04.01

Interpretation: Gaining clarification and meaning of measurement results

Understand the use of measurement results for the purpose of identifying educational needs

8.04.01.01   *Interpret measurement results for diagnosis and screening*

8.04.01.01.01   Utilize the measurement results for diagnosis and screening to refer individuals with disabilities for further assessment

8.04.01.01.02   Utilize measurement results for diagnosis and screening to write annual instructional goals

8.04.01.02   *Interpret norm-referenced, criterion-referenced, and content-referenced results for individuals with disabilities*

8.04.01.02.01   Utilize the results of norm-referenced, criterion-referenced, and content-referenced instruments in programming for individuals with disabilities

8.04.01.02.02   Utilize the results of norm-referenced, criterion-referenced, and content-referenced instruments in determining annual instructional goals

8.04.01.03   *Establish norm-referenced and criterion-referenced standards for qualifying students for placement in adapted physical education*

8.04.01.03.01   Utilize the entrance standards established to recommend adapted physical education services for individuals with disabilities

8.04.01.03.02   Explain the entrance standards to caregivers and other professionals during the IEP meeting

8.04

8.04.02

Interpretation: Gaining clarification and meaning of measurement results

Understand the use of measurement results for instructional planning

8.04.02.01   *Interpret measurement results for instructional planning*

8.04.02.01.01   Show evidence of the effect of measurements on the instructional plans

8.04.02.01.02   Modify expectations for student performance based on measurement results

8.04.02.02   *Interpret measurement results for monitoring progress in individuals with disabilities*

8.04.02.02.01   Incorporate the measurement results used to monitor progress in individuals with disabilities in program evaluation

8.04.02.02.02   Utilize measurement results in summative evaluation

8.04

8.04.03

Interpretation: Gaining clarification and meaning of measurement results

Understand the relationships between measures of physical and motor fitness, fundamental motor skills and patterns, skills in aquatics, dance and individual and group games and sports

8.04.03.01   *Incorporate integrated activities into the instructional plan*

8.04.03.01.01   Incorporate activities addressing reflex behavior, sensorimotor function, leisure skills, and functional skills into the educational plan (see Standard 9.03)

8.04.03.01.02	Include lifetime activities in the instructional plan based on the results of assessment
8.04.03.02	*Understand the importance of providing feedback for social, behavioral and language skills as they relate to and are demonstrated in a motor performance context*
8.04.03.02.01	Incorporate the necessary feedback concerning social, behavioral, and language skills into the student's overall physical education plan
8.04.03.02.02	Utilize both general and specific feedback when implementing the physical education plan
8.04.03.03	*Understand the connection between motor performance measures and self-help and mobility skills*
8.04.03.03.01	Incorporate self-help and mobility skills into the students physical education plan when appropriate
8.04.03.03.02	Identify changes in self-help and mobility skills
8.04.03.04	*Understand the importance of parental or guardians' input in the assessment process*
8.04.03.04.01	Actively seek parental or guardian input
8.04.03.04.02	Include parents or guardians in the delivery of services by encouraging family activities

8.04 8.04.04	**Interpretation: *Gaining clarification and meaning of measurement results*** Understand the importance of effectively communicating the results of assessment

8.04.04.01	*Communicate motor performance scores to parents or guardians*
8.04.04.01.01	Interpret motor performance scores to parents or guardians
8.04.04.01.02	Explain the relationship between motor performance scores and play behavior observed by parents or guardians
8.04.04.02	*Communicate motor performance scores to classroom teachers and other professionals*
8.04.04.02.01	Interpret motor performance scores to classroom teachers and other professionals
8.04.04.02.02	Work cooperatively with other professionals to determine the need to refer for further testing for additional instructional or related services
8.04.04.02.03	Explain the importance of providing general, specific, and corrective feedback for motor performance
8.04.04.03	*Communicate motor performance scores to individuals with disabilities as appropriate*
8.04.04.03.01	Interpret motor performance scores to individuals with disabilities as appropriate
8.04.04.03.02	Question individuals with disabilities on how they might improve their performance over the next review period

8.04 8.04.05	**Interpretation: *Gaining clarification and meaning of measurement results*** Understand measurement results that reach a criterion determining eligibility for adapted physical education

8.04.05.01	*Understand the local measurement criteria for determining eligibility for adapted physical education*
8.04.05.01.01	Interpret local criteria for determining eligibility for adapted physical education

8.04.05.01.02   Explain the difference between qualifying and non-qualifying performances relative to eligibility for adapted physical education

---

8.04

8.04.06

Interpretation: Gaining clarification and meaning of measurement results

Understand the choices of services available to students with disabilities in the school district or local educational agency

---

8.04.06.01   *Understand service delivery options for physical education in cooperation with a multi-disciplinary team*

8.04.06.01.01   Suggest the optimal service delivery option for physical education in cooperation with the multidisciplinary team

8.04.06.01.02   Agree upon the service delivery options for physical education in cooperation with the multi-disciplinary team

8.04.06.02   *Understand adaptations or modifications of activities based on the student's identified needs*

8.04.06.02.01   Provide suggestions for adaptations or modifications of activities based on the student's identified needs

8.04.06.02.02   Modify facilities and equipment as needed to accommodate the student's identified needs (see Standard 9.02.09-9.02.10)

8.04

8.04.07

Interpretation: Gaining clarification and meaning of measurement results

Recognize the need for staff training, additional administrative support and reallocation of resources for administration and interpretation

---

8.04.07.01   *Provide inservice for regular physical educators on measurement and interpretation of motor performance*

8.04.07.01.01   Offer assistance on assessment to other physical educators on an on-going basis

8.04.07.01.02   Attend inservices and workshops to keep current with assessment issues (see Standard 13.0)

8.04.07.02   *Recognize the need for classroom teacher involvement in motor performance assessment interpretation*

8.04.07.02.01   Offer inservice to classroom teachers about measurement and interpretation of motor performance as needed

8.04.07.02.02   Provide guidelines for referral to adapted physical education

---

8.05

8.05.01

Decision-Making: The process of making choices from alternatives

Knowledge of a theoretical framework with which to make comprehensive assessment decisions

---

8.05.01.01   *Understand the nature of decisions to be made regarding individuals with disabilities such as placement, diagnosis and programming*

8.05.01.01.01   Utilize the appropriate assessment instruments when making placement or programming decisions

8.05.01.01.02   Explain the use of assessment instruments for making placement and programming decisions

| 8.05 | **Decision-Making: The process of making choices from alternatives** |
| 8.05.02 | Understand the value of assessment as an on-going process |

8.05.02.01 *Understand how on-going assessment relates to programming decisions for individuals with disabilities*

8.05.02.01.01 Utilize on-going assessment in programming decisions for individuals with disabilities

8.05.02.01.02 Utilize annual goals as a means of on-going assessment

| 8.05 | **Decision-Making: The process of making choices from alternatives** |
| 8.05.03 | Understand instructional decisions based on measurements |

8.05.03.01 *Plan teaching based on assessment results*

8.05.03.01.01 Provide evidence of the effects of measurements on instructional decisions by changing teaching plans

8.05.03.01.02 Demonstrate that expectations for performance of students is based on the results of assessments

8.05.03.02 *Understand the difference between a full range of physical education services versus essential physical education service options for individuals with disabilities*

8.05.03.02.01 Explain the difference between the two service options to parents, guardians, and other professionals

8.05.03.02.02 Provide essential physical education services for individuals with disabilities

| 8.05 | **Decision-Making: The process of making choices from alternatives** |
| 8.05.04 | Knowledge of motor assessment resources available in the field |

8.05.04.01 *Locate names of local/state/regional resources for assistance with motor assessment issues*

8.05.04.01.01 Provide parents, guardians, and other professionals with names of local/state/regional resources for assistance with motor assessment issues

8.05.04.01.02 Explain to parents or guardians their rights to obtain assistance with motor assessment from sources outside the school environment

| 8.06 | **Skills Needed for Assessment Team Members: The ability to work together with other professionals in a multidisciplinary team (see Standard 15.0)** |
| 8.06.01 | Report the results of assessment procedures to parents, guardians and other professionals |

8.06.01.01 *Utilize the appropriate statements with regard to the individual with a disability when reporting assessment results*

8.06.01.01.01 Make statements of fact

8.06.01.01.02 Make statements of inference

8.06.01.01.03   Make statements of fact, inference and probability and distinguish among them

8.06.01.01.04   Utilize previous experience for establishing a context of reporting assessment results

8.06

> **Skills Needed for Assessment Team Members: The ability to work together with other professionals in a multidisciplinary team (see Standard 15.0)**
>
> 8.06.02   Record assessment results for use by members of the multidisciplinary team

8.06.02.01   *Understand the essential components of a comprehensive assessment report for use in making recommendations for programming*

8.06.02.01.01   State the essential dimensions of a summary report including demographics, overall summary of test results, specific behavioral observations during testing, specific subtest performances, and general recommendations regarding eligibility for services

8.06.02.01.02   Delineate between supportive data and opinion

8.06

> **Skills Needed for Assessment Team Members: The ability to work together with other professionals in a multidisciplinary team (see Standard 15.0)**
>
> 8.06.03   Understand the interface between the report of motor assessment, programming and the reports and programming of other team members

8.06.03.01   *Understand the potential for lesson plans and/or model lessons for regular physical education classes and inclusion experiences*

8.06.03.01.01   Write a task analysis that can be followed by a parent, guardian or aide

8.06.03.01.02   Demonstrate the use of a task analysis for teaching as it relates to assessment results

8.06.03.02   *Understand strategies which facilitate self-directed and independent participation of individuals with disabilities within the movement environment*

8.06.03.02.01   Plan community-based physical activity experiences

8.06.03.02.02   Coordinate community-based physical activity experiences with other professionals such as therapeutic recreation specialist or community nurse educator

8.06.03.03   *Understand how to collaborate and support other team members*

8.06.03.03.01   Engage other team members in discussion of the progress of individuals with disabilities at times other than formalized, planned meetings

8.06.03.03.02   Utilize multidisciplinary strategies as appropriate

9.01

9.01.01

> **Instructional Design: Understand the factors needed to develop a systematic overall curriculum plan of instruction**
> Analyze individual strengths/needs, goals and priorities

9.01.01.01
Understand individual needs, goals, and priorities specific to individuals with disabilities (see Standard 9.02.01, 9.03 and 9.04 and Standard 6.0)

9.01.01.01.01
Determine long term goals suitable for instruction given individuals' potential and time available to implement instructional programs such as the school year as well as considering such factors as equipment, space, and number of individuals per class

9.01.01.01.02
Determine the prerequisite behaviors and ancillary behaviors needed to complete the goals targeted for instruction such as demonstrating appropriate behavior

9.01.01.01.03
Evaluate individual's ability in the physical, cognitive and social domains based on the individual's assessment and evaluation of long term annual goals and behavioral objectives (see Standard 9.03)

9.01.01.01.04
Identify individual's preferences for activities

9.01.01.01.05
Consider individual's various learning modalities such as visual, kinesthetic or auditory

9.01.01.01.06
Establish and promote behaviors with the most immediate value such as those that allow individuals to function as independently as possible in the community and later in life

9.01.01.01.07
Identify behaviors that offer long term support and lifetime application

9.01

9.01.02

> **Instructional Design: Understand the factors needed to develop a systematic overall curriculum plan of instruction**
> Analyze resources, constraints, and alternate delivery systems

9.01.02.01
Understand resources, constraints, and alternate delivery systems and strategies specific to meeting the needs of individuals with disabilities (see Standard 7.0 and 15.03)

9.01.02.01.01
Develop support personnel to assist in planning for instruction such as the use of paraprofessionals and peer tutors (see Standard 15.03)

9.01.02.01.02
Develop community support services for developing instructional plan for individuals with disabilities such as Special Olympics, YMCA

9.01.02.01.03
Use existing resources in adapted physical education for instructional planning such as ABC (see Standard 7.0)

9.01.02.01.04
Advocate for accessibility to facilities and teaching areas such as ramps for individuals in wheelchairs and accessibility to playground equipment

9.01.02.01.05
Advocate for alternative placement in the least restrictive environment (see Standard 9.03.01.04)

9.01.02.01.06
Advocate for participation in intramural and interscholastic sport programs

| 9.01 | ***Instructional Design: Understand the factors needed to develop a systematic overall curriculum plan of instruction*** |
| 9.01.03 | Determine scope (goals and objectives) and sequence (when they will be taught) of the curriculum based on long term goals, which will serve as the basis for the IEP and IFSP (see Standard 9.03) |

9.01.03.01	*Understand the concept of "top-down planning" to establish long term goals for individuals with disabilities*
9.01.03.01.01	Select goals based on projected employment
9.01.03.01.02	Select goals based on living situation
9.01.03.01.03	Select goals based on leisure preferences
9.01.03.01.04	Select goals based on skill potential
9.01.03.01.05	Select goals based on access to facilities and equipment
9.01.03.02	*Understand the concept of instructional time and how it relates to planning functional curricula for individuals with disabilities*
9.01.03.02.01	Calculate the total time available in the program
9.01.03.02.02	Adjust the amount of time based on access to facilities and equipment
9.01.03.02.03	Adjust the amount of time based on student/teacher ratio
9.01.03.02.04	Adjust the amount of time based on teacher competency
9.01.03.02.05	Adjust the amount of time based on outside practice opportunities
9.01.03.03	*Understand how to delimit the number of goals that can be achieved in the program by individuals with disabilities based upon the amount of instructional time and the resources available*
9.01.03.03.01	Determine goal emphasis
9.01.03.03.02	Establish time needed to achieve mastery of objectives (see Standard 9.02 and 9.03)
9.01.03.03.03	Plan time needed for retention and maintenance
9.01.03.04	*Understand how to delineate and sequence the objectives across the years of the program, based upon the attributes of the learner's disability, so that the program goals can be achieved in the time available*
9.01.03.04.01	Sequence objectives based on age appropriateness
9.01.03.04.02	Sequence objectives based on developmental level
9.01.03.04.03	Sequence objectives based on social ability such as interacting with others
9.01.03.04.04	Determine when instruction should begin
9.01.03.04.05	Determine when achievement is expected
9.01.03.04.06	Determine what objectives should be included in the IEP
9.01.03.05	*Understand how to use the scope and sequence of the objectives in the curriculum as the basis for program evaluation of individuals with a disability (see Standard 12.0)*

9.01.03.05.01   Evaluate whether the program is progressing as planned

9.01.03.05.02   Determine when program revisions are needed

9.01.03.05.03   Communicate the program purpose

9.01.03.05.04   Communicate the individual's progress

9.01.03.05.05   Monitor IEP progress using the curriculum scope and sequence

---

9.02   **Organization: Design units and lesson plans to maximize instruction**

9.02.01   Plan to accommodate for learner characteristics and individual background

---

9.02.01.01   *Understand that individuals with disabilities exhibit a unique array of characteristics such as limited attention span, distractibility, and hyperactivity (see Standard 6.0)*

9.02.01.01.01   Plan structured program, class routines and activities such as including instructional learning cues to maintain attention (see Standard 10.04)

9.02.01.01.02   Select equipment that maintains attention such as considering color, size, and shape

9.02.01.01.03   Plan a variety of presentations so that specific tasks are altered if needed in order to maintain interest and attention

9.02.01.01.04   Understand that the readiness level of individuals with disabilities may vary

9.02.01.01.05   Plan a variety of teaching styles that will meet the needs of individuals with disabilities (see Standard 10.01)

9.02.01.02   *Understand that the readiness level of individuals with disabilities may vary*

9.02.01.02.01   Plan programs to include appropriate modifications for individuals with disabilities who learn at slower or different rates

9.02.01.02.02   Plan programs to include appropriate skills and activities based on individual's readiness level

9.02.01.03   *Understand motivation levels of individuals with disabilities*

9.02.01.03.01   Plan programs with consideration of the teaching behaviors to promote and motivate the learner (see Standard 10.02)

9.02.01.03.02   Plan programs with consideration to what the individual finds reinforcing to promote and motivate the learner

9.02.01.04   *Understand the wide variety of individual differences among and within different types of individuals with disabilities*

9.02.01.04.01   Plan programs to account for individual differences among individuals with disabilities such as using various teaching styles

9.02.01.04.02   Plan programs to modify games and activities (see Standard 9.02.08)

9.02.01.04.03   Plan programs for appropriate use of environment, equipment, rules, materials and activities (see Standard 10.01)

| 9.02 | **Organization: Design units and lesson plans to maximize instruction** |
| 9.02.02 | Accommodate the medical history of the individual in instructional design |

9.02.02.01 — *Understand the effect certain medical conditions may have when planning physical activity for an individual with a disability*

9.02.02.01.01 — Check individual's medical records (file) and be aware of current medical condition and medication being taken such as by individuals with seizures

9.02.02.01.02 — Consult with a physician and other medical staff regarding recommended and contraindicated activities as a result of the individual's medical condition/medication

9.02.02.01.03 — Plan for recommended activities and exercises and avoid activities and exercises that are contraindicated such as butterfly swim stroke and diving activities for individuals with atlantoaxial instability

9.02.02.01.04 — Keep a schedule for medication and chart the effect certain medications (type, dosage) have on movement performance such as fatigue or errors in movement and distractibility or hypoglycemia in individuals with diabetes

9.02.02.01.05 — Organize the learning environment so that disabilities are not aggravated or exacerbated such as the removal of strobe lights, flickering fluorescent lighting, or sounds to prevent the inducement of seizures

9.02.02.02 — *Understand the effect medication (type and dosage) may have on the behavior and performance of an individual with a disability when planning activities*

9.02.02.02.01 — Plan programs based on the effect the medication has on the individual's motor skill abilities and physical work capacity

9.02.02.02.02 — Plan programs based on the effect the medication has on the length of time the individual is able to remain on task

| 9.02 | **Organization: Design units and lesson plans to maximize instruction** |
| 9.02.03 | Plan for safety and risk management |

9.02.03.01 — *Understand proper safety techniques and principles specific to individuals with disabilities*

9.02.03.01.01 — Plan activities by taking into account the amount of risk involved by considering such factors as space available, floor surfaces, appropriate equipment, and types of activities offered

9.02.03.01.02 — Plan for such safety procedures as handling wheelchair transfers, securing and strapping techniques, negotiating stairs, inclines, bracing, reinsertion of tracheotomy tube, and guiding techniques

9.02.03.01.03 — Identify and post safety procedures for specific emergency procedures

9.02.03.01.04 — Be aware of national, state, and community agencies that have health and safety information including voluntary health organizations and associations related to a specific condition and government office/agency

| 9.02 | **Organization: Design units and lesson plans to maximize instruction** |
| 9.02.04 | Plan for proper supervision following school policies |

9.02.04.01 — *Understand potentially dangerous situations and activities specific to individuals with disabilities*

9.02.04.01.01	Identify and share information and procedures with regular physical education teacher and others regarding individuals with disabilities and special needs such as individuals who have seizures and other conditions
9.02.04.01.02	Develop and post emergency plan specific to individuals with a disability such as procedures to follow for an individual having a seizure
9.02.04.01.03	Plan for directional, visual, auditory and tactile signals for potentially dangerous activities and emergencies
9.02.04.01.04	Develop specific supervision and spotting procedures
9.02.04.02	*Understand LEA policies with regard to safety of individuals and staff*
9.02.04.02.01	Implement safety policies specific to individuals with disabilities
9.02.04.02.02	Fill out appropriate forms with regard to safety of individuals and staff

9.02	**Organization: Design units and lesson plans to maximize instruction**
9.02.05	Consider teacher/individual ratio

9.02.05.01	*Understand certain individuals with disabilities may need a lesser teacher/individual ratio*
9.02.05.01.01	Plan for activities using paraprofessionals and peer tutors for individuals who require greater attention for such reasons as being disruptive to others, short attention span or assistance with learning a skill
9.02.05.01.02	Plan for activities with and without assistance of teacher such as use of station or reciprocal style teaching (see Standard 10.0)
9.02.05.01.03	Plan for training of paraprofessionals and volunteers to assist individuals with disabilities (see Standard 15.03.07)

9.02	**Organization: Design units and lesson plans to maximize instruction**
9.02.06	Consider class size and composition

9.02.06.01	*Understand the effect the arrangement of the class and various formations will have when planning activities specific to individuals with disabilities*
9.02.06.01.01	Design for smaller group formations such as shorter relay lines with individuals who are easily distracted and/or display difficulty staying on task
9.02.06.01.02	Design class formation for individuals who need to be near the teacher such as deaf or hard of hearing
9.02.06.01.03	Structure the class composition to be free of extraneous stimuli
9.02.06.01.04	Design for the grouping of individuals with and without disabilities

9.02	**Organization: Design units and lesson plans to maximize instruction**
9.02.07	Plan for physical education classroom management, organization and routines

9.02.07.01	*Understand the importance of developing class management rules, routines, transition and consequences specific to individuals with disabilities (see Standard 10.04)*

9.02.07.01.01   Develop signals for getting the classes' attention, starting, and stopping the class taking into account various characteristics of learners

9.02.07.01.02   Design consistent routines and transitional procedures that can be used with individuals with disabilities such as tangible markings, like cones, for individuals who are easily distracted and display difficulty following directions

9.02.07.01.03   Plan to use peer tutors to assist in class management

---

9.02

9.02.08

Organization: Design units and lesson plans to maximize instruction

Plan for appropriate use of environment, equipment, rules, materials, and activities

---

9.02.08.01   *Understand how to plan the environment, equipment, rules, materials, and activities specific to individuals with disabilities*

9.02.08.01.01   Use equipment that is developmentally appropriate and accommodates the needs of individuals with disabilities

9.02.08.01.02   Plan for such games as beep baseball or goal ball to accommodate such individuals with disabilities who are visually impaired or blind (see Standard 9.02.09 - 9.02.12)

9.02

9.02.09

Organization: Design units and lesson plans to maximize instruction

Plan for modifications of environment

9.02.09.01   *Understand the concepts and strategies necessary to plan for the modification of the environment specific to individuals with disabilities such as the play area*

9.02.09.01.01   Reduce the playing area for individuals who have limited mobility

9.02.09.01.02   Use hard surfaces or play indoors for individuals such as those in wheelchairs

9.02.09.01.03   Lower the basket or net to varying heights in such games as basketball or volleyball for individuals with low stamina or deficient skill levels

9.02.09.01.04   Use sound devices, bright equipment, hand signals or flags, mark goals and boundaries for individuals with visual disabilities

9.02.09.01.05   Increase the size of the goal for individuals with an eye-hand deficit

9.02.09.01.06   Provide visual cues on wall to assist such individuals with short term memory or language barriers

---

9.02

9.02.10

Organization: Design units and lesson plans to maximize instruction

Plan for modifications of equipment

9.02.10.01   *Understand the concepts and strategies necessary to plan for the modifications of equipment specific to individuals with disabilities such as weight, size, color, and texture*

9.02.10.01.01   Use different size balls for individuals who are clumsy

9.02.10.01.02   Use a contrasting background to equipment such as when catching a ball outside or when performing dynamic balance activities (visual figure ground)

9.02.10.01.03   Use activities and equipment that are motivational such as brightly colored balls

9.02.10.01.04	Use equipment that will attract attention such as beep baseball or bell ball for individuals who are blind
9.02.10.01.05	Decrease the speed of a moving object such as adding or reducing weight, deflating a ball or putting a tail on the object
9.02.10.01.06	Shorten the length of the handle on a striking implement such as a racket, bat, or golf club
9.02.10.01.07	Use large visual targets for individuals with visual deficits
9.02.10.01.08	Use soft and light equipment such as Nerf Frisbee or ball for individuals who have difficulty handling objects
9.02.10.01.09	Make objects stationary such as using a batting tee for individuals who have difficulty striking a moving object
9.02.10.01.10	Use Velcro mitts and balls for children who have difficulty catching
9.02.10.01.11	Change the texture of the object such as using a foam ball for such individuals who are fearful of the object

---

| 9.02 | **Organization: Design units and lesson plans to maximize instruction** |
| 9.02.11 | Plan for modifications of rules |

9.02.11.01	*Understand the concepts and strategies necessary to plan for modification of rules specific to individuals with disabilities*
9.02.11.01.01	Use rules from various sports for disabled associations and organizations such as Challenger Little League Baseball, National Wheelchair Basketball Association (e.g., use two pushes in wheelchair basketball)
9.02.11.01.02	Play with different number of players on the floor than the rules permit to make the game more challenging or fair such as three players on a side for tennis or badminton
9.02.11.01.03	Use modifications such as having individuals move closer to the net or over the serving line when serving in games like volleyball or badminton
9.02.11.01.04	Reduce the number of rules to simplify game or activity
9.02.11.01.05	Preserve purpose of the game when modifying rules

---

| 9.02 | **Organization: Design units and lesson plans to maximize instruction** |
| 9.02.12 | Plan for modifications of activities and games |

9.02.12.01	*Understand the concepts and strategies necessary to plan for modification of activities and games specific to meet the needs of individuals with disabilities by incorporating such concepts as cooperative games or game intervention*
9.02.12.01.01	Avoid elimination games
9.02.12.01.02	Keep collective score among teams by combining points for both teams
9.02.12.01.03	Do not always keep score during games
9.02.12.01.04	Emphasize cooperation over winning among teammates as well as opponents
9.02.12.01.05	Plan games and activities that stress participation for everyone

9.02	**Organization: Design units and lesson plans to maximize instruction**
9.02.13	Plan for appropriate time spent in lesson

9.02.13.01   *Understand the importance of planning to maximize learning time with individuals with disabilities*

9.02.13.01.01   Maximize learning time by matching the difficulty of the task with the unique ability levels of individuals with disabilities (see Standard 9.02.01)

9.02.13.01.02   Plan for individuals with disabilities who require more time to complete tasks and need time for review

9.02.13.01.03   Sequence lesson plan activities according to unique needs of individuals with disabilities (see Standard 9.02.01)

9.02.13.01.04   Modify lesson plan format and activities according to unique needs of individuals with disabilities such as providing frequent rest periods for individuals with low physical vitality

9.02.13.01.05   Plan for individuals who need time to determine how best they will modify such factors as equipment or rules

9.02.13.02   *Understand the importance of planning to optimize instruction time with individuals with disabilities*

9.02.13.02.01   Teach individuals using optimal communication mode such as total communication for deaf or hard of hearing

9.02.13.02.02   Keep instructions to a minimum for individuals with mental or cognitive disabilities such as mental retardation

9.02.13.02.03   Use key words or commands to elicit the desired response or behavior with individuals with disabilities

9.02.13.03   *Understand the importance of planning to reduce transition time for individuals with disabilities*

9.02.13.03.01   Arrange environment to allow for smooth and quick transition from one activity to another when working with individuals who have limited attention spans or who need a longer period of time to move from one activity to another

9.02.13.03.02   Allow for adequate time for individuals to change in and out of physical education clothes, and who require assistance in changing such as individuals with orthopedic disabilities and/or multiple disabilities

9.02	**Organization: Design units and lesson plans to maximize instruction**
9.02.14	Determine individual progression through a formative evaluation plan (i.e., evaluates unit & lesson plans)

9.02.14.01   *Understand the importance of evaluating the progress of individuals with disabilities (see Standards 4.0 and 8.0)*

9.02.14.01.01   Chart progress on the individual's IEP or IFSP (see Standard 9.03)

9.02.14.01.02   Plan for the evaluation standards unique to individuals with disabilities that determine the mastery of a skill or activity such as using task analysis

9.02.14.01.03   Plan for the evaluation of individual program progression from dependent supervised training to independent completion of the activity

9.02.14.02   *Understand the importance of selecting realistic lesson plan goals and objectives that can be successfully attained by individuals with disabilities*

9.02.14.02.01   Include individuals with disabilities as part of the planning process of goals and objectives selected

9.02.14.02.02   When appropriate, include individuals with disabilities in recording progress using charts and tables

9.02.14.02.03   Select functional skills for instruction and evaluation that match the needs of individuals with disabilities

9.02.14.03   *Understand the importance of evaluating the functional aspects of performance for individuals with disabilities*

9.02.14.03.01   Evaluate performance in the environments in which individuals with disabilities will perform the skill

9.02.14.03.02   Evaluate performance based on criteria determined as needed for successful participation in the community such as being able to bowl at a bowling center

---

9.02   **Organization: Design units and lesson plans to maximize instruction**
9.02.15   Plans for paraprofessionals, volunteers & peer tutors

---

9.02.15.01   *Understand the importance of planning for paraprofessionals, volunteers and peer tutors to assist with teaching individuals with disabilities*

9.02.15.01.01   Establish a system of recruiting, training, communicating, and providing feedback with paraprofessionals, volunteers and peer tutors such as providing training in techniques used in data based physical education like monitoring behaviors with a checklist

9.02.15.01.02   Provide individuals with disabilities with tasks that are compatible with their ability level

---

9.03   **IEP and IFSP: Understand federal mandates involved in planning programs of physical education for individuals with disabilities**
9.03.01   Knowledge of IEP process

9.03.01.01   *Understand present level of performance such as knowledge of the movement skill development in individuals 3-21 years old with disabilities that includes physical fitness, fundamental skills, games, sport, and leisure*

9.03.01.01.01   Write present level of performance statement based on assessment information such as using normative test scores, criterion referenced test scores, and informal test methods (see Standard 4.0)

9.03.01.01.02   Write present level of performance statement based on information from records, parent, and other professional's information

9.03.01.02   *Understand annual physical education outcomes statements based on developmentally appropriate activities specific to individuals with disabilities and their needs*

9.03.01.02.01   Write annual motor outcomes statements based on present level of performance information

9.03.01.02.02   Write clear and concise annual motor outcomes statements

9.03.01.03   *Understand that short term motor instructional objectives include the components mandated by law such as specific skills, condition under which the skills are to be performed, and degree to which skills should be performed to indicate mastery*

9.03.01.03.01   Write instructional objectives in behavioral terms based on present level of performance information

9.03.01.03.02   Match objectives to previously established annual goals

9.03.01.03.03   Write instructional objectives while establishing a priority of need based on the individual

9.03.01.04   *Understand that a continuum of least restrictive environments in physical education exists*

9.03.01.04.01   Provide various physical education and adapted physical education delivery services to individuals with disabilities to meet specific learner needs

9.03.01.04.02   Work with other physical education service delivery providers to meet the needs of individuals with disabilities

9.03.01.04.03   Provide and advocate for each individual to receive full inclusion services when appropriate

9.03.01.05   *Understand that related services such as PT and OT are available based on the individual's needs*

9.03.01.05.01   Communicate and work with the related service providers in meeting the individual's established goals and objectives

9.03.01.05.02   Monitor the effectiveness of the related service to the individual's overall physical education goals and objectives

9.03.01.06   *Understand how to project dates for the initiation and duration of physical education services such as knowledge of establishing realistic dates for the implementation of the program*

9.03.01.06.01   Coordinate the individual's physical education program with all service providers

9.03.01.06.02   Monitor and sequence program progress and make sure service providers implement the individual's established physical education program for the duration of needed services

9.03.01.06.03   Monitor program progress for the duration of the established physical education program and until goals/objectives are met

9.03.01.07   *Understand physical education transition from school to community by demonstrating knowledge of the similarities & differences between physical education needs within the school structure to needs within the community*

9.03.01.07.01   Coordinate the transition skills needed within the existing physical education structure with community services

9.03.01.07.02   Collaborate with the support services and service providers in implementing the transition plan

9.03.01.07.03   Write age and ability transition goals and objectives according to the individual's ability within the physical education environment

9.03 | **IEP and IFSP: Understand federal mandates involved in planning programs of physical education for individuals with disabilities**
9.03.02 | Knowledge of IFSP process

9.03.02.01   *Understand child's present level of performance by identifying family's knowledge of their child's motor skills through various data collection methods including formal assessment, verbal communication, and observation*

9.03.02.01.01   Record the information collected from the family concerning child's motor skills

9.03.02.01.02   Write present level of performance based on information gathered from assessment, verbal communication, and observations

9.03.02.02   *Understand family's motor outcomes by developing a sequential instructional plan of motor skill activities that includes realistic goals & objectives for the family to implement with their child*

9.03.02.02.01   Write realistic annual goals for the child that include the needs of the family

9.03.02.02.02   Write objectives that reflect the present level of performance

9.03.02.02.03   Write a motor program that the family can implement that matches the stated goals and objectives

9.03.02.03   *Understand how to determine family timelines to meet motor outcome progress*

9.03.02.03.01   Write timelines that incorporate the child's motor needs to stated goals and objectives

9.03.02.03.02   Write timelines that are monitored by family and instructor

9.03.02.04   *Understand how to plan for services to meet family motor needs*

9.03.02.04.01   Monitor various services for the family to meet the established goals and objectives including community service, educational support, and other private and public services

9.03.02.04.02   Coordinate various early intervention services that meet the motor development needs of the child so that cooperation occurs, and not duplication of services

9.03.02.04.03   Monitor the various services which the family has in order to assess their contribution to the child's progress in motor development

9.03.02.05   *Understand how to establish dates for the implementation and evaluation of an IFSP*

9.03.02.05.01   Write dates for the implementation of the program, including gathering or purchasing of equipment, amount of time involved in training, and time to provide adequate space

9.03.02.05.02   Coordinate the child's motor program with the family, child, and early intervention service providers

9.03.02.05.03   Monitor motor development skill sequence and acquisition timeline

9.03.02.05.04   Monitor program progress and service providers' ability to implement the child's established motor program for the duration of the needed service

9.03.02.05.05   Monitor program progress and families' ability to implement the child's established program for the duration of the needed service

9.03.02.06   *Understand how to plan for motor transition from early intervention to school*

9.03.02.06.01   Determine the similarities and differences between the early intervention environment and that of the educational setting

9.03.02.06.02   Determine the similarities and differences between available early intervention services

9.03.02.06.03   Determine the similarities and differences between the individual's motor needs in the home in contrast to those same motor needs in school

9.04 9.04.01	**_Technology Applications: Demonstrate knowledge of communication systems sanctioned by the American Speech-Language-Hearing Association (ASHA)_** Understand verbal communication is a medium of oral communication that employs a linguistic code (language)

9.04.01.01   *Express thoughts, ideas, and feelings using oral communication in physical education class to individuals with language disabilities*

9.04.01.01.01   Rephrase thoughts or ideas during communication

9.04.01.01.02   Use appropriate vocabulary

9.04 9.04.02	**_Technology Applications: Demonstrate knowledge of communication systems sanctioned by the American Speech-Language-Hearing Association (ASHA)_** Understand nonverbal (alternative/augmentative) communication is any approach designed to support, enhance or supplement the communication of individuals who are not independent verbal communicators

9.04.02.01   *Understand how non-technical aides augment communication for individuals with speech and language disorders such as the deaf and hard of hearing*

9.04.02.01.01   Demonstrate a proficiency in communicating in physical education using sign language

9.04.02.01.02   Demonstrate a proficiency in communicating in physical education using Blissymbolics

9.04.02.01.03   Demonstrate a proficiency using Rebus

9.04.02.01.04   Demonstrate a proficiency in communicating in physical education using communication boards

9.04.02.01.05   Demonstrate a proficiency in communicating in physical education using facilitated communication

9.04.02.01.06   Demonstrate a proficiency in communicating in physical education using typing

9.04.02.01.07   Demonstrate a proficiency in communicating in physical education using writing

9.04.02.02   *Understand how technical aides augment communication for individuals with speech and language impairments such as orthopedic, autistic, and the traumatic brain injured*

9.04.02.02.01   Demonstrate a proficiency in communicating in physical education using a Touch Talker

9.04.02.02.02   Demonstrate a proficiency in communicating in physical education using a Light Talker

9.04.02.02.03   Demonstrate a proficiency in physical education using a Wolf

9.04.02.02.04   Demonstrate a proficiency in communicating in physical education using a Canon Communicator

9.04.02.02.05   Demonstrate a proficiency in communicating in physical education using a laptop computer as a computer based speaking and writing system

9.05 9.05.01	**_Assistive Devices: Knowledge of adaptation of assistive devices to enhance participation in physical education_** Understand how physical positioning can facilitate movement in physical education

9.05.01.01   *Identify types of equipment used to position individuals with disabilities such as cerebral palsy*

9.05.01.01.01	Use bolsters for positioning to facilitate movement
9.05.01.01.02	Use wedges for positioning to facilitate movement
9.05.01.01.03	Use side lying wedges for positioning to facilitate movement
9.05.01.01.04	Use strapping to maintain appropriate body alignment during physical education activities
9.05.01.01.05	Use standing frame for positioning to facilitate movement
9.05.01.02	*Understand how modified seating can enhance movement for individuals with disabilities such as cerebral palsy and spinal cord injuries*
9.05.01.02.01	Utilize adaptations to the wheelchair such as removal of arm rests to facilitate movement
9.05.01.02.02	Utilize alternative seating such as on a bench or on the floor to enhance movement in physical education

9.05	**Assistive Devices: Knowledge of adaptation of assistive devices to enhance participation in physical education**
9.05.02	Understand how canes enhance mobility in physical education

9.05.02.01	*Identify types of canes used by individuals with lower limb disabilities such as hemiplegia*
9.05.02.01.01	Incorporate use of a quad cane to enhance mobility
9.05.02.01.02	Incorporate use of an ice gripper cane to enhance mobility

9.05	**Assistive Devices: Knowledge of adaptation of assistive devices to enhance participation in physical education**
9.05.03	Understand how crutches enhance mobility in physical education

9.05.03.01	*Identify types of crutches that are most often used by individuals with disabilities such as amputees, long leg brace users, and individuals with a temporary disability*
9.05.03.01.01	Incorporate use of the Lofstrand crutch during physical education activities
9.05.03.01.02	Incorporate use of the forearm support crutch during physical education activities
9.05.03.01.03	Incorporate use of the platform crutch during physical education activities
9.05.03.01.04	Incorporate use of the underarm crutch during physical education activities

9.05	**Assistive Devices: Knowledge of adaptation of assistive devices to enhance participation in physical education**
9.05.04	Understand how walkers can provide more stability than crutches during physical education activities

9.05.04.01	*Identify types of walkers that are most often used by individuals with lower extremity disabilities*
9.05.04.01.01	Incorporate use of the pick up walker during physical education activities
9.05.04.01.02	Incorporate use of the rolling walker during physical education activities

9.05.04.01.03   Incorporate use of the forearm support walker during physical education activities

9.05.04.01.04   Incorporate use of the Kaye posture control walker during physical education activities

---

9.05

Assistive Devices: Knowledge of adaptation of assistive devices to enhance participation in physical education

9.05.05

Understand an orthosis is a positioning device for support or immobilization, and is used to prevent or correct a deformity, or to assist or restore function

---

9.05.05.01   *Identify types of orthotic devices for individuals with lower extremity disabilities such as cerebral palsy*

9.05.05.01.01   Accommodate the use of ankle-foot orthoses (AFO) during physical education activities

9.05.05.01.02   Accommodate the use of hip-knee-ankle-foot orthoses (HKAFO) during physical education activities

9.05.05.01.03   Accommodate the use of knee-ankle-foot orthoses (KAFO) during physical education activities

9.05.05.01.04   Accommodate use of reciprocating gait orthoses (RGO) during physical education activities

9.05.05.02   *Identify types of orthotic devices for individuals with upper extremity disabilities such as cerebral palsy*

9.05.05.02.01   Incorporate the use of Hand Oppens Orthoses during physical education activities

9.05.05.02.02   Incorporate the use of serpentine splints during physical education activities

---

9.05

Assistive Devices: Knowledge of adaptation of assistive devices to enhance participation in physical education

9.05.06

Understand a prosthesis is a substitute for a missing extremity

---

9.05.06.01   *Identify prosthetic devices for lower extremity amputees*

9.05.06.01.01   Incorporate the use of foot prostheses such as the Seattle Foot during physical education activities

9.05.06.01.02   Incorporate the use of lower limb prostheses during physical education activities

9.05.06.02   *Identify prosthetic devices for upper extremity amputees*

9.05.06.02.01   Incorporate the use of a Myoelectric arm during physical education activities

9.05.06.02.02   Incorporate the use of upper extremity prostheses during physical education activities

---

9.05

Assistive Devices: Knowledge of adaptation of assistive devices to enhance participation in physical education

9.05.07

Understand adaptations of equipment used for sport and recreational activities

---

9.05.07.01   *Understand specific adaptations of equipment for individuals with visual impairments*

9.05.07.01.01   Utilize beepers to help locate a target

9.05.07.01.02   Utilize handrails to adjust body posture

| 9.05.07.01.03 | Utilize beeper or bell balls in throwing, rolling, or catching activities |

9.05.07.02   *Understand specific adaptations of equipment for individuals with physical impairments*

9.05.07.02.01	Utilize strapping such as Velcro to attach striking implements to the arms of amputees or individuals who cannot grasp the implement
9.05.07.02.02	Enlarge the handle for grasping striking implements
9.05.07.02.03	Utilize Velcro gloves or mitts for students with upper extremity involvement to make catching easier
9.05.07.02.04	Use modified skis such as sit skis to enable individuals with lower extremity involvement to ski
9.05.07.02.05	Modify a walker by adding skis to enable individuals with lower extremity involvement to stand and ski

9.06

Mobility Devices: Knowledge of various mobility aids to enhance participation in physical education

9.06.01   Understand that wheelchairs either enhance individuals' mobility or provide total means of mobility for those who have lower extremity physical disabilities

9.06.01.01   *Understand types of manual wheelchairs such as medical model, lightweight or sports, and racing or track wheelchairs*

9.06.01.01.01	Incorporate the use of stainless steel manual wheelchairs in physical education
9.06.01.01.02	Incorporate safety travel/lift in space wheelchairs designed for individuals with severe physical disabilities in physical education
9.06.01.01.03	Incorporate lightweight or sport wheelchairs in physical education activities
9.06.01.01.04	Incorporate track or racing wheelchairs for racing

9.06.01.02   *Understand components of manual wheelchairs*

9.06.01.02.01	Demonstrate use of locks and brakes to facilitate participation in physical activity
9.06.01.02.02	Demonstrate the adjustment of armrests to facilitate participation in physical activity
9.06.01.02.03	Demonstrate adjustment of footrests to facilitate participation in physical activity
9.06.01.02.04	Suggest modifications to casters, wheels, and handrims to facilitate participation in physical activity
9.06.01.02.05	Suggest modifications to chair backs and seats to facilitate participation in physical activity

9.06.01.03   *Understand components of power or motorized wheelchairs used by individuals with disabilities*

9.06.01.03.01	Accommodate the use of standard upright powerchairs to facilitate participation in physical education activities
9.06.01.03.02	Demonstrate use of control box mechanism to facilitate participation in physical education activities
9.06.01.03.03	Demonstrate use of battery to facilitate participation in physical education activity
9.06.01.03.04	Explain procedure to engage/disengage motors

9.06	**Mobility Devices: Knowledge of various mobility aids to enhance participation in physical education**
9.06.02	Understand scooters are a means for increasing mobility and participation in physical education

9.06.02.01   *Identify a variety of scooter boards for individuals with disabilities such as lower extremity involvement*

9.06.02.01.01   Incorporate use of regular and long scooter boards to facilitate participation in physical education activities

9.06.02.01.02   Incorporate use of modified scooters to facilitate participation in physical education

9.06	**Mobility Devices: Knowledge of various mobility aids to enhance participation in physical education**
9.06.03	Understand bicycles and tricycles increase mobility in physical education

9.06.03.01   *Identify various bicycles and tricycles used by individuals with physical impairments*

9.06.03.01.01   Attach unicycle to front of wheelchair to convert to a tricycle

9.06.03.01.02   Incorporate the use of hand crank cycle to facilitate participation in physical education activities

9.06.03.01.03   Incorporate the use of standard adult tricycle to facilitate participation in physical education activities

9.06.03.02   *Identify adaptations made to cycles to accommodate individuals with physical impairments*

9.06.03.02.01   Incorporate the use of footsandals to facilitate participation in physical education activities

9.06.03.02.02   Incorporate the use of hip and chest straps to facilitate participation in physical education activities

9.06.03.02.03   Incorporate the use of back and neck supports to facilitate participation in physical education activities

9.06	**Mobility Devices: Knowledge of various mobility aids to enhance participation in physical education**
9.06.04	Understand how the use of mobility aids for the visually impaired enhances their participation in physical education

9.06.04.01   *Identify types of mobility aids for individuals with visual impairments*

9.06.04.01.01   Incorporate cane walking to enhance participation in physical education

9.06.04.01.02   Incorporate sighted guide techniques to enhance participation in physical education

9.06.04.01.03   Incorporate partner assists to enhance participation in physical education

9.06.04.01.04   Incorporate guide wire or rope assists to enhance participation in physical education

10.01	**_Teaching Styles: Demonstrate various teaching styles in order to promote learning in physical education_**
10.01.01	Understand the command style of teaching

10.01.01.01   *Understand the effectiveness of using command style teaching with individuals with disabilities in order to promote learning in physical education*

10.01.01.01.01   Provide clear, concise, and simple language when needed

10.01.01.01.02   Use specific, clear, concise verbal cues to highlight points

10.01.01.01.03   Use total communication as needed

10.01.01.01.04   Use visual cues to demonstrate skill such as colored sock to show kicking foot

10.01.01.02   *Understand the effectiveness of demonstrating an activity using a command style approach for individuals with disabilities*

10.01.01.02.01   Secure students' attention through a command or other communication means before demonstrating

10.01.01.02.02   Perform demonstrations in an environment which minimizes distractions for individuals who have short attention spans or who are easily distracted

10.01.01.02.03   Perform demonstrations with verbal cues to maximize sensory information input

10.01.01.02.04   Perform demonstration in a position that allows the individual to best receive information such as individuals who are deaf or hard of hearing

10.01.01.03   *Understand the effectiveness on class organization and control using the command style of teaching*

10.01.01.03.01   Organize the class so that individuals with disabilities such as autism or mental retardation, perform skills under structured class rules and conditions

10.01.01.03.02   Structure the class so that individuals with disabilities complete assigned skills on command

10.01.01.03.03   Establish a physical activity environment that remains the same in terms of format, procedures, & routines for individuals with disabilities such as autism, mental retardation and blindness

10.01.01.03.04   Teach class so that individuals with a variety of disabilities practice the activity together under the direct supervision of the teacher

10.01	**_Teaching Styles: Demonstrate various teaching styles in order to promote learning in physical education_**
10.01.02	Understand the reciprocal style of teaching

10.01.02.01   *Understand the effectiveness of using reciprocal style teaching with individuals with disabilities in order to promote learning in physical education*

10.01.02.01.01   Guide students to be peer tutors or partners to teach individuals with disabilities

10.01.02.01.02   Design activities that allow individuals to work together in pairs

10.01.02.01.03   Design activities so peer tutors can see progress

10.01.02.02   *Understand the importance of training peer instructors to effectively participate in reciprocal teaching environment with individuals with disabilities in order to promote learning*

10.01.02.02.01   Train peer tutors in providing a continuum of prompts from minimum to maximum prompting and assistance for individuals with disabilities

10.01.02.02.02   Train peer tutors how to communicate effectively with individuals with disabilities

10.01.02.02.03   Train peer tutors to provide appropriate feedback to individuals with disabilities

10.01.02.02.04   Train peer tutors to use their initiative and provide alternative progressions and skill techniques when their partner is not experiencing success with the activity being attempted

10.01.02.03   *Understand what qualities to look for when selecting and assigning peer tutors to work with individuals with disabilities*

10.01.02.03.01   Identify peer tutors with a tolerant positive nature and mature disposition

10.01.02.03.02   Identify peer tutors with good communication skills, preferably in more than one mode of communication, such as ability to use communication boards or an additional language such as sign language, Spanish, etc.

10.01.02.03.03   Identify peer tutors with ability to model skills correctly

10.01   **Teaching Styles: Demonstrate various teaching styles in order to promote learning in physical education**

10.01.03   Understand the task teaching style

10.01.03.01   *Understand the effectiveness of using task style teaching with individuals with disabilities in order to promote learning in physical education*

10.01.03.01.01   Design activities and instructions to the ability level of the individuals with disabilities such as using picture activity cards to depict the desired skill to be performed

10.01.03.01.02   Design for a variety and modification of equipment in each activity to ensure successful completion of each assigned task

10.01.03.01.03   Select tasks that can be performed by the individual with a disability individually and safely

10.01.03.01.04   Identify and create goal levels for each skill or activity that will allow all individuals with disabilities to achieve levels of success at the same task

10.01.03.02   *Understand how to organize a class environment to promote a task style teaching method for individuals with disabilities*

10.01.03.02.01   Design the class activities in a circuit type or station arrangement

10.01.03.02.02   Arrange the class so that individuals with disabilities can move quickly and safely from one task to the next

10.01.03.02.03   Arrange the class so that individuals with disabilities can perform tasks individually and safely

10.01.03.02.04   Design tasks with multiple successful outcomes to allow individuals with disabilities to develop coping and adapting strategies

10.01.03.03   *Understand how to effectively analyze progress and provide feedback to individuals with disabilities using task style teaching method*

10.01.03.03.01   Identify goals and objectives specific to the individual with disabilities needs and abilities and to match IEP

10.01.03.03.02   Use self-recording to allow individuals with disabilities to monitor their own progress and assess their own gains

10.01

Teaching Styles: Demonstrate various teaching styles in order to promote learning in physical education

10.01.04   Understand individualized style of teaching

10.01.04.01   *Understand the effectiveness of using individualized style teaching with individuals with disabilities in order to promote learning in physical education*

10.01.04.01.01   Design physical activities based on the individual with disabilities' specific needs

10.01.04.01.02   Create an individualized education program based on the specific needs of individuals with disabilities

10.01.04.01.03   Use individualized charts and reports to determine the progress of individuals with disabilities

10.01.04.01.04   Create activity opportunities with variable levels of success to enable all individuals to achieve some measure of success in the same activity (e.g., using stations)

10.01.04.01.05   Provide instruction and feedback to the individual with disability in that individual's prime mode of communication

10.01.04.02   *Understand how to assess individuals with disabilities to determine present level of performance and IEP*

10.01.04.02.01   Select appropriate assessment tools specific to the individual with disabilities (see Standard 4.0 & 8.0)

10.01.04.02.02   Develop tools or instruments based on the task analysis of behaviors

10.01.04.02.03   Determine the level of independence for each individual based on assessment information

10.01.04.03   *Understand how to provide effective feedback using an individualized style of teaching*

10.01.04.03.01   Provide personal recording methods such as self-recording progress cards and charts

10.01.04.03.02   Design tasks and activities that provide individualized feedback of results and information on the successful completion of the task such as lights and buzzers that sound when the ball has gone through the hoop

10.01

Teaching Styles: Demonstrate various teaching styles in order to promote learning in physical education

10.01.05   Understand the guided discovery style of teaching

10.01.05.01   *Understand the effectiveness of using guided discovery style teaching with individuals with disabilities in order to promote learning in physical education*

10.01.05.01.01   Develop problem solving techniques involving challenging questions and tasks to promote adaptation and coping strategies for individuals with disabilities

10.01.05.01.02	Develop problem solving techniques based on naturally occurring obstacles and challenges that occur in the everyday environment
10.01.05.01.03	Guide the student, when appropriate, to efficient task completion
10.01.05.01.04	Develop a hierarchy of problem solving from single to multiple tasks

10.01	**Teaching Styles: Demonstrate various teaching styles in order to promote learning in physical education**
10.01.06	Understand the divergent or exploratory style of teaching

10.01.06.01	*Understand the effectiveness of using divergent or exploratory style teaching with individuals with disabilities in order to promote learning in physical education*
10.01.06.01.01	Select tasks for instruction that have multiple methods of successful completion for individuals with disabilities
10.01.06.01.02	Choose activity areas that are appropriate for the future needs of the individuals with disabilities
10.01.06.01.03	Use praise and feedback to foster alternative methods of completing the skill or task
10.01.06.01.04	Use the concept of generalization to challenge the individual with disabilities to complete a specific task under different environmental conditions and circumstances
10.01.06.01.05	Encourage and praise effort and creativity in addition to task completion
10.01.06.02	*Understand how to present tasks using a divergent or exploratory style of teaching that is appropriate for the individual with disabilities*
10.01.06.02.01	Identify tasks and skills that are developmentally as well as age appropriate for individuals with disabilities
10.01.06.02.02	Use group activities to promote cooperative learning and development
10.01.06.03	*Understand how to effectively use feedback and praise when using a divergent or exploratory style of teaching for individuals with disabilities*
10.01.06.03.01	Use corrective feedback which provides information that indicates the correct way to perform the task for individuals with disabilities
10.01.06.03.02	Use comments that promote alternative variations to completing the task that fosters independent coping and adapting strategies for the individual with disabilities

10.01	**Teaching Styles: Demonstrate various teaching styles in order to promote learning in physical education**
10.01.07	Understand the cooperative learning style of teaching

10.01.07.01	*Understand the effectiveness of using cooperative learning style of teaching with individuals with disabilities in order to promote learning in physical education*
10.01.07.01.01	Use group activities to foster incidental learning such as social values and interaction skills in individuals with disabilities
10.01.07.01.02	Use noncompetitive tasks and environments to promote cooperation and interaction among individuals with disabilities and individuals without disabilities in a non-threatening environment

10.01.07.01.03   Use group activities that include individuals with disabilities to challenge current concepts on how some tasks should be performed and to promote variations that allow everyone to successfully complete the task

10.01.07.01.04   Provide culminating activities which reinforce cooperation

10.02

Teaching Behaviors: Understand the various teaching behaviors needed to promote learning

10.02.01   Understand various instructional cues such as verbal directions, demonstrations, and physical guidance

10.02.01.01   *Understand the importance of using various instructional cues to prompt certain individuals disabilities to complete tasks*

10.02.01.01.01   Implement instructional and environmental cues based on the needs of individuals with disabilities from least to most intrusive

10.02.01.01.02   Implement instructional and environmental cues based on the unique needs of the individual with a disability such as having an individual with mental retardation step in a hoop in order to cue them to step with opposition while throwing

10.02.01.01.03   Avoid unknowingly eliciting abnormal reflexes when providing physical guidance

10.02.01.01.04   Use other types of instructional cues if one is not effective in communicating to the individual's unique needs or disability such as braille for an individual who is blind

10.02.01.01.05   Use peers to demonstrate instructional cues such as demonstrating a skill to an individual with a disability

10.02.01.01.06   Avoid over cuing or over demonstrating in the selected modality for an individual with a disability such as an individual with an attention deficit disorder (ADD)

10.02.01.01.07   Transition individual reliance on instructional cues to independent completion of the task

10.02

Teaching Behaviors: Understand the various teaching behaviors needed to promote learning

10.02.02   Understand the process of task analysis (see Standard 10.02.04)

10.02.02.01   *Understand the use of task analysis procedures to promote skill learning into teachable parts with individuals with disabilities*

10.02.02.01.01   Break skills down along a hierarchy in order to meet the unique needs of individuals with disabilities

10.02.02.01.02   Provide the prerequisite and ancillary skills needed to complete the skill targeted for instruction

10.02.02.01.03   Develop an ecological task analysis that includes the unique needs of the learner and their environment such as teaching the skill in various settings (school and community)

10.02.02.01.04   Assess skill development and progress using a skill/student specific task analysis testing tool (qualitative) that also accounts for level of independence/dependence during evaluation and teaching (see Standard 8.0)

10.02	***Teaching Behaviors: Understand the various teaching behaviors needed to promote learning***
10.02.03	Understand the concept of time on task

10.02.03.01   *Understand the importance of providing maximal time on task in each lesson to maximize learning for individuals with disabilities in physical education*

10.02.03.01.01   Plan lessons allowing the individual with disabilities to receive as many opportunities to perform the task as possible

10.02.03.01.02   Organize the teaching environment so that transition time between task responses and activities is kept to a minimum

10.02.03.01.03   Utilize behavior management such as incentives/rewards for completing the task and teaching environment strategies such as removing other items or activities that may distract the student in order to sustain student performance during time on task

10.02.03.01.04   Keep instructional information concise such as focusing on key words and phrases

10.02	***Teaching Behaviors: Understand the various teaching behaviors needed to promote learning***
10.02.04	Understand qualitative skill teaching (see Standard 10.02.02)

10.02.04.01   *Understand the importance of teaching qualitative aspects of skills and activities to individuals with disabilities*

10.02.04.01.01   Teach the correct form necessary to perform the skill

10.02.04.01.02   Promote qualitative aspects of skills that facilitate normalization and are socially inconspicuous for individuals with disabilities such as pedalling an exercise bike correctly

10.02.04.01.03   Promote generalization such as how to correctly and safely use a stair climber exercise machine at the local gymnasium or health club

10.02.04.01.04   Use modified equipment to enable the individual with disabilities to complete the task in as close to normal manner as possible or on a functional skill level

10.02	***Teaching Behaviors: Understand the various teaching behaviors needed to promote learning***
10.02.05	Understand quantitative skill teaching

10.02.05.01   *Understand the importance of using quantitative aspects of skills to teach individuals with disabilities in physical education*

10.02.05.01.01   Emphasize the product outcome of a skill such as scoring a basket in basketball

10.02.05.01.02   Use group cooperation activities in integrated settings to promote task completion

10.02.05.01.03   Emphasize outcome aspects of skill instruction which allow the individual with disabilities to successfully participate in socially normal environments such as hitting a tennis ball back over the net and into the court in a game of tennis

10.02.05.01.04   Use adapted equipment that allows the individual with disabilities to participate successfully in socially normal environment such as using a bowling ramp to bowl (see Standard 9.02.08)

10.02

Teaching Behaviors: Understand the various teaching behaviors needed to promote learning

10.02.06   Understand teacher monitoring and pacing of lesson

---

10.02.06.01   *Understand the importance of pacing activities to meet the unique needs of the individual with a disability such as timing activities to maintain interest*

10.02.06.01.01   Plan additional activities in a lesson for individuals such as those with a short attention span

10.02.06.01.02   Plan frequent rest breaks in a lesson for individuals with disabilities such as those with low fitness levels or obesity

10.02.06.01.03   Establish lesson activity sequence that alternates high and low intensity activities to foster fitness improvement

---

10.02

Teaching Behaviors: Understand the various teaching behaviors needed to promote learning

10.02.07   Understand how to communicate learner expectations and content

---

10.02.07.01   *Understand the importance of using various means of communication to provide teacher expectations to individuals with disabilities such as the latest communication technology (see Standard 9.04)*

10.02.07.01.01   Communicate to individuals in their primary learning modality (e.g., total communication with individuals who are deaf)

10.02.07.01.02   Keep communication simple for those students who are limited in cognition (e.g., posting pictures of class rules for children who cannot read)

10.02.07.01.03   Allow individuals with disabilities to record their own results so they can monitor their progress toward the established goals (see Standard 10.01.04.03.02)

10.02.07.01.04   Allow individuals with disabilities to be part of program planning and where applicable have them sign the program plan

---

10.02

Teaching Behaviors: Understand the various teaching behaviors needed to promote learning

10.02.08   Understand the type of social climate which promotes interaction

---

10.02.08.01   *Understand how to use peer tutors to promote social interaction and normal social values with individuals with disabilities*

10.02.08.01.01   Select peer tutors with appropriate communication skills, social skills and maturity level

10.02.08.01.02   Select peer tutors from the community who demonstrate skills needed by individuals with disabilities

10.02.08.01.03   Train peer instructors to communicate and interact with individuals with disabilities

10.02.08.01.04   Provide partner and group activities that foster appropriate interactions for individuals with and without disabilities

10.02.08.01.05   Play cooperative games which foster social interaction and trust for individuals with and without disabilities (see Standard 9.02.12)

10.02   **Teaching Behaviors: Understand the various teaching behaviors needed to promote learning**

10.02.09   Understand knowledge of feedback (knowledge of performance such as the movement and knowledge of results such as the outcome)

10.02.09.01   *Understand the importance of providing positive specific immediate feedback to individuals with disabilities*

10.02.09.01.01   Provide feedback that individuals with disabilities can understand and comprehend such as using short action word statements with individuals with mental retardation

10.02.09.01.02   Design activities for individuals with disabilities that provide knowledge of performance through auditory and visual feedback

10.02.09.01.03   Provide immediate feedback for individuals with disabilities to establish a response consequence relationship between the feedback and the performed behavior

10.02.09.01.04   Provide the majority of feedback for individuals with disabilities in a positive way such as providing positive specific feedback and how to correct performance

---

10.02   **Teaching Behaviors: Understand the various teaching behaviors needed to promote learning**

10.02.10   Understand how to determine progress and make changes to fit individual needs

---

10.02.10.01   *Understand the importance of monitoring progress specific to individuals with disabilities*

10.02.10.01.01   Use appropriate assessment that is relevant to the specific individual and their disability (see Standard 8.0)

10.02.10.01.02   Conduct informal and formal assessment of the progress of individuals with disabilities on a regular basis

10.02.10.01.03   Use multiple tests and assessment methods and criteria to determine the progress of individuals with disabilities

10.02.10.02   *Understand how to make changes in teaching to meet the needs of individuals with disabilities based on assessment data*

10.02.10.02.01   Re-evaluate goals and objectives (program, student, teacher) on a regular basis for individuals with disabilities

10.02.10.02.02   Develop task analysis checklists with sequential steps that are appropriate to the needs and developmental level for individuals with disabilities

10.02.10.02.03   Use task analysis breakdowns to determine intermediate steps for skills that have not been attained at the end of the teaching period for individuals with disabilities

10.02.10.02.04   Use adapted equipment and/or alternative teaching techniques to make immediate changes during the lesson when an individual with disabilities continually fails to complete a task or activity with existing teaching methods

---

10.03

ABA Principles: Understand the principles of adapted behavior analysis to promote learning

10.03.01   Understand how to select and define specific behaviors to be changed or maintained

---

10.03.01.01   *Understand that individuals with disabilities may exhibit more severe and unique behaviors (see Standard 6.0)*

10.03.01.01.01   Identify self-injurious behaviors that may be exhibited by individuals with autism, depression, serious emotional behaviors and other rare syndromes

10.03.01.01.02   Identify lack of motivation to perform activities such as those exhibited by individuals with mental retardation

---

10.03

ABA Principles: Understand the principles of adapted behavior analysis to promote learning

10.03.02   Understand how to observe, chart, and analyze the behavior to be changed

---

10.03.02.01   *Understand how to systematically observe, chart, and analyze the unique behaviors exhibited by individuals with disabilities*

10.03.02.01.01   Use members of multidisciplinary team to assist with observing, charting, and analyzing the behaviors exhibited by individuals with disabilities

10.03.02.01.02   Analyze student information from a variety of formal and informal settings

10.03.02.01.03   Use frequency, duration, and interval recording procedures when needed (see Standard 4.11.01.02.01.-03.)

10.03

ABA Principles: Understand the principles of adapted behavior analysis to promote learning

10.03.03   Understand a variety of strategies for changing behaviors

---

10.03.03.01   *Understand that individuals with disabilities may require the application of a number of unique behavior change strategies and programs*

10.03.03.01.01   Implement a continuum of behavior change strategies depending on the needs of the individual with a disability from prevention to punishment (see Standards 10.04-10.06)

10.03.03.01.02   Implement consistent behavior change strategies with other team members and when possible across various settings such as the classroom, physical education, and home

10.03.03.01.03   Implement a variety of behavior change strategies when necessary

---

10.03

ABA Principles: Understand the principles of adapted behavior analysis to promote learning

10.03.04   Understand how to evaluate the behavior change plan

---

10.03.04.01   *Understand the importance of evaluating the behavior change plan in individuals with disabilities in order to meet the unique needs necessary to change behavior*

| 10.03.04.01.01 | Include behavior plan information with the individual's IEP, teaching units, lesson plans and other progress reports |
| 10.03.04.01.02 | Communicate behavior change plan results with other team members who work with the individual |

| 10.04 | **Preventive Strategies: Understand preventive management strategies in order to promote learning** |
| 10.04.01 | Understand how to use signals for getting the class's attention, starting, and stopping the class |

10.04.01.01	*Understand the use of specific signals to get the attention of individuals with disabilities*
10.04.01.01.01	Use sound signals (i.e., tambourine, whistle) for individuals with disabilities such as those who are blind
10.04.01.01.02	Use visual and tactile signals for individuals with disabilities such as those who are deaf

| 10.04 | **Preventive Strategies: Understand preventive management strategies in order to promote learning** |
| 10.04.02 | Understand routines and transitional procedures from one activity to the next |

10.04.02.01	*Understand the use of routines and transitional procedures that can be used with individuals with disabilities*
10.04.02.01.01	Communicate class routines in a meaningful way such as posting schedules or using flip charts
10.04.02.01.02	Communicate clear concise transitional procedures such as rotating clockwise from one activity to the next activity

| 10.04 | **Preventive Strategies: Understand preventive management strategies in order to promote learning** |
| 10.04.03 | Understand how to organize the class into groups and formations based on the activity |

10.04.03.01	*Understand that certain individuals with disabilities may need a lesser teacher/individual ratio (e.g., distribution of students)*
10.04.03.01.01	Use paraprofessionals and peer tutors for individuals who require greater attention
10.04.03.01.02	Use station or reciprocal teaching style (see Standard 10.01.02)
10.04.03.01.03	Use small group formations (e.g., only one or two individuals at a station)

| 10.04 | **Preventive Strategies: Understand preventive management strategies in order to promote learning** |
| 10.04.04 | Understand how to deal with interruptions while teaching |

| 10.04.04.01 | *Understand that certain individuals with disabilities such as those with attention span deficits may seek constant attention and interrupt class* |

10.04.04.01.01   Identify cause(s) of interruption(s) which may be specific to an individual with a disability

10.04.04.01.02   Implement specific plans, strategies, and signals such as proximity control, extinction or timeout procedures for dealing with interruptions and confrontations

---

10.04

Preventive Strategies: Understand preventive management strategies in order to promote learning

10.04.05
Understand how to teach individual goal setting strategies

10.04.05.01   *Understand the importance of setting realistic goals based on the limitations, needs, and strengths of individuals with disabilities*

10.04.05.01.01   Use goal setting to motivate individuals with disabilities to participate in adapted and regular physical education

10.04.05.01.02   Implement realistic sequential steps to achieve goals

---

10.04

Preventive Strategies: Understand preventive management strategies in order to promote learning

10.04.06
Understand how to teach self-management and maintenance procedures

---

10.04.06.01   *Understand the importance of self-control at a developmentally appropriate level for individuals with disabilities*

10.04.06.01.01   Identify the most appropriate community settings in which to implement self-management behaviors

10.04.06.01.02   Have individual perform behaviors in a variety of settings over a number of different trials

---

10.05

Increasing Behaviors: Knowledge of positive teaching methods for maintaining and increasing student behavior in order to promote learning

10.05.01
Understand modeling as a teaching method

10.05.01.01   *Understand the importance of the teacher and individuals without disabilities modeling appropriate behavior to individuals with disabilities*

10.05.01.01.01   Model appropriate instructional behavior to individuals with disabilities

10.05.01.01.02   Use peer tutor models to demonstrate appropriate behavior to individuals with disabilities

---

10.05

Increasing Behaviors: Knowledge of positive teaching methods for maintaining and increasing student behavior in order to promote learning

10.05.02
Understand prompting as a teaching method

10.05.02.01   *Understand the use of prompts such as verbal, demonstration, and physical guidance and the hierarchy of prompts from less intrusive to more intrusive based on the individual's disability (see Standard 10.02.01.01)*

10.05.02.01.01   Select prompts based upon individual needs (e.g., physical prompts for individuals who are blind)

10.05.02.01.02	Use more intrusive prompts as needed
10.05.02.01.03	Avoid physical guidance for individuals with tactile sensitivity

10.05	***Increasing Behaviors: Knowledge of positive teaching methods for maintaining and increasing student behavior in order to promote learning***
10.05.03	Understand shaping as a teaching method

10.05.03.01	*Understand how to use shaping strategies such as task analysis and successive approximation with individuals with disabilities (see Standard 10.02.02, 10.02.04, and 10.02.05)*
10.05.03.01.01	Teach and reinforce only those parts of the skill that are necessary
10.05.03.01.02	Use qualitative and quantitative aspects in developing a shaping plan for individuals with disabilities (see Standard 10.02.02, 10.02.04, and 10.02.05)

10.05	***Increasing Behaviors: Knowledge of positive teaching methods for maintaining and increasing student behavior in order to promote learning***
10.05.04	Understand chaining as a teaching method

10.05.04.01	*Understand when to use forward chaining, reverse chaining, and total task presentation depending on the individual's disability*
10.05.04.01.01	Use total task presentation prior to forward or backward chaining
10.05.04.01.02	Implement different forms of progressive forward and reverse chaining of skills depending on the needs of the individual
10.05.04.01.03	Use reverse chaining when needed

10.05	***Increasing Behaviors: Knowledge of positive teaching methods for maintaining and increasing student behavior in order to promote learning***
10.05.05	Understand social reinforcement as a teaching method

10.05.05.01	*Understand how to use various social nonverbal and verbal reinforcement strategies based on the individual's disability*
10.05.05.01.01	Identify a variety of social reinforcers that may appeal to individuals with disabilities, such as age appropriate social reinforcer (e.g., smile, high five, shaking hands)
10.05.05.01.02	Use verbal reinforcement at a level the individual with a disability can comprehend such as using action words or simple two word statements
10.05.05.01.03	Use mercury switches to activate reinforcers

10.05	***Increasing Behaviors: Knowledge of positive teaching methods for maintaining and increasing student behavior in order to promote learning***
10.05.06	Understand tangible reinforcement as a teaching method

10.05.06.01	*Understand the use of tangible reinforcers with individuals with disabilities*

10.05.06.01.01	Select reinforcers that are highly reinforcing to each individual
10.05.06.01.02	Provide age appropriate tangible reinforcers
10.05.06.01.03	Continue social reinforcement and fade tangible reinforcers as appropriate

10.05	**_Increasing Behaviors: Knowledge of positive teaching methods for maintaining and increasing student behavior in order to promote learning_**
10.05.07	Understand physical activity reinforcement as a teaching method

10.05.07.01	_Understand the use of physical activity reinforcers with individuals with disabilities_
10.05.07.01.01	Use physical activity reinforcers to assist individuals with disabilities to make progress toward IEP goals and objectives
10.05.07.01.02	Use physical activity reinforcers to develop leisure and recreational choices for community involvement

10.05	**_Increasing Behaviors: Knowledge of positive teaching methods for maintaining and increasing student behavior in order to promote learning_**
10.05.08	Understand reinforcement menus, token economy, and point systems as a teaching method

10.05.08.01	_Understand the use of reinforcement menus, token economy, and contingency point systems with individuals with disabilities_
10.05.08.01.01	Match system (e.g., token economy) to the individuals comprehension level
10.05.08.01.02	Utilize age appropriate items on reinforcement menu
10.05.08.01.03	Identify individual reinforcers that are highly reinforcing

10.05	**_Increasing Behaviors: Knowledge of positive teaching methods for maintaining and increasing student behavior in order to promote learning_**
10.05.09	Understand written contracts as a teaching method

10.05.09.01	_Understand the value of written contracts when developing accountability in individuals with disabilities_
10.05.09.01.01	Utilize written contracts modified to the comprehension level of the individual
10.05.09.01.02	Include essential components of a written contract such as behavior, reinforcement and consequences

10.05	**_Increasing Behaviors: Knowledge of positive teaching methods for maintaining and increasing student behavior in order to promote learning_**
10.05.10	Understand group and individual contingencies as teaching methods

10.05.10.01	_Understand value of group and individual contingencies in changing behaviors in individuals with disabilities_

10.05.10.01.01	Use group contingencies when peer pressure is effective in changing behavior such as with individuals with a behavior disorder
10.05.10.01.02	Provide contingencies which are achievable for the lowest functioning individual within a group
10.05.10.01.03	Develop different individual contingencies for those individuals who can not conform to the group contingency

10.05	***Increasing Behaviors: Knowledge of positive teaching methods for maintaining and increasing student behavior in order to promote learning***
10.05.11	Understand reinforcement schedules as a teaching method

10.05.11.01	*Understand the hierarchy of reinforcement schedules to use with individuals with disabilities*
10.05.11.01.01	Provide immediate reinforcement to those individuals who require such reinforcement
10.05.11.01.02	Provide more sophisticated reinforcement schedules such as ratio and interval reinforcement to assist individuals with disabilities who are learning to maintain or generalize a behavior over time
10.05.11.01.03	Implement a ratio schedule of reinforcement in applying reinforcement for the number of responses to a target behavior
10.05.11.01.04	Implement an interval schedule of reinforcement in applying reinforcement for the number of times performing a target behavior

10.05	***Increasing Behaviors: Knowledge of positive teaching methods for maintaining and increasing student behavior in order to promote learning***
10.05.12	Understand differential reinforcements (DR) as a teaching method

10.05.12.01	*Understand that DR is a method of manipulating the reinforcement schedule and may be used to increase or decrease the rate at which an individual with a disability exhibits a behavior*
10.05.12.01.01	Identify DR as a viable strategy for individuals who require a powerful reinforcement strategy such as those with severe disabilities
10.05.12.01.02	Use DR to increase a behavior by choosing methods which are positive when appropriate
10.05.12.01.03	Describe examples of using DR to reinforce alternative and incompatible behaviors

10.06	***Decreasing Behaviors: Use different methods, along a continuum from less to more intrusive, only after positive methods have been ineffective***
10.06.01	Understand extinction as a teaching method

10.06.01.01	*Understand the importance of using extinction for individuals with disabilities*
10.06.01.01.01	Ignore mild forms of inappropriate behavior with individuals who are constantly seeking attention while reinforcing alternate forms of appropriate behaviors
10.06.01.01.02	Avoid using extinction with such severe behaviors as self-abuse
10.06.01.01.03	Recognize that extinction is effective when attention is acting as the reinforcer

10.06

10.06.02

> **_Decreasing Behaviors: Use different methods, along a continuum from less to more intrusive, only after positive methods have been ineffective_**
> Understand response cost as a teaching method

10.06.02.01   *Understand response cost as a technique which removes reinforcement and may be effectively used with individuals with disabilities*

10.06.02.01.01   Withdraw extrinsic earned reinforcers contingent upon the occurrence of the inappropriate behavior

10.06.02.01.02   Use response cost as an alternative to physical or psychological aversive strategies

10.06.02.01.03   Use reinforcement of an appropriate behavior in conjunction with response cost to deter an inappropriate behavior

10.06.02.01.04   Use response cost effectively with both individuals and groups

10.06

10.06.03

> **_Decreasing Behaviors: Use different methods, along a continuum from less to more intrusive, only after positive methods have been ineffective_**
> Understand overcorrection as a teaching method

10.06.03.01   *Understand the value of overcorrection in teaching appropriate behavior while eliminating inappropriate behavior in individuals with disabilities*

10.06.03.01.01   Allow the individual to experience the effort required by others to restore the damaged environment such as cleaning gymnasium walls

10.06.03.01.02   Use potential restitutional and positive practice overcorrection procedures appropriate for adapted physical education settings

10.06

10.06.04

> **_Decreasing Behaviors: Use different methods, along a continuum from less to more intrusive, only after positive methods have been ineffective_**
> Understand time out procedures as a teaching method

10.06.04.01   *Understand that different time out procedures are effective for individuals with disabilities such as contingent observation, seclusion, and isolation*

10.06.04.01.01   Identify legal aspects involved with time out procedures

10.06.04.01.02   Administer the proper mechanics for using time out procedures with individuals with disabilities

10.06.04.01.03   Use contingent observation timeout with the individual placed in timeout and allowed to continue to observe the activity

10.06

10.06.05

> **_Decreasing Behaviors: Use different methods, along a continuum from less to more intrusive, only after positive methods have been ineffective_**
> Understand paired stimuli (pairing primary and secondary reinforcers) as a teaching method

10.06.05.01   *Understand that paired stimuli may be used for both increasing and decreasing behaviors in individuals with disabilities*

10.06.05.01.01	Use paired stimuli to reinforce incompatible behaviors
10.06.05.01.02	Combine reinforcement or punishment techniques to increase the effectiveness of a form of punishment that is not effective in reducing a behavior
10.06.05.01.03	Use pairing techniques (e.g., with individuals with more severe disabilities)

10.06

10.06.06

> ***Decreasing Behaviors: Use different methods, along a continuum from less to more intrusive, only after positive methods have been ineffective***
> Understand strong punishers (corporal punishment) as a teaching method

10.06.06.01	*Understand that the use of strong punishers with individuals with disabilities such as aversives, physical restraints, and corporal acts are very controversial and may not be allowed in many school districts*
10.06.06.01.01	Modify management techniques based on the knowledge that the administration of strong punishers is usually not a behavior builder
10.06.06.01.02	Modify management techniques based on knowledge that administration of strong punishers is usually considered beyond the expertise of the adapted physical educator and should only be used with proper training and documentation of the technique

10.07

10.07.01

> ***Other Methods: Use other management methods/models for increasing, maintaining and decreasing student behavior in order to promote learning***
> Understand Value Responsibility Model as a teaching method

10.07.01.01	*Understand that most individuals with disabilities can benefit from programs that promote self control of behaviors*
10.07.01.01.01	Develop social skills by using the Value Responsibility Model hierarchy of levels (e.g., irresponsibility, self-control, involvement, self-responsibility, and caring)
10.07.01.01.02	Use appropriate strategies such as modeling, contracts, goal setting, reflection time, student sharing, and journal writing to implement the different levels of the Value Responsibility Model

10.07

10.07.02

> ***Other Methods: Use other management methods/models for increasing, maintaining and decreasing student behavior in order to promote learning***
> Understand Teacher Effectiveness Training as a teaching method

10.07.02.01	*Understand the value of effective communication between the teacher and individuals with disabilities*
10.07.02.01.01	Use effective communication methods with the individual such as active listening
10.07.02.01.02	Use two way communication to enhance learning and minimize behavioral problems in adapted physical education setting such as using a chalkboard to foster communication and questioning between instructor and an individual who is deaf
10.07.02.01.03	Modify using teacher effectiveness training with individuals with limited communication skills

10.07	**_Other Methods: Use other management methods/models for increasing, maintaining and decreasing student behavior in order to promote learning_**
10.07.03	Understand Reality Therapy as a teaching method

10.07.03.01   *Understand that many individuals with disabilities can be taught to accept responsibility for their behavior*

10.07.03.01.01   Teach individuals with disabilities to acknowledge their behavioral deviations and be responsible for developing a plan to change

10.07.03.01.02   Help individuals with disabilities address the here-and-now, develop a plan to achieve goals, and keep the individual on track

10.07.03.01.03   Use questions and classroom meetings as potential methods for certain individuals with disabilities

10.07	**_Other Methods: Use other management methods/models for increasing, maintaining and decreasing student behavior in order to promote learning_**
10.07.04	Understand Social Discipline as a teaching method

10.07.04.01   *Understand that interactions between the teacher and individuals with disabilities involves social interaction*

10.07.04.01.01   Modify styles of interaction because misbehaviors may be the result of inappropriate needs such as attention, power, revenge, proving inadequacy

10.07.04.01.02   Utilize student reflection to identify antecedent behaviors

10.07.04.01.03   Encourage and apply logical consequences as viable tools for developing appropriate behavior in individuals with disabilities

11.01	***Motivation: Understand how motivation influences behavior***
11.01.01	Understand Maslow's theory as the basis for planning consultation and staff development

11.01.01.01   *Understand the motivation of general practitioners teaching individuals with disabilities*

11.01.01.01.01   Use a survey instrument to determine teachers needs prior to inservice

11.01.01.01.02   Utilize techniques to reduce intimidation and fear

11.01.01.01.03   Provide successful experiences for teachers so they feel capable of teaching individuals with disabilities

11.02	***Administrative Skills: Knowledge of program organization and administrative hierarchy***
11.02.01	Understand administrative organizational structure of education agencies/services

11.02.01.01   *Understand how decisions are made in the educational agency*

11.02.01.01.01   Identify who are key personnel players in the decision making process

11.02.01.01.02   Implement strategies to change organizational behavior

11.02.01.01.03   Encourage administrator's interaction with teachers during inservice presentation

11.02	***Administrative Skills: Knowledge of program organization and administrative hierarchy***
11.02.02	Understand program organization

11.02.02.01   *Understand how curriculum decisions are made for teaching individuals with disabilities*

11.02.02.01.01   Explain the program planning, assessment, prescription, teaching, evaluation, and modification (PAPTEM) strategy

11.02.02.01.02   Monitor implementation of individualized education program plan in general physical education class

11.02	***Administrative Skills: Knowledge of program organization and administrative hierarchy***
11.02.03	Understand effects of living environment and parent and guardian intervention

11.02.03.01   *Understand strategies for communication with living environments*

11.02.03.01.01   Instruct parents and guardians on how to teach motor skills at home

11.02.03.01.02   Encourage parents and guardians to be proactive in providing sport and leisure opportunities on a segregated and integrated basis

11.02.03.02   *Describe legal rights and responsibilities of parents and guardians of individuals with disabilities*

11.02.03.02.01   Identify advocates to assist parents and guardians in assuring appropriate physical education programming

11.02.03.02.02   Inform parents and guardians of their right to due process

| 11.02 | **Administrative Skills: Knowledge of program organization and administrative hierarchy** |
| 11.02.04 | Understand the role of community based activity programs |

11.02.04.01   *Identify community resources for individuals with disabilities*

11.02.04.01.01   Facilitate transportation possibilities for individuals to participate in community programming

11.02.04.01.02   Develop motor skills that facilitate transition to community recreation facilities

| 11.02 | **Administrative Skills: Knowledge of program organization and administrative hierarchy** |
| 11.02.05 | Understand identification of funding sources |

11.02.05.01   *Describe how funds can be obtained at various levels*

11.02.05.01.01   Seek funding from community service organizations

11.02.05.01.02   Contact grants officer for local education agency

11.02.05.01.03   Contact grants officer with state education agency

11.02.05.01.04   Contact foundations that fund programs and equipment for individuals with disabilities

| 11.03 | **Group Dynamics: Demonstrate knowledge of team approaches for providing educational programs for all individuals** |
| 11.03.01 | Understand the team approach for providing educational programs |

11.03.01.01   *Understand the multidisciplinary team process related to individuals with disabilities (see Standard 15.04)*

11.03.01.01.01   Establish a working relationship with members of motor team such as physical therapists, occupational therapists, and speech therapists

11.03.01.01.02   Utilize communication skills to enhance cooperation and mutual respect among team members

11.03.01.04   *Understand the ecological approach related to individuals with disabilities*

11.03.01.04.01   Include families in the decision making process (see Standard 15.01.01)

11.03.01.04.02   Collaborate with the community to provide physical education services to individuals with disabilities

11.03.01.04.03   Utilize the available expertise when planning a physical education program for individuals with disabilities

11.03	**Group Dynamics: Demonstrate knowledge of team approaches for providing educational programs for all individuals**
11.03.02	Understand the nature of group cohesiveness

11.03.02.01   *Understand the forces acting upon members to remain in group to improve physical education services provided to individuals with disabilities*

11.03.02.01.01   Create incentives for providing physical education services to individuals with disabilities

11.03.02.01.02   Establish group goals so there is an expectancy of outcomes related to improving physical education services to individuals with disabilities

11.03.02.01.03   Plan group activities that are valuable to the members and will improve physical education to individuals with disabilities

11.03.02.01.04   Evaluate success of group related to the expected outcomes of improving physical education services for individuals with disabilities

11.03	**Group Dynamics: Demonstrate knowledge of team approaches for providing educational programs for all individuals**
11.03.03	Understand situational leadership

11.03.03.01   *Understand human relationships related to working with others to provide physical education services to individuals with disabilities*

11.03.03.01.01   Develop positive interaction with teachers who have effective teaching behaviors

11.03.03.01.02   Use teachers with effective teaching behaviors to mentor teachers who are less effective

11.03.03.02   *Understand task orientation related to working with others to provide physical education services to individuals with disabilities*

11.03.03.02.01   Use explicit communication related to expectations in terms of performance in teaching physical education to individuals with disabilities

11.03.03.02.02   Provide physical education teachers with the information they need to acquire the technical competence to teach physical education to individuals with disabilities

11.03	**Group Dynamics: Demonstrate knowledge of team approaches for providing educational programs for all individuals**
11.03.04	Understand cultural issues related to group dynamics

11.03.04.01   *Understand differences in the behavior and lifestyle of other cultures*

11.03.04.01.01   Appreciate and accommodate differences in the behavior and lifestyle of other cultures

11.03.04.01.02   Determine what language is spoken in the home environment

11.03.04.01.03   Refrain from stereotyping individuals who look similar

11.03.04.01.04   Establish rapport with ethnically diverse individuals by being sensitive to their cultural belief systems related to sport and exercise

11.04

Interpersonal Communication Skills: Knowledge of the ability to interact with, discuss and write about individuals

11.04.01
Understand active listening as a communication skill

11.04.01.01 *Identify components of active listening useful in communication as an adapted physical education consultant*

11.04.01.01.01 Establish a physical education environment that will allow for good communication between the teacher and the consultant

11.04.01.01.02 Use active listening when communicating with teachers

11.04

Interpersonal Communication Skills: Knowledge of the ability to interact with, discuss and write about individuals

11.04.02
Understand the dynamics of advocacy groups

11.04.02.01 *Identify strategies used by advocacy groups for individuals with disabilities*

11.04.02.01.01 Teach individuals with disabilities about the laws that govern their right to access quality physical education, recreation, and sport

11.04.02.01.02 Promote and defend the rights of individuals with disabilities to have access to public recreation facilities

11.05

Psychological Dimensions: Knowledge of the cognitive processes that affect behavior

11.05.01
Understand attitude theories

11.05.01.01 *Understand Contact theory as related to individuals with disabilities*

11.05.01.01.01 Establish contact between individuals with and without disabilities that includes cooperative physical activities

11.05.01.01.02 Establish contact between individuals with and without disabilities in a physical education setting that emphasizes the similarities between individuals with and without disabilities

11.05.01.02 *Understand Mediated Generalization theory as related to individuals with disabilities*

11.05.01.02.01 Organize successful experiences in game and movement situations in which individuals with and without disabilities participate together

11.05.01.02.02 Select game activities that all individuals in an integrated physical activity program can perform and be successful at

11.05.01.03 *Understand Assimilation-Contrast theory as related to individuals with disabilities*

11.05.01.03.01 Use inservice training to promote positive attitudes toward individuals with disabilities

11.05.01.03.02 Prepare the physical education class to receive a new student who has a disability

11.05.01.04 *Understand Stigma theory as related to individuals with disabilities*

11.05.01.04.01   Integrate individuals with disabilities into physical education activities with the support they need relative to type and degree of disability

11.05.01.04.02   Integrate individuals with disabilities into activities that utilize abilities and strengths

11.05.01.05   *Understand Interpersonal Relations theory as related to individuals with disabilities*

11.05.01.05.01   Design a peer tutoring program for physical education that is structured and long term (see Standard 10.01.02)

11.05.01.05.02   Provide opportunities for individuals to observe highly competitive sporting events for individuals with disabilities, such as a wheelchair track meet

11.05.01.06   *Understand Group Dynamics theory as related to individuals with disabilities*

11.05.01.06.01   Provide input to teachers as to how their attitude toward individuals with disabilities affect others' attitudes

11.05.01.06.02   Empower teachers to plan lessons that facilitate success and stress equity

11.05.01.07   *Understand Cognitive Dissonance as related to individuals with disabilities*

11.05.01.07.01   Conduct activities that simulate disabling conditions during physical education

11.05.01.07.02   Provide new experiences for students without disabilities such as using a wheelchair for a day

11.05.01.08   *Understand Reasoned Action theory as related to individuals with disabilities*

11.05.01.08.01   Provide a clear purpose and value for participation in adapted physical activities for all students before beginning the activity

11.05.01.08.02   Provide a motivation for all students to participate together in an integrated physical activity setting

---

11.06   **Consulting Models: Knowledge of how to utilize various consulting models**
11.06.01   Understand prescription mode

11.06.01.01   *Understand that adapted physical education consultants provide plans or aid in the selection of strategies for predetermined problems*

11.06.01.01.01   Conduct assessment and write the IEP for the direct service provider (see Standard 8.0)

11.06.01.01.02   Provide one-to-one consulting sessions with the direct service provider

---

11.06   **Consulting Models: Knowledge of how to utilize various consulting models**
11.06.02   Understand provision mode

11.06.02.01   *Understand that adapted physical education consultants provide direct services to individuals as needed*

11.06.02.01.01   Provide direct physical education services to individuals with disabilities when appropriate

11.06.02.01.02   Model desired teaching behaviors

11.06

11.06.03

> **Consulting Models: Knowledge of how to utilize various consulting models**
> Understand collaboration mode

11.06.03.01   *Understand that adapted physical education consultants respond to requests by engaging in mutual efforts to understand the problem, devise an action plan, and implement the plan*

11.06.03.01.01   Engage in a problem solving relationship with the direct service provider

11.06.03.01.02   Work with the direct service provider to select mutually agreeable strategies and ways to implement them

11.06

11.06.04

> **Consulting Models: Knowledge of how to utilize various consulting models**
> Understand mediation mode

11.06.04.01   *Understand that adapted physical education consultants respond to requests from two or more consultees to help them accomplish an agreement or reconciliation by serving as a facilitator*

11.06.04.01.01   Facilitate solutions for quality physical education services for students with disabilities when teachers and administrators are in disagreement

11.06.04.01.02   Facilitate positive relationships between parents and guardians and direct service providers when disagreements occur, without dictating solutions

Standard **12** PROGRAM EVALUATION

12.01	**Student Outcomes: Understand the value to program evaluation of measuring student achievement**
12.01.01	Monitor the effectiveness of the assessment plan and make appropriate revisions

12.01.01.01	*Recognize different methods for evaluating program effectiveness*
12.01.01.01.01	Utilize student progress on goals and objectives as an indicator of program effectiveness
12.01.01.01.02	Utilize unanticipated outcomes as an indication of program effectiveness
12.01.01.02	*Discuss the advantages and limitations of formal testing*
12.01.01.02.01	Describe how the attributes of learners influence formal testing procedures
12.01.01.02.02	Explain the effect on formal testing procedures of the preferred learning style(s) of individuals with disabilities
12.01.01.02.03	Select instruments that are valid for the age and suspected disability of the individual being tested
12.01.01.02.04	Modify formal testing procedures to accommodate the preferred learning styles of individuals with disabilities
12.01.01.03	*Discuss the advantages and limitations of informal testing*
12.01.01.03.01	Utilize evaluation in the assessment process of determining motor performance needs of individuals with disabilities
12.01.01.03.02	Utilize formative evaluation techniques and apply them to individuals with disabilities
12.01.01.03.03	Utilize summative evaluation techniques and apply them to individuals with disabilities
12.01.01.03.04	Modify evaluation instruments and explain the effect of these modifications on validity and reliability
12.01.01.03.05	Write realistic and functional goals for individuals with disabilities utilizing appropriate standards of performance
12.01.01.03.06	Explain the differences in validity and reliability between instruments that are used for making placement decisions and instruments used for determining student progress
12.01.01.04	*Utilize available resources to evaluate a student's needs for modified equipment and/or learning materials*
12.01.01.04.01	Project and justify appropriate modification of equipment or materials
12.01.01.04.02	Seek outside funding to supplement available resources as needed

12.01	**Student Outcomes: Understand the value to program evaluation of measuring student achievement**
12.01.02	Utilize existing criteria for quality physical education programs in terms of curriculum accessibility, appropriateness, frequency and duration of program delivery

12.01.02.01	*Compare curriculum with existing criteria for quality physical education programs*

12.01.02.01.01	Use developmentally and functionally appropriate curriculum for individuals with disabilities

12.01.02.01.02   Use developmentally appropriate curriculum for individuals with disabilities

12.01.02.02   *Justify program content based on evaluation standards*

12.01.02.02.01   Write goals and instructional objectives that are measurable and justifiable based on evaluation standards

12.01.02.02.02   Discuss goals and instructional objectives with other professionals

12.01.02.02.03   Utilize developmentally and functionally appropriate goals and instructional objectives for individuals with disabilities

12.01.02.03   *Monitor the effectiveness of the program plan and make appropriate revisions in program content*

12.01.02.03.01   Select a timeline for implementing revised content for a smooth and easy transition for individuals with disabilities into regular classes

12.01.02.03.02   Document intended program outcomes

12.01.02.04   *Match program content with program components of activities addressing physical and motor fitness, fundamental motor skills and patterns, skills in aquatics, dance and individual and group games and sports as well as functional living skills*

12.01.02.04.01   Compare duration of time spent on program components with needs of individuals with disabilities

12.01.02.04.02   Compare the developmental and functional appropriateness of program components with needs of individuals with disabilities

12.01.02.05   *Measure the effectiveness of program implementation based on the plan and make appropriate revisions*

12.01.02.05.01   Distinguish between effective and ineffective service delivery for each individual with a disability

12.01.02.05.02   Modify the service delivery model to meet the individualized needs of the student

12.01.02.06   *Evaluate the effectiveness of various service delivery models such as collaboration, consultation, inclusion and integration*

12.01.02.06.01   Discuss the strengths and weaknesses of various service delivery models as they relate to meeting the unique needs of individuals with disabilities

12.01.02.06.02   Discuss the degree to which different models are being implemented in the LEA

12.02   **Program Operations: Understand the importance of monitoring the quality of program operations**

12.02.01   Understand the legal requirements for accessibility of physical education facilities for individuals with disabilities (see Standards 5.02 and 5.06)

12.02.01.01   *Recognize and utilize tools for evaluating accessibility of physical education facilities*

12.02.01.01.01   Evaluate accessibility of physical education facilities using architectural standards to accommodate individuals with disabilities

12.02.01.01.02   Recommend modifications or retrofitting where needed to aid facility accessibility for individuals with disabilities

| 12.02 | **_Program Operations: Understand the importance of monitoring the quality of program operations_** |
| 12.02.02 | Recognize the importance of properly functioning wheelchairs and orthopedic appliances |

12.02.02.01   *Demonstrate the ability to evaluate the functional operation of wheelchairs and other orthopedic appliances (see Standard 9.06)*

12.02.02.01.01   Describe adjustments for wheelchairs enabling sport participation by individuals with disabilities

12.02.02.01.02   Describe adjustments for braces and other appliances enabling sport participation by individuals with disabilities

12.02.02.01.03   Recommend available resources for the repair of wheelchairs and other orthopedic appliances

| 12.02 | **_Program Operations: Understand the importance of monitoring the quality of program operations_** |
| 12.02.03 | Recognize the need for staff training, additional administrative support and reallocation of resources for assessment |

12.02.03.01   *Contribute to staff training by submitting ideas for programs to meet the needs of personal development*

12.02.03.01.01   Conduct sessions for staff training addressing needs of colleagues

12.02.03.01.02   Participate in staff training to improve skills and competencies in adapted physical education (see Standard 13.0)

12.02.03.02   *Contribute to training of parents and families by submitting ideas for presentations (see Standard 15.01)*

12.02.03.02.01   Develop video tapes for parent and family training on issues related to adapted physical education

12.02.03.02.02   Conduct training sessions for parents and families on how to work with their children in physical activity

| 12.02 | **_Program Operations: Understand the importance of monitoring the quality of program operations_** |
| 12.02.04 | Understand various methods of describing and registering the results of measurement and evaluation |

12.02.04.01   *Familiarity with systematic observational techniques for recording academic learning time (ALT)*

12.02.04.01.01   Utilize event recording techniques to observe behavior

12.02.04.01.02   Utilize duration recording techniques to observe behavior

12.02.04.01.03   Utilize interval recording techniques to observe behavior

12.02.04.01.04   Explain the uses and limitations of systematic observational techniques

12.02.04.01.05   Use unobtrusive measures such as rating scales, case studies and anecdotal records

12.02.04.01.06   Graph baseline data which has been collected over a pre-set interval of time

12.02.04.02   *Understand how to use student self-report and/or peer evaluation data*

12.02.04.02.01   Use student self-report data when appropriate in formulating individualized program plans and goals

12.02.04.02.02   Use peer evaluation data when appropriate in formulating individualized program plans and goals

---

12.02   **Program Operations: Understand the importance of monitoring the quality of program operations**

12.02.05   Utilize performance profiles in reporting student achievement

---

12.02.05.01   *Interpret performance profiles in reporting student achievement*

12.02.05.01.01   Utilize age appropriate award systems in rewarding and motivating achievers

12.02.05.01.02   Utilize forms of recognition other than awards for student achievement

---

12.02   **Program Operations: Understand the importance of monitoring the quality of program operations**

12.02.06   Use grades to report student progress

12.02.06.01   *Understand how letter grades can be supplemented to report progress of students with disabilities*

12.02.06.01.01   Interpret letter grades with an accompanying narrative

12.02.06.01.02   Utilize a performance profile to interpret letter grades

---

12.02   **Program Operations: Understand the importance of monitoring the quality of program operations**

12.02.07   Recognize the need for staff training, additional administrative support and reallocation of resources for reporting and recording

---

12.02.07.01   *Awareness of resources available to support staff training*

12.02.07.01.01   Locate and confirm presenters for staff training

12.02.07.01.02   Obtain additional resources for staff training

---

12.02   **Program Operations: Understand the importance of monitoring the quality of program operations**

12.02.08   Demonstrate the ability to evaluate the degree to which a program meets professional standards of quality

---

12.02.08.01   *Conduct a self study of program strengths and weaknesses*

12.02.08.01.01   Study the quality of the school-community environment in terms of mission, philosophy, climate, recognition of accomplishments, parent involvement, communication and public relations

12.02.08.01.02	Study the quality of the physical education program in terms of goals and objectives, curriculum organization, IEPs, equity, program evaluation process, program implementation and dissemination of evaluation results
12.02.08.01.03	Study the quality of the instruction in physical education in terms of student characteristics, teacher characteristics, teacher-student interactions, classroom management, discipline and student evaluation
12.02.08.01.04	Study the quality of personnel including qualifications of teachers, resource and support staff, district leadership, school leadership, teacher evaluation and staff development
12.02.08.01.05	Study the quality of facilities, equipment and safety practices, safety considerations, school medical records and procedures (see Standard 9.02.02)

12.03 **Consumer Satisfaction: Monitor indications of consumer satisfaction**
12.03.01 Knowledge of the caregivers' role in gathering information regarding students' attitudes toward physical education

---

12.03.01.01	*Communicate with parents and guardians regarding students' attitudes toward physical education*
12.03.01.01.01	Recommend community resources for parents and guardians
12.03.01.01.02	Explain methods used to communicate with parents and guardians to other professionals
12.03.01.01.03	Establish an on-going communication with parents and guardians to obtain their input
12.03.01.02	*Survey parents or guardians on their satisfaction with the physical education program*
12.03.01.02.01	Explain how the results of a parent or guardian survey can be used
12.03.01.02.02	Recommend physical activity resources for parents or guardians that they can use or make

---

12.03 **Consumer Satisfaction: Monitor indications of consumer satisfaction**
12.03.02 Recognize the value of student opinions in program evaluation

---

12.03.02.01	*Understand how to use different methods of soliciting feedback from students with disabilities regarding program merit and weaknesses*
12.03.02.01.01	Question students regarding their attitudes toward physical education
12.03.02.01.02	Use critical incidence surveys
12.03.02.02	*Survey students for suggestions on curriculum offerings in physical education*
12.03.02.02.01	Explain how the results of a student survey can be used
12.03.02.02.02	Utilize student survey results to influence curricular offerings

---

12.03 **Consumer Satisfaction: Monitor indications of consumer satisfaction**
12.03.03 Monitor students' behavior relative to approaching or avoiding physical activity as an indication of their enjoyment or dissatisfaction with the movement medium

---

12.03.03.01	*Use non-verbal indicators of students' satisfaction with curricular offerings*

12.03.03.01.01	Record how frequently students initiate physical activity given a choice to select a physical activity
12.03.03.01.02	Provide recognition for students who engage in physical activity outside of school programs
12.03.03.02	*Survey students about the vigorousness of their leisure time activities*
12.03.03.02.01	Explain how survey results may be used
12.03.03.02.02	Refer students to programs for leisure time participation

Standard **13** CONTINUING EDUCATION

13.01	**Understand how to remain current of issues and trends that influence the field of physical education**
13.01.01	Understand the impact of federal statutes and mandates on the provision of physical education service delivery

13.01.01.01 *Understand how to find the Federal Register in order to access information related to individuals with disabilities*

13.01.01.01.01 Apply information found in the Federal Register to maintain compliance with current legislation related to individuals with disabilities such as in Individuals with Disabilities Education Act (IDEA) and Americans with Disabilities Act (ADA)

13.01.01.01.02 Synthesize information with local practices pertaining to individuals with disabilities such as making reasonable accommodations within physical education programs

13.01.01.02 *Understand information provided in the U.S. Department of Education Annual Report to Congress related to individuals with disabilities*

13.01.01.02.01 Access a copy of the Annual Report to Congress related to individuals with disabilities

13.01.01.02.02 Interpret statistics relative to the implementation of IDEA in State Education Agency (SEA) and Local Education Agency (LEA)

13.01.01.02.03 Compare LEA's implementation of IDEA with other LEA's within a region of the state

13.01.01.02.04 Compare state statistics on implementation of IDEA with other states

13.01.01.02.05 Assess LEA's program to determine compliance with IDEA

13.01.01.03 *Understand the current federal nomenclature related to individuals with disabilities*

13.01.01.03.01 Interpret federal abbreviations and acronyms such as Office of Special Education and Rehabilitative Services (OSERS), Free and Appropriate Public Education (FAPE), Regular Education Initiative (REI)

13.01.01.03.02 Use federal abbreviations and acronyms in communications pertaining to compliance with federal regulations in physical education for individuals with disabilities

13.01	**Understand how to remain current of issues and trends that influence the field of physical education**
13.01.02	Understand how to access information through local offices of congressional leadership who are influential on matters related to individuals with disabilities

13.01.02.01 *Know how to obtain the names of state and local legislators who are instrumental in the passage of issues related to individuals with disabilities*

13.01.02.01.01 Contact legislators who are instrumental in the passage of issues related to individuals with disabilities

13.01.02.01.02 Participate in advocacy groups that attempt to lobby legislators who are instrumental in the passage of legislation related to individuals with disabilities

13.01.02.02   *Identify how legislators vote on critical issues related to individuals with disabilities*

13.01.02.02.01   Access information through newspapers or the Congressional Record

13.01.02.02.02   Use information on the voting records of decisions at the local, state, and federal levels regarding adapted physical education

13.01.02.03   *Know current changes of Public Laws and how these changes affect adapted physical education*

13.01.02.03.01   Use information about current changes in Public Laws to influence LEA policies and procedures related to the provision of adapted physical education

13.01.02.03.02   Use information about current changes in Public Laws to influence best practice in adapted physical education

---

13.01   **Understand how to remain current of issues and trends that influence the field of physical education**

13.01.03   Understand how to access information through State Departments of Education

---

13.01.03.01   *Know how to access SEA's state plan for the implementation of IDEA*

13.01.03.01.01   Evaluate whether state plan includes procedures for implementing physical education for individuals with disabilities

13.01.03.01.02   Evaluate procedures for implementing physical education mandates for students with disabilities

13.01.03.02   *Know how to access LEA plans for the implementation of IDEA*

13.01.03.02.01   Evaluate whether local districts have developed procedures for implementing physical education for individuals with disabilities

13.01.03.02.02   Evaluate and compare procedures for implementing physical education mandates for individuals with disabilities

13.01.03.03   *Understand current state and local nomenclature related to individuals with disabilities*

13.01.03.03.01   Interpret state and local terminology related to individuals with disabilities

13.01.03.03.02   Use state and local terminology in communications pertaining to compliance with regulations that affect physical education for individuals with disabilities

---

13.01   **Understand how to remain current of issues and trends that influence the field of physical education**

13.01.04   Understand governance as it is conducted by the LEA

13.01.04.01   *Understand how school boards or their equivalent operate on issues related to individuals with disabilities including the provision for adapted physical education*

13.01.04.01.01   Help LEA monitor compliance with legislation designed to assure adapted physical education for individuals requiring such services

13.01.04.01.02   Advocate for adapted physical education services when issues requiring public hearing are necessary

13.01	**Understand how to remain current of issues and trends that influence the field of physical education**
13.01.05	Understand the positions of various professional organizations and groups on issues related to individuals with disabilities

13.01.05.01	*Understand how to access information through professional organizations related to individuals with disabilities*
13.01.05.01.01	Attend local and state meetings to acquire legislative updates on issues related to individuals with disabilities
13.01.05.01.02	Discuss current issues related to individuals with disabilities with other professionals in adapted physical education
13.01.05.02	*Understand how to access information through individuals with disabilities*
13.01.05.02.01	Discuss current issues with parents/guardians or other advocacy groups for individuals with disabilities
13.01.05.02.02	Discuss current issues with friends or colleagues with disabilities
13.01.05.03	*Understand the nature of parent-professional communication to assist in the development of parent understanding of adapted physical education (see Standard 15.01)*
13.01.05.03.01	Involve parents/guardians in adapted physical education by making presentations or otherwise keeping them informed about their child's rights under IDEA
13.01.05.03.02	Disseminate information to parents/guardians and community to assist them in determining if the provision for adapted physical education is appropriate
13.01.05.03.03	Organize parents/guardians to advocate for appropriate adapted physical education services in the community

13.02	**Keep up to date with current literature in physical education**
13.02.01	Subscribe to and read journals in physical education

13.02.01.01	*Review literature regarding physical education for individuals with disabilities*
13.02.01.01.01	Implement new teaching strategies and methods for use in adapted physical education
13.02.01.01.02	Support and use innovative ideas
13.02.01.01.03	Communicate with other professionals who work with individuals with disabilities relative to current literature on adapted physical education

13.02	**Keep up to date with current literature in physical education**
13.02.02	Read journals from allied fields that publish current research related to the field of adapted physical education

13.02.02.01	*Understand the implications for adapted physical education as it pertains to the literature from allied fields*
13.02.02.01.01	Apply multidisciplinary teaching methods to improve quality physical education programming

13.02.02.01.02   Utilize most recent information on medically restricted conditions to enhance the quality of adapted physical education programming

---

13.03

> ## *Interact with professional organizations that address issues involving physical education*
>
> **13.03.01**   Support the activities of state, regional, and national organizations that promote physical education

---

13.03.01.01   *Demonstrate professional commitment through attendance at regional, state, and national meetings sponsored by AAHPERD and the National Consortium for Physical Education and Recreation for Individuals with Disabilities*

13.03.01.01.01   Make presentations related to adapted physical education

13.03.01.01.02   Serve on committees that support the efforts of the organization as they relate to adapted physical education

13.03.01.02   *Demonstrate professional commitment through service to local, state, and national organizations involving adapted physical education*

13.03.01.02.01   Chair or serve on committees involved in influencing policies and procedures concerning issues and concerns about individuals with disabilities

13.03.01.02.02   Chair or serve on committees involved in the planning and conduct of professional development activities

13.03.01.02.03   Provide consultation with community members regarding adapted physical education

13.03.01.02.04   Provide workshops to community leaders and professionals in the area of adapted physical education

---

13.03

> ## *Interact with professional organizations that address issues involving physical education*
>
> **13.03.02**   Support activities of other organizations that may address issues directly or indirectly related to physical education such as the Council for Exceptional Children

---

13.03.02.01   *Know how to contact the State Department of Education to obtain necessary information regarding professional development activities related to individuals with disabilities*

13.03.02.01.01   Attend workshops/courses that address issues indirectly related to adapted physical education

13.03.02.01.02   Present at workshops/courses that address issues related to adapted physical education

13.03.02.02   *Join associations or organizations that deal with research and practice in special and remedial education*

13.03.02.02.01   Provide professional development to school personnel and members of the community regarding adapted physical education

13.03.02.02.02   Instruct other professionals about the benefits of adapted physical education

13.04

Understand how to use technology as a tool to disseminate information pertaining to physical education

13.04.01
Know how to utilize electronic bulletin boards as a means of posting and retrieving information pertaining to physical education

13.04.01.01
Understand how colleagues in LEAs, SEAs and other professional organizations can access information related to individuals with disabilities

13.04.01.01.01
Stay informed of current and new developments in special education and adapted physical education

13.04.01.01.02
Share information with colleges and universities, special education centers, and schools

13.04.01.01.03
Share information with local recreation centers, parks, and public facilities that provide community recreation programs for individuals with disabilities

13.04

Understand how to use technology as a tool to disseminate information pertaining to physical education

13.04.02
Know how to access a variety of information retrieval systems such as ERIC

13.04.02.01
Disperse information obtained from information retrieval systems to assist professionals and others to understand professional practice in adapted physical education

13.04.02.01.01
Use information obtained from information retrieval systems to improve the quality of adapted physical education programming

13.04.02.01.02
Use information obtained from information retrieval systems to assist professionals and others to remain updated with current theories, concepts, trends, and practices in adapted physical education

13.04

Understand how to use technology as a tool to disseminate information pertaining to physical education

13.04.03
Know how to use computers to facilitate record keeping and data storage

13.04.03.01
Know how computers can assist IEP management

13.04.03.01.01
Use computers to manage and analyze IEP assessment data

13.04.03.01.02
Use computers to generate adapted physical education IEP goals and objectives

13.04.03.01.03
Use computers to generate IEP progress reports to be given to students and parents

13.04

Understand how to use technology as a tool to disseminate information pertaining to physical education

13.04.04
Understand how to use computers to disseminate information to others regarding the effectiveness of your physical education program

13.04.04.01
Know how to use commercial database programs as they relate to adapted physical education

13.04.04.01.01   Use word processing programs to create adapted physical education newsletter

13.04.04.01.02   Use word processing programs to produce personalized form letters pertaining to issues related to adapted physical education

13.04.04.02   *Know how to use commercial electronic spreadsheet programs as they relate to adapted physical education*

13.04.04.02.01   Use a spreadsheet program to manage and calculate student grades in adapted physical education

13.04.04.02.02   Use a spreadsheet program to manage the adapted physical education budget

13.04.04.03   *Know how to use commercial database programs as they relate to adapted physical education*

13.04.04.03.01   Use a database program to manage student performance data such as fitness and motor skill data in adapted physical education

13.04.04.03.02   Use a database program to create and maintain mailing lists of adapted physical education professionals

13.05   ## Understand the need to maintain current teaching certifications
13.05.01   Understand what mechanisms are available to maintain current teaching certifications

13.05.01.01   *Know how to access professional development activities related to physical education for individuals with disabilities*

13.05.01.01.01   Enroll in adapted physical education course work at local colleges/universities

13.05.01.01.02   Participate in adapted physical education workshops offered by non-degree granting agencies

Standard 14 ETHICS

14.01 **Understand the need for professional standards**

14.01.01 Understand and respect the roles and responsibilities of educators and other school-related professionals (see Standard 15.03)

14.01.01.01 *Understand the need for standards for professionals who work closely with adapted physical educators, including special educators and related personnel such as occupational and physical therapists*

14.01.01.01.01 Apply the professional and ethical standards associated with training and certification as adapted physical educators

14.01.01.01.02 Uphold the standards associated with certification as a teacher and adapted physical educator

14.01.01.01.03 Respect the need to monitor and enforce professional standards for teachers of adapted physical education

---

14.02 **Understand and value appropriate professional conduct**

14.02.01 Accept the need for standards for a professional engaged in the education of children, youth, and adolescents

---

14.02.01.01 *Accept the responsibility for developing and providing appropriate adapted physical education experiences*

14.02.01.01.01 Develop and implement programs that are based on research findings and acknowledged best practices as related to the education of individuals with disabilities

14.02.01.01.02 Respect confidentiality and right to privacy in all matters related to the education of individuals with disabilities, including evaluation, assessment outcomes, and report writing

14.02.01.02 *Understand the need to be respectful of all students, parents, advocates, and other professionals*

14.02.01.02.01 Interact with students with disabilities, parents, surrogates, advocates and others in a professional and courteous manner

14.02.01.02.02 Use appropriate terminology such as person-first language

---

14.02 **Understand and value appropriate professional conduct**

14.02.02 Understand the need for continuous professional development

---

14.02.02.01 *Recognize opportunities to participate in meetings, seminars, and conferences related to the education of individuals with disabilities (See Standard 13.03)*

14.02.02.01.01 Attend courses, conferences, seminars, and other continuing education experiences on a regular basis

14.02.02.01.02 Provide and share professional information with others, including parents, guardians, and related personnel, that is accurate, current, and free of personal bias (See Standard 15.01.01)

14.02

14.02.03

Understand and value appropriate professional conduct

Understand the responsibility to advocate for the educational needs of individuals with disabilities

14.02.03.01

Understand issues confronting individuals with disabilities and the relationship of these to programs designed to provide needed physical activity opportunities

14.02.03.01.01

Articulate the challenges individuals with disabilities experience in accessing health-related facilities and programs

14.02.03.01.02

Support and promote individuals and organizations that provide physical activity programs for individuals with disabilities

14.02.03.01.03

Cooperate with parent and guardian organizations and professional societies in promoting the health and fitness of individuals with disabilities (see Standard 15.01.02.03)

14.02

14.02.04

Understand and value appropriate professional conduct

Understand the need to maintain credentials and professional standards

14.02.04.01

Understand the responsibility to hold credentials as an adapted physical educator as required by the state and/or professional society

14.02.04.01.01

Adhere to the requirements of professional standards and credentials in the practice of providing adapted physical education services

14.02.04.01.02

Suggest changes or modifications to professional standards or procedures for assessing standards to state and/or professional society

14.03

14.03.01

Understand the need to advance the knowledge base

Understand the need to conduct and support various forms of research (e.g., action, field, laboratory, qualitative) designed to expand the knowledge base

14.03.01.01

Understand the need to support research endeavors which advance programs and services for individuals with disabilities

14.03.01.01.01

Engage and support research with special populations if it adheres to appropriate standards (i.e., approved by human subject's board)

14.03.01.01.02

Utilize an informed consent process and respect the rights of students with and without disabilities to choose to participate in research studies

14.03.01.01.03

Report findings of studies with special populations consistent with research outcomes

14.03.01.01.04

Accept responsibility to conduct research relevant to the needs of individuals with disabilities (e.g., field based, socially valid)

14.03.01.01.05

Acknowledge the contributions of others, including subjects, to the research endeavor

14.03

14.03.02

> ## *Understand the need to advance the knowledge base*
> ### Understand the responsibility to incorporate research findings into practice

14.03.02.01

Identify journals that provide current information about latest research regarding programs and activities for individuals with disabilities

14.03.02.01.01

Utilize research findings and incorporate promising practices into adapted physical education programs and activities

14.03.02.01.02

Evaluate new program ideas incorporated from research to assess their effectiveness on student outcomes

14.04

14.04.01

> ## *Advance the Profession*
> ### Serve on professional committees

14.04.01.01

Be aware of adapted education professional organizations and their committee structure

14.04.01.01.01

Volunteer to serve on committees and actively contribute

14.04.01.01.02

Respond to requests for assistance from professional organizations such as completion of a survey data form

14.04.01.01.03

Retain the rights to agree and disagree over professional matters, recognizing the need to do so in a courteous and professional manner

14.04.01.01.04

Accept leadership opportunities consistent with talent, available time, and other responsibilities

Standard **15** COMMUNICATION

	Parents and Families: Communication with parents and families
15.01	
15.01.01	Understand the importance of parent and family intervention

---

15.01.01.01 *Understand the importance of family support during the Individualized Education Program (IEP) and Individualized Family Service Plan (IFSP) and other parent/teacher conferences/meetings*

15.01.01.01.01 Explain the motor components of the IFSP to family members

15.01.01.01.02 Assist family members with the transition of the motor component from the IFSP to the IEP

15.01.01.01.03 Explain physical education service plan (IEP) to family members

15.01.01.02 *Understand the management skills needed to encourage families to participate in play, sport and physical activity for individuals with disabilities*

15.01.01.02.01 Develop a management plan specific to family's needs

15.01.01.02.02 Train families in the specific management skills needed to implement a play, sport or physical activity program

15.01.01.02.03 Provide families with strategies and teaching techniques to increase their effectiveness as instructors

---

	Parents and Families: Communication with parents and families
15.01	
15.01.02	Be a family advocate and counselor of physical activity

---

15.01.02.01 *Understand the importance of family advocacy meetings where parents can meet and learn about physical activity programs for individuals with disabilities*

15.01.02.01.01 Advocate for programs by working closely with the press and media such as writing in newsletters

15.01.02.01.02 Volunteer to be a speaker at parent advocacy meetings

15.01.02.02 *Knowledge about already developed home-based physical activity programs such as Data-Based Gymnasium*

15.01.02.02.01 Design family home-based physical activity programs

15.01.02.02.02 Teach parents to implement a plan that includes long range goals, behavioral objectives, lesson plans, teaching cues, and strategies for charting child progress

15.01.02.02.03 Provide homework assignments or home-based activity programs

15.01.02.03 *Knowledge of national agencies, organizations and community programs to assist families in play, sport and physical activity such as Special Olympics, United States Association for Blind Athletes, and American Occupational Therapy Association*

15.01.02.03.01 Assist families in contacting and getting involved in such national agencies, organizations and community programs

15.01.02.03.02 Assist families in appropriate assessment procedures for placement in play, sport and physical activity

15.01.02.03.03 Assist families in utilizing and adapting equipment

| 15.02 | **Public Relations: Communicating the role of physical education (see Standards 5.09 and 13.01)** |
| 15.02.01 | Knowledge of physical education and ability to communicate the importance of the profession |

15.02.01.01 *Understand and communicate the importance of physical activity for individuals with disabilities in the schools and community*

15.02.01.01.01 Integrate the adapted physical education program with other subject areas including regular physical education

15.02.01.01.02 Plan and implement programs that promote adapted physical education for parents and other groups

15.02.01.01.03 Take community based educational trips and provide feedback relative to body and space management for individuals with disabilities

15.02.01.01.04 Take integrated groups to such community based activities as ice skating, bowling and fitness centers

15.02.01.01.05 Advocate consulting role for adapted physical education person on transition teams

15.02.01.01.06 Communicate with local physicians regarding the importance of adapted physical education programs

15.02.01.01.07 Involve oneself in assessment and IEP/placement process

15.02.01.01.08 Advocate for inclusion of individuals with disabilities in intramural and athletic programs

15.02.01.01.09 Communicate with local business and municipal recreation leaders about the need to market recreational activities for all individuals, including those with disabilities; offer to help/consult

15.02.01.01.10 Speak to civic organizations about the rights to recreate for individuals with disabilities such as addressing specific community needs to offer inclusive recreation/leisure opportunities

| 15.03 | **Job Positions: Understand other professionals who work with adapted physical educators and serve individuals with disabilities** |
| 15.03.01 | Awareness of the roles and responsibilities of occupational therapy (OT) |

15.03.01.01 *Adapted physical educators understand how OT can assist in programs of physical activity for individuals with disabilities*

15.03.01.01.01 Confer with OT on activities of daily living (ADL)

15.03.01.01.02 Meet regularly about progress of individuals with disabilities relative to self-care, work skills, and daily activities to ensure that work toward goals are congruent

15.03.01.01.03 Observe OT working with individuals with disabilities and invite OT to observe physical education/adapted physical education classes where children receiving OT are present

15.03.01.01.04 Assist individuals with disabilities in identifying special interests in recreation/physical education which may require OT services

15.03.01.01.05 Assist individuals with disabilities in identifying future vocational skills which would require adapted physical education/OT collaborative services

15.03	**Job Positions: Understand other professionals who work with adapted physical educators and serve individuals with disabilities**
15.03.02	Awareness of the roles and responsibilities of physical therapy (PT)

15.03.02.01   *Adapted physical educators understand how the PT can assist in programs of physical activity for individuals with disabilities*

15.03.02.01.01   Confer with PT on such activities as use and safety of wheelchairs and orthotics, wheelchair transfers, and positioning of children with reflexive movements

15.03.02.01.02   Communicate with PT regarding assistive devices such as sport wheelchair for active and least restrictive involvement of individuals with disabilities

15.03.02.01.03   Collaborate with PT for most appropriate stretching exercises for individuals with specific physical disabilities

15.03	**Job Positions: Understand other professionals who work with adapted physical educators and serve individuals with disabilities**
15.03.03	Awareness of the roles and responsibilities of therapeutic recreation (TR)

15.03.03.01   *Adapted physical educators understand how the TR can assist in community based leisure activities for individuals with disabilities*

15.03.03.01.01   Confer with TR to identify leisure needs

15.03.03.01.02   Confer with TR to identify what community recreation/leisure opportunities exist

15.03.03.01.03   Confer with TR regarding ecological inventory and task analysis of community recreation/ leisure activities

15.03.03.01.04   Accompany individuals with disabilities on recreation/leisure trips to assess adapted physical education needs

15.03.03.01.05   Contact agencies such as Easter Seals with the intent to cooperatively expand recreation activities such as horseback riding

15.03.03.01.06   Confer with TR regarding camping, climbing, and canoe paddling activity options for individuals with disabilities

15.03	**Job Positions: Understand other professionals who work with adapted physical educators and serve individuals with disabilities**
15.03.04	Awareness of the roles and responsibilities of vocational specialist (VS)

15.03.04.01   *Understand the importance of physical fitness to enhance job skills and productivity*

15.03.04.01.01   Design fitness and physical activity programs on vocational work site

15.03.04.01.02   Accompany the VS to study work site to assess physical abilities needed

15.03.04.01.03   Collaborate with VS to teach proper posture and body mechanics during manual labor

15.03.04.01.04   Explore how fitness activities can be combined with work experiences such as walk or bike to work; stretch during work breaks; perform low back exercises during break

15.03	**Job Positions: Understand other professionals who work with adapted physical educators and serve individuals with disabilities**
15.03.05	Awareness of the roles and responsibilities of regular physical education teacher (RPE)

15.03.05.01   *Adapted physical educators understand how the regular physical education teacher can assist in curricular and scheduling decisions for individuals with disabilities*

15.03.05.01.01   Consult with regular physical educator to make appropriate adaptations to activities

15.03.05.01.02   Observe individuals with disabilities in inclusive settings

15.03.05.01.03   Collaborate with regular physical educator during assessment, writing goals and objectives, and any placement recommendations

15.03.05.01.04   Confer with regular physical educator to identify and access appropriate community recreation opportunities

15.03.05.01.05   Work with regular physical educator to include individuals with disabilities in intramural programs

15.03.05.01.06   Write grants cooperatively to improve programs such as acquiring sport wheelchairs to be used in physical education classes by individuals who ambulate with crutches

15.03	**Job Positions: Understand other professionals who work with adapted physical educators and serve individuals with disabilities**
15.03.06	Awareness of the roles and responsibilities of special education classroom teacher (SP ED)

15.03.06.01   *Adapted physical educators understand how the SP ED teacher can assist in the appropriate placement of individuals with disabilities in such least restrictive environments as regular or special education*

15.03.06.01.01   Collaborate with SP ED regarding written work required

15.03.06.01.02   Collaborate with SP ED regarding behavior management in order to keep management techniques consistent across settings

15.03.06.01.03   Inform SP ED when routines or activities of individuals with disabilities will be changed in physical education classes

15.03.06.01.04   Assist in establishing community recreation/leisure involvement

15.03.06.01.05   Assist with prerequisite physical skills needed for transitioning to community work force

15.03.06.01.06   Assist in developing activities for SP ED and regular education classroom teacher for individuals with disabilities to work on in the classroom, during recess, at home, or in the community

15.03	**Job Positions: Understand other professionals who work with adapted physical educators and serve individuals with disabilities**
15.03.07	Awareness of the roles and responsibilities of paraprofessionals and other volunteers (PP/V)

15.03.07.01   *Adapted physical educators understand how the paraprofessionals and other volunteers can assist in the adapted physical education program*

15.03.07.01.01   Demonstrate for PP/V how to physically assist individuals with disabilities

15.03.07.01.02   Model for PP/V regarding how to sufficiently challenge individuals with disabilities during programming

15.03.07.01.03   Teach PP/V how to encourage peer partners

15.03.07.01.04   Ask PP/V to assist during assessments

15.03.07.01.05   Train PP/V to take a lead role in teaching when adapted physical educator is absent due to involvement in assessments or IEP meetings (depending on LEA policy)

15.03.07.01.06   Teach PP/V how to use specialized equipment

15.03.07.01.07   Evaluate the effectiveness of the PP/V

15.03   **Job Positions: Understand other professionals who work with adapted physical educators and serve individuals with disabilities**

15.03.08   Awareness of the roles and responsibilities of other school based professionals

15.03.08.01   *Adapted physical educators understand how to collaborate with these professionals toward providing the most appropriate educational services for individuals with disabilities*

15.03.08.01.01   Communicate with other professionals regarding assessment and programming for individuals with disabilities

15.03.08.01.02   Maintain communication between adapted physical educator and SP ED Director to keep communication lines open about whether regular physical education is appropriately meeting the needs of individuals

15.03.08.01.03   Meet with SP ED Director to clarify legal documents or legal procedures

15.03.08.01.04   Discuss with other professionals referral procedures for assessment if adapted physical education is needed

15.03.08.01.05   Collaborate with principal in following school policies

15.03.08.01.06   Consult with psychologist to determine the appropriateness of assessment instruments

15.03.08.01.07   Collaborate with athletic director (AD) in accommodating individuals with disabilities in interscholastic athletics and intramurals

15.03.08.01.08   Work with AD to identify a variety of methods other than athletic participation to involve individuals with disabilities, such as managers, scorers, timers

15.03.08.01.09   Speak to regular education students about how they can be effective peer tutors

15.03.08.01.10   Ask regular education classroom teacher what special topics are being studied and then offer to complement topics with activities in adapted physical education/physical education

15.03.08.01.11   Offer programming methods to maximally involve individuals with disabilities in regular education setting

15.03.08.01.12   Inform speech/language professionals of new vocabulary introduced in adapted physical education/physical education classes

15.03.08.01.13   Learn basic signs from speech/language professional such as stop, go, run, throw, catch

15.03.08.01.14	Determine from speech/language records the extent of residual hearing of individuals with disabilities
15.03.08.01.15	Join rhythm lesson in music class and observe body movements of individuals with disabilities
15.03.08.01.16	Collaborate with music teacher to accompany basic fundamental movements such as lessons with rhythm sticks
15.03.08.01.17	Collaborate with music teacher to orchestrate movements to holiday music for individuals with disabilities
15.03.08.01.18	Guide the observation of individuals with disabilities as they watch musical videos to identify such basic movements as jumps, hops, slides
15.03.08.01.19	Plan movements which traditionally have specific speeds (sustained, short and choppy, explosive) and help music teacher match sport movements to these rhythms
15.03.08.01.20	Assist music teacher in choreographing movements for a musical drama
15.03.08.01.21	Assist individuals with disabilities in art projects such as drawing sport figures, photographing, or videotaping athletes
15.03.08.01.22	Assist individuals with disabilities to think of recreational ideas to draw or paint such as horseback riding, campfire at night, and fishing
15.03.08.01.23	Assist in involving individuals with disabilities in such activities as school plays, holiday pageants, and other shows
15.03.08.01.24	Consult with counselor for motor skills needed in transition to work place
15.03.08.01.25	Inform counselor of any inappropriate behavior or behavioral concerns such as depression, talk of suicide, low self-esteem of individuals with disabilities
15.03.08.01.26	Attend inservice on catheterization procedures
15.03.08.01.27	Consult with nurse and other medical professionals about any concerns/questions regarding problems and contraindications or medicine side effects
15.03.08.01.28	Discuss with nurse and other medical professionals how surgeries that individuals with disabilities have will affect movement capabilities (see Standard 9.02.02)

15.04	### Team Approach: Communicate effectively in a team approach
15.04.01	Knowledge of differences among various team approaches

15.04.01.01	*Adapted physical educators understand which team approach is used in school district where they teach such as multidisciplinary and transdisciplinary, motor development team approach (preschool 0-2 years) (see Standard 11.0)*
15.04.01.01.01	Work with the primary intervention agent on behalf of the team and share information among team members
15.04.01.01.02	Communicate and work effectively in a team approach by using such methods as consensus forming with the various members of the team
15.04.01.01.03	Communicate individual's goals and objectives to other professional team members
15.04.01.01.04	Communicate how adapted physical education contributes toward the total growth of individuals with disabilities

15.04.01.01.05   Communicate how such services as adapted physical education, OT, and PT can complement activities to meet the needs of individuals with disabilities

15.04.01.01.06   Avoid the duplication of such activities for individuals with disabilities such as adapted physical education, OT, and PT

15.04.01.01.07   Assume a primary role in promoting physical activity

EVALUATION AND REVIEW COMMITTEE MEMBERS

Pamela Abeling
Hezi Aharoni
Lisa Ash
Mary Kay Baker
Elizabeth Bayuk
Eileen Bender
Cynthia Berrol
John Boeltar
Peanuts Boyer
Sally Bruce
Louise Burbank
Sharon Burton
Ellen Campbell
Denise Chang
Penny Christensen
Jan Collings
Erin Coolman
Connie Custer
Ron Davis
Debby Dearden
John Dlabal
Carl Eichstaedt
Lorri Engstrom
Elizabeth Evans
Manny Felix
Susan Floethe
Pat Giebink
Joanne Gonzalez
Hollis Green
Linda Gunning
Jerry Harris
John Hassenzahl
Betty Heising
Michele Herzing

John Adair
Constance Alchus
Peter Aufsesser
Karen Barnhart
Kristi Beach
Jim Bennink
Maria Bertolucci
Aaron Bond
Gail Brevig
Juan Bruno
Teresa Burgess
Howard Cadenhead
Stacey Carniglia
Jo Chew
Kara Christian
Sue Combs
Kathleen Cooney
John Dagger
Jennifer Davis
Jim Decker
Victor Dominocieo
Janice Elix
Catherine Erhard
Jean Evans-Kent
Beverly Fillingin
Mary Frampton
Kris Gilmore
Mary Goodwin
Ann Griffin
Christine Guzzo
Lois Harris
Ruth Haynes
Nancy Henderson
Kathy Hixon

Beverly Adam
Elizabeth Anderson
Brad Bacaro
Joe Barry
Christine Belanger
Walt Bergman
Heidi Bickel
Donald Bornell
Dawn Bridges
Cathy Bryan
Lee Burkett
Kittie Callaway
Marcia Carrillo
Rose Chew
Gail Clark
Gail Conrad
Jill Corti
Denise Darvel-Citana
Cindy Dawley
Frank Degnan
Ann Dorrance
Cindy Elrod
Julie Erickson-Hines
Gretta Fahey
Janet Fisher
Rikki Gans
Pamela Glueck
Craig Gordon
Dale Grupe
Carlton Hansen
Virginia Harris
Marsha Heath
Tina Herring
Chris Hopper

Jeff Adams
Kim Anderson
Cindia Badger
Greg Bayley
Kathy Bell
Alice Berkner
William Bishop
Wayne Boudreau
Kathy Brinker
Joy Bryceson
Allen Burton
Sal Caminada
Sam Cerceres
Christine Chiodo
Doug Collier
Judy Conroy
Judy Cox
Tim Davis
Michelle De Lorm
Brenda Dessauer
Anne Duncan
Marne Engleking
Glendora Estacion
Anita Farnholtz
Ann Fleury
Tom Gentry
Elly Goldman
Glen Graham
Nancy Guggenheim
Karen Happke
Aleita Hass-Holcombe
Paul Heine
Todd Herrington
Jane Horner

Denise Horpedahl	Charles Howe	Carol Huettig	Linda Huntimer
Diane Hursky	Patsy Jackson	Paul Jansma	Melanie Jernigan
Leon Johnson	Edwin Johnson	Steve Johnston	Jean Jones
Phyllis Jorgensen	Jennifer Kahaian	Lyn Kalinowski	Susan Kasser
Billy Keel	Chuck Keller	Brian Kelly	Diane Kime
Pamela Kissler	Kirk Klucznik	Barbara Knipe	Karl Knopf
Deborah Konar	Sharon Kounas	Claire Kzeski	Luigi Lettieri
Kim Lewolt	Ingrid Loen	Carol Lynch	Rose Lyon
Kay Mabry	Julienne Maeda	Raye Maero	Doug Malay
Shelley Mallue	Susan Mangel	Brent Mangus	Jean Margolis
Michael Marsallo	Larry Martin	Janet McCauley	Deann McCormick
Skip McCrory	Jana McKinley	Linda McMorran	Nancy McNamee
Gail Meacham	Nancy Megginson	Howard Menton	Corine Meyer
Mike Miley	Glenn Mills	Jerri Miner	Linda Mitchell
Ron Moon	Kathleen Morland	Dennis Morrow	Kimble Morton
Paul Motley	Ginny Mott	Sue Moucha	Eugene Mulcahy
Peggy Munten	Nathan Murata	Terry Murray	Diana Nelson
Sue Nestor	Gerry O'Brien	Rita O'Loughlin	Carolyn Oborny
Robin Olberding	Stephanie Ontiveros	John Oppliger	Brad Osato
Linda Osborn	Patricia Osborne	Patty Osborne	Carol Outhier
Stephen Overby	Shelia Owen	Patricia Owens	George Pacheco
Ann Page	Chris Pappas	Jocelyn Paré	Lee Parks
Bill Payret	Steve Peak	Peter Pedroza	Randi Perkins
Karlene Peterson	Jeannie Phillips	Lisa Picini-Asman	David Poretta
David Potter	Richard Powell	Kathy Powell	Joan Pylman
Doreen Ramsey	Linda Raphael	Terrie Rauzon	Tim Ray
Belinda Rector	Patricia Reed	Helen Rehm	Barbara Rethans
Peter Richter	Jim Rimmer	Terry Rizzo	Ted Robertson
Pat Robinson	Robert Roesch	Jessica Rogers	Trish Rogers-McIntyre
Monica Rogerson	Barbara Rohleder	Robynn Rome	Jody Rose-Dressler
Susan Rosenthal	Debe Rougeau	Mary Ann Rounds	Mark Runac
Ronda Runyon	Kathryn Russell	Carol Ryan	Jack Sage
Susan Schakel	Leigh Schmidt	Roger Schoonover	Lisa Schreeder
Steven Seymour	Bill Shannahan	Carolyn Sharp	Vicky Sheesley
Carol Shenosky	Marge Shively	Susie Shurmur	Lisa Silliman
Bob Sinibaldi	Linda Skinner	Janet Sklenar	Marie Slusser
Carolyn Snyder-Sain	Chet Spencer	David Stabelfeldt	Allan Stanbridge
Alex Streltzov	Diane Swanson	Jayne Swercinski	James Sylvis
Diane Symons	Sue Tarr	Terri Taylor	Noel Teichman
Mary Thompson	Margery Thompson	Debbie Tillett	Joan Tomaszewski
Michelle Trujillo	Deb Turner	Louise Van Zee	Elinor Vandegrift
Joanie Verderber	Paul Vogel	Patty VonOhlen	Julie Wally
Debbie Watson	Diane Wetherill	Sue Wheeler-Ayres	Nancy Whitehurst
Nancie Whiteside	Bettie Wickersham	Ann Wilber	Kathy Wildermuth
Debbie Williams	Beverly Williamson	Susan Williford	Penny Wills
Gwen Wilson	Pam Witzmann	Pamela Wolosky	Joanne Woodruff
Lynde Woolace	Joan Worley	Jennifer Wright	Marnie Young
Julia Young	John Zerkle	Hedy Zikratch-Marches	

ADAPTED PHYSICAL EDUCATION NATIONAL STANDARDS PROJECT EVALUATION AND REVIEW COMMITTEE APPLICATION FORM

Name: _____

Preferred Mailing Address: _____

_____

_____

Work Phone: _____ **Home Phone:** _____

Fax: _____

For reporting purposes, we need to be able to summarize demographic and educational data requested below on all committee members. All of your responses will be held confidential and no references will ever be made to individuals in any reports. The only reference to your name will be in the list of professionals that served on the Evaluation and Review Committee.

Age: _____   Gender: _____

Race: _____   Do you have a disability: _____

Education—Check the degrees you hold and the major area(s) of study for each degree:

	Degree	Year Earned	Major	Minor
( )	Undergraduate	_____	_____	_____
( )	Masters	_____	_____	_____
( )	Doctorate	_____	_____	_____
( )	Other	_____	_____	_____

Title of your current position: _____

Percentage of your current job that is related to providing physical education services to students with disabilities? _____%

Total number of years of teaching experience in adapted physical education? _____ years

Please return to: Dr. Luke E. Kelly, Health & Physical Education, 221 Memorial Gymnasium, University of Virginia, Charlottesville, VA 22903

ADAPTED PHYSICAL EDUCATION NATIONAL STANDARDS FEEDBACK REPORTS

As discussed in the introduction, the current standards represent the initial attempt to delineate the scope and sequence of the content practicing adapted physical educators should know. While the focus of the next three years of the project will be on developing and validating a national examination, the project director and NCPERID are interested in receiving feedback on these standards. Your input will be used by future NCPERID committees in revising the standards.

All input is welcome. We are particularly interested in your feedback related to:

1. The introduction—was enough information provided regarding the purpose of the project and how the standards were created?

What additional information would you recommend be included in future reports?
2. The content of the standards—editorial corrections, omissions, recommended additions, questions or concerns?
3. Major changes—are there any broad content areas that you feel should be considered in future revisions or do you have any suggestions regarding the format of the content presented in the standards?

Send all feedback reports to: Luke E. Kelly, APENS Project Director, Health & Physical Education, 221 Memorial Gymnasium, University of Virginia, Charlottesville, VA 22903

National Consortium for Physical Education and Recreation for Individuals with Disabilities

The purpose of the National Consortium for Physical Education and Recreation for Individuals with Disabilities (NCPERID) is to promote, stimulate, and encourage the conduct of service delivery, professional preparation and research in physical education and recreation for individuals with disabilities. The NCPERID provides public information and education, promotes the development of programs and services and disseminates professional and technical information. The organization succeeded the National Committee on Physical Education and Recreation for Handicapped Children and Youth, formed in 1973. Members of the organization are primarily professionals in adapted physical education and therapeutic recreation employed in colleges and universities throughout the United States. Other members include individuals and organizations that advocate for people with disabilities.

Related to the areas stated in the purpose of the organization, the membership works diligently to stimulate and/or conduct research efforts directed toward improving the lifestyle and well being of individuals with disabilities through physical education and recreation. In part, the membership works to monitor available research funding from governmental agencies by articulating current needs and collectively advocating for funding related to our mission. In addition, the membership works to serve as liaison to legislative organizations at the national, state and local levels. An essential function of the NCPERID is to develop and/or foster the adoption of standards related to staff qualifications, services facilities and recommended levels of support for recreation and physical education programs for persons with disabilities at national, state and local levels.

An additional goal of the NCPERID is to serve as a professional voice and collective force in support of physical education and recreation for all people. This may be articulated through the development of national policy and position statements reflecting the contribution of physical education and recreation on the lives of people with disabilities. Efforts are made to communciate effectively within the membership of NCPERID and with other professional organizations that advocate for the rights of people with disabilities.

GLOSSARY

APE with Collaboration: Physical education services provided and/or implemented jointly with parents and other staff (California Department of Education, 1993).

APE with Consultation: Ideas and suggestions communicated between the APE specialist and other service providers for individualizing physical education instructional strategies, equipment, and curriculum.

Academic Learning Time (ALT): A unit of time in which students are engaged in tasks related to the class objectives.

Achievement-Based Curriculum (ABC): A model for integrating the processes of program planning, assessing, prescribing, teaching, and evaluating so that the physical education needs of all individuals can be addressed.

Activities of Daily Living (ADL): Those skills which are necessary to perform everyday functions such as eating and dressing.

Adapted Physical Education (APE):
1. The art and science of assessment and prescription within the psychomotor domain to ensure that an individual with a disability has access to programs designed to develop physical and motor fitness, fundamental motor skills and patterns, and skills in aquatics, dance, and individual and group games and sports so that the individual can ultimately participate in community-based leisure, recreation, and sport activities and as such, enjoy an enhanced quality of life.
2. A diversified program of physical education having the same goals and objectives as regular physical education, but modified when necessary to meet the unique needs of each individual.

Administrative Feasibility: The practicality and ease of administering a test.

Afterload: An additional load placed on the muscle during contraction (Mohrman & Heller, 1986).

Agonist: A muscle that is the principle mover or one of the principle movers of a lever.

Allied Educators: All individuals who provide instruction to individuals with disabilities.

Alternate Communication Modes: See Alternative/Augmentative Communication.

Alternative/ Augmentative Communication: Refers to supplemental communication techniques that are used in addition to whatever naturally acquired speech and vocalization exists, to include such things as sign language and gestures.

American Sign Language: Primary language of the Deaf, using hand signs and finger spelling. Signs are concept based and are grammatically and symbolically different than English.

Amplitude: The distance between two target centers in an aiming task.

Annual Goals:	General statements of student outcomes projected over the school year (Eichstaedt & Lavay, 1992).
Antagonist:	A muscle that in contracting tends to produce movement opposite to that of the agonist.
Antecedent Stimuli:	Any stimulus that occurs prior to a response.
Anticipation:	The ability to predict what is going to happen in the environment and when it will occur, and then perform various information-processing activities in advance of the event.
Applied Behavior Analysis:	Procedures derived from the principles of behavior are systematically applied to enhance socially significant behavior to a meaningful degree and demonstrate experimentally that the procedures employed caused the improved behavior (Cooper, Heron, & Heward, 1987).
Appropriate Education:	Education that is specifically designed to meet the unique needs of an individual with a disability.
Arousal:	An internal state of alertness or excitement.
Assessment:	Interpretation of measurements for the purpose of making decisions about placement, program planning and performance objectives; any procedures employed by appropriately trained professionals during the period of eligibility.
Assessment Plan:	Predetermined procedures and instruments for gathering, interpreting, and reporting data gathered in the assessment process.
Ataxia (Cerebral Palsy):	A type of cerebral palsy that is characterized by hypotonia, poor coordination and poor balance.
Atlantoaxial Instability:	Misalignment of the first and second cervical vertebrae which can cause permanent damage to the spinal cord during hyperflexion or hyperextension of the head or neck.
Attention:	In motor learning, a limited capacity, or set of capacities, to process information.
Augmented Feedback:	Extrinsic Feedback.
Automatic Processing:	A mode of information processing that is fast, done in parallel, not attention demanding, and often involuntary.
Automaticity:	The process of dealing with information that is (a) fast; (b) not attention demanding, in that such processes do not generate (very much) interference with other tasks; (c) parallel, occurring together with other processing tasks; and (d) involuntary, often unavoidable.
Axes:	Imaginary lines or points about which a body or a segment rotates (Kreighbaum & Barthels, 1981).
Backward Chaining:	Selectively reinforcing a desired behavior by beginning with the last behavioral link in the chain of behaviors.
Balance:	A process whereby the body's state of equilibrium is controlled for a given purpose (Kreighbaum & Barthels, 1981).
Baseline Data:	Behaviors or scores used to set goals and establish criteria for measuring change.
Behavior Disorders:	See Seriously Emotionally Disturbed.

Behavior Management: Encompasses all of the strategies that educators utilize to develop effective and appropriate student behaviors (Dunn & French, 1982). See Applied Behavior Analysis.

Biomechanics: The area of study wherein knowledge and methods of mechanics are applied to the structure and function of the living human system (Kreighbaum & Barthels, 1981).

Bleed: A characteristic of individuals with hemophilia in which bleeding occurs into joints or muscles, most commonly into the knee, ankle and elbow, leading to joint damage.

Blind: Visual impairment so severe that, even with correction, educational performance is adversely affected. Legal definition states that 20/200 or poorer in the better eye, after maximum correction, or field of vision of 20 degrees or less.

Blissymbolics: Graphic, meaning-based communication system capable of conveying aspects of human experience; basic symbol elements, pictographs and ideographs, can be used to construct compound symbols, giving the system the potential to provide a large vocabulary.

Blood Pressure: The force that moves the blood through the circulatory system. Blood pressure has two components: systolic pressure, which is the higher pressure, is created when the heart ejects the blood into the arterial system; diastolic pressure, which is the lower pressure, is the pressure between heart beats (systoles) (Fox, Kirby, & Fox, 1987).

Body Composition: The component parts of the body—mainly fat and fat-free weight (Fox, Kirby, & Fox, 1987).

Brittle Diabetes: A condition that is not well controlled and has increased potential for symptoms to occur at any time such as dizziness and nausea.

Calorimetry: Measurement of heat expressed in calories.

Canon Communicator: A portable tape typewriter, in which the control display contains the letters of the alphabet, and the interface consists of multiple switches or keys which the user depresses as selections are made.

Carbohydrates: Chemical compounds containing carbon, hydrogen, and oxygen. Some important carbohydrates are the starches, celluloses, and sugars. Carbohydrates are one of the basic foodstuffs (Fox, Kirby, & Fox, 1987).

Caregiver: Guardian of an individual with a disability who provides care, including parents, supervisors, or full time home staff.

Chain: The sequencing of a series of learned behaviors presented in a fixed order to achieve a more complex terminal response (French & Jansma, 1978).

Child Kinship: The relationships between a child and significant persons in his/her life, including natural and adopted parents, and other adults who assume responsibility for the child.

Choice Reaction Time: Time involved in choosing one response from a collection of possible movements selected in advance.

Circuit or Station Type of Teaching: The creation of discrete learning areas within the general teaching area where students work on activities independently and at their own rates. Very conducive to a group that possess a wide range of abilities.

Closed Loop Control: A mode of system control involving feedback and error detection and correction which is applicable to motor behavior.

Closed Skill: A skill for which the environment is stable and predictable, allowing advance organization of movement.

Collaboration: Working jointly with others to accomplish a common goal such as making decisions or implementing programs and assessment plans.

Command Style Teaching: A style in which the teacher makes all of the decisions regarding the organization of the lesson (starting, stopping, activities to be performed, how they are performed, etc.), and the student is only required to respond to the teacher's command signals (Mosston & Ashworth, 1994).

Communication: Any means by which an individual relates experiences, ideas, knowledge, and feelings to another (includes speech, sign language, gestures, writing).

Communication Board: Apparatus upon which the alphabet, numbers, and commonly used words are represented; used when oral expression is difficult or cannot be obtained.

Community Resources: Personnel, materials, services, and facilities available in the community for use by educators to enrich IEP's, facilitate IFSP's, and actualize transition plans for individuals with disabilities.

Consistent Mapping: The process of having the same stimulus always leading to the same response.

Consultation: Working through others to accomplish a common goal such as advising classroom or physical educators on activity modifications, suggesting techniques for modifying behavior or providing inservice education.

Contained Choices: Giving a limited amount of choices to an individual.

Content-Referenced Standards: Established expectations in terms of the content of components of the task to be mastered.

Contingency: A relationship between the target behavior to be changed and the events or consequences which follow that particular behavior (Kazdin, 1980).

Contingent Observation Timeout: Combines modeling and timeout procedures as the individual is removed from the group but is left near enough to observe peers demonstrating appropriate behavior.

Continuous Reinforcement: Schedule of reinforcement based on the individual being rewarded immediately and each time the target behavior is successfully met.

Continuous Skill: A skill in which the action unfolds continuously, without a recognizable beginning or end.

Continuum of Placement: The concept of ensuring that individuals with disabilities are afforded an opportunity to be placed in education programs along a continuum from least to more restrictive educational settings.

Continuum of Prompts: Varying degrees of assistance offered to the individual with a disability by the instructor to enable that student to complete the assigned task (Snell & Zirpoli, 1987).

Contractibility: The muscles' ability to contract or shorten (Fox, Kirby, & Fox, 1987).

Contraindicated: Conditions, activities or tasks known to aggravate or exacerbate a condition or disability.

Controlled Processing: A mode of information processing that is slow, serial, attention demanding, and voluntary.

Cooperative Learning: Individual students learn from other students in the class by working in groups that allow those with abilities in specific areas to help others in the group. The outcome is that the group and not the individual achieves the goal giving all members of the group a feeling of success (Dunn & Fait, 1989).

Coping and Avoiding Strategies: Methods and techniques employed by individuals with disabilities to avoid practicing/learning the objectives being taught.

Corrective Physical Education: Used to denote physical education of a prescriptive nature, involving a body part(s), posture and/or remediation or correction of specific weaknesses.

Criterion-Referenced Standards: A description of an explicitly defined task or behavior to be mastered.

Cues: Stimulus used by the performer to make a discrimination (Anshel, 1991). See Prompt.

Curriculum-Embedded: The ongoing and continuous process of data gathering as part of the instructional phase of a program. See also Content-Referenced Standards.

Data-Based Gymnasium: A systematic approach used to teach physical education to individuals with severe disabilities developed by Dunn, Morehouse, and Fredericks (1986). The system requires the use of cues, consequences, and data analyses.

Demonstrations: A more intrusive level of cuing or prompting involving the instructor exhibiting the behavior so that individuals may respond and complete the task. The demonstration is often accompanied by verbal cues. May also be referred to as modeling.

Developmental Delay: A discrepancy between an individual's chronological age and functional age in the cognitive, language, motor, or affective domains.

Developmentally Appropriate Activities: Program of activities suited to the developmental needs, capacities, and limitations of students in physical education.

Differential Reinforcement: Reinforcing an appropriate response in the presence of one stimulus while extinguishing an inappropriate response in the presence of another stimulus.

Direct Measures: Data gathering techniques that measure movement parameters directly through the use of instrumentation that often does not require the performance of a skill or pattern.

Direct Service (physical education): Delivery of physical education services by the adapted physical education specialist including screening, evaluation, assessment, and individualized education plans.

Discrete Skill: A skill in which the action is usually brief and with a recognizable beginning and end.

Discrimination Reaction Time: Time required to respond to a simple stimulus given multiple stimuli.

Distributed Practice: A practice schedule in which the amount of rest between practice trials is long relative to the trial length.

Divergent or Exploratory Teaching Styles: A teaching style in which the learner is encouraged to come up with multiple responses to a single question or problem (Mosston & Ashworth, 1994).

Domain-Referenced:	Assessment that uses tests which measure a general ability from which inferences are made about a student's general capability. See also Performance Sampling.
Due Process:	A legally defined set of procedures available to individuals with disabilities to assure that their rights are not violated. These procedures include mediation hearings and court actions.
Duration Recording:	Recording the number of minutes (duration) the behavior occurs during a predetermined period of time. For example, the number of minutes a student is exhibiting on task behavior.
Dwarfism:	A form of short stature syndrome in which the trunk is average sized with unusually short arms and legs or all body parts are proportionate but abnormally short.
Dynamic Lung Volume:	Lung volume measured during exercise.
Dynamic Systems Theory:	The belief in coordinative structures including those simple voluntary motor tasks such as reaching or stepping movements, which result from a systematic relationship among muscle structures established at the spinal cord.
Dynamics:	The study of mechanical factors associated with systems in motion (Kreighbaum & Barthels, 1981).
ERIC:	The Educational Resources Information Center.
Ecological Task Analysis:	The subskills and progressions needed to complete tasks and skills that are appropriate to the individual with a disability within the specific environment in which these skills will be conducted (Snell & Grigg, 1987). Also referred to as Ecological Inventories.
Ecological Theory:	Pertains to interactions between the individual and everything in the individual's environment; in teaching and learning this suggests that environmental factors as well as personal factors must be considered.
Economy (of Measurement Instruments):	A desirable test characteristic having minimal cost in terms of time, personnel and equipment needed to administer. See also Administrative Feasibility.
Encephalitis:	An infection resulting in inflammation of the brain.
Endocrine Control:	Controlled by hormones.
Endurance:	The ability to continue performance of a movement activity (Kreighbaum & Barthels, 1981).
Equilibrium:	The state of a system whose motion is not being changed, accelerated or decelerated (Kreighbaum & Barthels, 1981).
Equilibrium Reactions:	Automatic reactions which the body uses for maintaining or controlling its center of gravity.
Ergometry:	Technique of measuring work output by means of an apparatus that is usually calibrated such as an arm crank ergometer (Anshel, 1991).
Error Detection Capability:	The learned capability to detect one's own error through analyzing response-produced feedback.
Evaluation:	The process that uses measurements to compare with predetermined standards to facilitate rational decisions; used in Standard 12 to refer only to program evaluation.

Event Recording: Recording the number of times the behavior (event) occurs during a predetermined period of time.

Extinction: The process of eliminating or reducing a conditioned response by not administering any form of reinforcement.

Extrinsic Feedback: Feedback provided artificially over and above that received naturally from a movement.

Extrinsic Reinforcers: Those reinforcers not naturally occurring in the environment in which the behavior is being performed.

Facilitated Communication: Method of enabling individuals with disabilities to communicate, using an alphabet board, a hand held typewriter (e.g., a Canon Communicator) or a computer. The student or adult types or points to letters with the help of the touch of another person.

Fading: The gradual removal of a cue, prompt or reinforcer.

Fats: The soft tissue of the body other than that making up the skeletal muscle mass and the viscera. Also foods such as oils, butter, margarine, and animal fats that form an important part of the diet (Fox, Kirby, & Fox, 1987).

Feedback:
1. A verbal, gestural, and/or physical consequence given immediately after the individual responds to a cue (Dunn, Morehouse & Fredericks, 1986).
2. The difference between the state of a system and its goal, often meaning augmented or extrinsic feedback in motor learning.

Flexibility: The range of motion of a joint (static flexibility); opposition or resistance of a joint to motion (dynamic flexibility) (Fox, Kirby, & Fox, 1987).

Fluid Mechanics: The effects that a fluid environment (i.e., air, water) have on the motion of a body (Hay, 1978).

Force: Work= force × distance. The force length applied to a body multiplied by the relationships' distance through which that force is applied (Kreighbaum & Barthels, 1981).

Formative Evaluation: Measurement and evaluation of an individual's performance using a predetermined standard; usually at the beginning of an instructional unit.

Functional Skills: Those skills which possess everyday relevance for that individual. See also Activities of Daily Living.

Functionally Appropriate: Motor activities or tests that have everyday relevance for an individual.

Game Intervention or Cooperative Games: Designing alternative approaches to the game in order to effectively accommodate and include rather than exclude all participants.

Generalization: The process of applying what is learned in a class of tasks to other, unpracticed tasks of the same class.

Generalization Activities: Activities that allow the student with a disability to apply newly learned behaviors and skills in other settings and environments (Auxter, Pyfer, & Heuttig, 1993).

Gestational Disorders: Various anomalies that occur during the period of time when the developing human organism is in the uterus.

Group Contingency: The presentation of a highly desired reinforcer to a group of individuals based on the behavior of one person or the group as a whole. An example is the good behavior game in which the entire group may earn points toward a predetermined reward (Vogler & French, 1983).

Guidance: A procedure used to reduce errors in practice in which the learner is physically or verbally directed through the performance to reduce errors.

Guided Discovery Teaching Style: The learning environment is arranged by the teacher to lead the individual to the learning outcome.

Heart Rate: The number of times the heart beats per minute (Fox, Kirby, & Fox, 1987).

Hemiplegia: Paralysis of the arm and leg on the same side of the body.

Heredegenerative: A condition in which a congenital disorder becomes evident later in life.

Home-Based Physical Activity: Caregivers and/or siblings providing physical activity for individuals with disabilities outside the school physical education setting.

Hydrocephalus: An abnormally large head caused by an accumulation of cerebrospinal fluid.

I-CAN: An extensive set of preprimary, primary, and secondary teaching resources based upon the ABC model composed of performance objectives, assessment items, instructional activities, and games.

Ideographs: Symbols representing ideas.

Impulsivity: The tendency to move without carefully considering the alternatives (Sherrill, 1993).

Incidental Learning: Learning that occurs from general interaction with the environment and not as a result of formal instruction (Auxter, Pyfer & Heuttig, 1993).

Inclusion: The placement of an individual with a disability (even a severe disability) into regular classes with peers in their neighborhood school. The individual is not an occasional visitor, but a viable member of the class with appropriate support services.

Individualized Education Program (IEP): A written statement of instruction based on a multidisciplinary assessment of each student receiving education services according the mandates of IDEA.

Individualized Family Service Plan (IFSP): A written plan of instruction and services based on a multidisciplinary assessment of each infant and toddler's needs which includes an evaluation of family needs.

Individualized Teaching Style: Focuses on the concept of student-centered learning through an individualized and personalized curriculum (Pangrazi & Dauer, 1992).

Integrated Settings: Physical education class settings that include individuals with disabilities learning alongside nondisabled individuals. See Inclusion.

Integration: The process of incorporating individuals with disabilities into society in general and regular schools in particular.

Interaction Skills: Personal skills such as communication and social behavior required by individuals to enable them to successfully work with and relate to others around them.

Interdisciplinary: A philosophical approach that facilitates a sharing of information among professionals for the purpose of increased service to individuals with disabilities.

Intertrial Interval: The time separating two trials of a task.

Interval Recording: Dividing the observation of the behavior into small intervals of time and observing when that behavior occurred during the designated interval.

Interval Reinforcement: A schedule of reinforcement based on the individual being rewarded over a certain period of time for performance of the target behavior.

Intoxicants: Refers to chemical toxins such as alcohol and cocaine that when ingested during pregnancy place the developing fetus at high risk for brain related disorders.

Intrinsic Feedback: Feedback naturally received from producing a movement. See also Extrinsic Feedback.

Involuntary: Muscle not under voluntary control (Spence & Mason, 1992).

Karvonen Formula: A method for determining heart rate reserve (Fox, Kirby, & Fox, 1987).

Kinematics: An area of study that is concerned with time and space factors in the motion of a system (Kreighbaum & Barthels, 1981).

Kinesiology: The study of human movement from an anatomical and/or mechanical perspective (Kreighbaum & Barthels, 1981).

Kinesthesis: The sense derived from muscular contractions during purposeful movements; related to proprioception.

Kinetics: An area of study that is concerned with the forces that act on a system (Kreighbaum & Barthels, 1981).

Knowledge of Performance: Augmented feedback that describes a feature of the movement pattern produced.

Knowledge of Results: Augmented, postresponse, verbalizable information about success in meeting the movement goal.

Lactate Threshold: Point at which lactate accumulates at rates faster than expected.

Least Intrusive Level of Prompts: A continuum of prompts ranging from physical assistance (most intrusive) to natural cues in the environment (least intrusive) (Block, 1994).

Least Restrictive Environment (LRE): The educational setting in which the individual can most adequately function and meet their potential.

Leisure Counseling: Counseling involving the knowledge and understanding of leisure, the importance of leisure lifestyles, personal concepts of leisure choices and the exploration of personal resources including skills, finances, experiences, and home/community resources.

Lifespan: The continuous and cumulative process of development originating at birth and ending at death.

Light Talker: An augmentative device similar to the Touch Talker which uses a scanning device activated by a switch for individuals who cannot directly select symbols.

Local Education Agency (LEA): The educational agency responsible, such as school, school district or county, under the law, for the education of a given individual.

Long Term Goals: Broad general statements of student outcomes.

Long Term Memory: Contains information that has been collected over a lifetime; it may be essentially limitless in capacity.

Metabolic Equivalent (MET): The resting energy requirement, estimated to be 3.5ml of oxygen per kilogram of body weight per minute (Fox, Kirby, & Fox, 1987).

Massed Practice: A practice schedule in which the amount of rest between trials is short relative to the trial length.

Mechanical: The ability of the human body for producing efficient mechanical work such as walking, running and cycling.

Medical Gymnastics: A system popularized by Dudley Sargent in the early 1900's in which exercise was prescribed for various problems.

Meningitis: An infection resulting in an inflammation of the covering of the brain (meninges).

Mental Practice: A practice procedure in which the learner imagines successful action without overt physical practice.

Mercury Switch: A device involving the use of a mercury switch attached by Velcro to the individual's body or clothes. When the individual performs the desired movement the mercury switch completes the electrical circuit, allowing a reinforcer such as a light, music, or toy to be activated (French, Folsom-Meek, Cook, & Smith, 1987).

Metabolic Rate: The energy expended by the body per unit time (Spence & Mason, 1992).

Metabolism: The sum total of all chemical reactions that occur in the body during the production of energy for work (Fox, Kirby, & Fox, 1987).

Microcephalus: An abnormally small head.

Mineralization: Normal or abnormal deposition of minerals in the tissues (Taber's, 1989).

Modeling: A practice procedure in which another person demonstrates the correct performance of the skills to be learned.

Modified Physical Education: Regular physical education, with appropriate modifications or adjustments suited to the needs, capacities and limitations of individuals with disabilities.

Moral Development: A process whereby humans progress from behaving in a way that gets rewards and avoids punishment to the desired stage of unselfish concern for human rights; cognitive thought process and moral reasoning are believed to be parallel.

Motor Fitness: Components of physical performance such as agility, coordination, speed and power that contribute to success in various physical activities.

Motor Program: A centrally located structure that defines the essential details of skilled action.

Multidisciplinary: The broad term indicating that many disciplines are involved in the service delivery process; involves separate evaluations and prescriptions by different specialists (various team members).

Multidisciplinary Model: Involves separate evaluations and prescriptions by different specialists assigned to identify the individual's specific problem.

Muscular Endurance: The ability of a muscle or muscle group to perform repeated contractions against a light load for an extended period of time (Fox, Kirby, & Fox, 1987).

Muscular Strength: The amount of force exerted or resistance overcome by a muscle for a single repetition (Fox, Kirby, & Fox, 1987).

Myoelectric Arm: A particular type of prosthesis for individuals who have had a portion of their arms amputated. The arm, which operates by means of a small battery-driven motor, obeys signals received from electric energy produced by movement of the remaining muscle groups. This allows control of elbow or hand strength of motion.

Negative Reinforcement: The removal of an aversive event as a consequence of a behavior in order to increase the frequency of the behavior (Henderson & French, 1989).

Negative Transfer: Occurs when the experience with a previous skill hinders or interferes with the learning of a new skill.

Neuro-developmental Theory: Suggests that (a) delayed or abnormal motor development is the result of interference with normal brain maturation, (b) this interference is manifested as an impairment of the postural reflex mechanism, (c) abnormal reflex activity produces abnormal degree and distribution of postural and muscle tone, and (d) righting and equilibrium reactions should be used to inhibit abnormal movements while simultaneously simulating and facilitating normal postural responses.

Non-Technical Aides: Unaided: Approaches that rely on gestural communication, (e.g., American Manual Alphabet, American Sign Language, American Indian Sign Language, Finger-spelling). Aided: Approaches that depend on a system or device of some kind, (e.g., Blissymbolics, Rebus, Communication Boards, Facilitated Communication, typing and writing).

Nonverbal Communication: Any approach designed to support, enhance, or supplement the communication of individuals who are not independent verbal communicators in all situations.

Normalization: The principle of instructing persons with disabilities in community settings so that the activity can be generalized to the setting in which it will normally be performed. In this principle, socially acceptable ("normal") behavior is emphasized to reduce the obviousness of a disability and allow more natural blending in with others.

Normalization Theory: This theory was introduced to the USA from Sweden by Bengt Nirge and expanded by Wolf Wolfensberger. The theory emphasizes that individuals with disabilities should be afforded the opportunity to experience a pattern of living, learning, and working that is as close to normal as possible.

Objective-Taxonomic: An approach to specifying curriculum content that focuses on how the learner acquires knowledge, skills, attitudes, normative social behaviors, and values.

Occupational Therapy: Primarily concerned with the components of performance to maintain the individual's self care, work, and leisure activities. Major components: motor functioning, sensory integrative functioning, and cognitive functioning.

Open Loop Control: A mode in which instructions for the effector system are determined in advance and run off without feedback.

Open Skill: A skill for which the environment is unpredictable or unstable, preventing advance organization of movement.

Operant Conditioning: The use of a consequence to increase the probability that a behavior will be strengthened, maintained, or weakened (Dunn & French, 1982).

Opportunity to Respond: Number of appropriate learning trials (opportunities) a student had during a lesson.

Order Effect: The influence of other test items on the performance of a test item as a result of the order in which the performances were sampled.

Organizing Centers: The focal points for the curriculum and learning; they are the frame of reference, emphasis, or theme around which the subject matter is designed.

Orientation and Mobility Training: Training provided to blind and individuals who are partially sighted in order to assist in independent travel, movement and orientation to surroundings.

Orthoptic Vision: Refers to activity of the six external muscles of the eye which move the eyes up, down, in, out, and in diagonal directions.

Orthosis: The straightening or correction of a deformity or disability.

Orthotics: Splinting or bracing that may begin in infancy to facilitate upright or functional positioning as near normal as possible.

Outcome Based Goals and Objectives: Goals and objectives that focus on the result or outcome of the completed task and not the way in which the task is completed.

Overcorrection: A method of reducing inappropriate behavior while also providing training for appropriate alternative behaviors (Cooper, Heron, & Heward, 1987).

Overfat: Having a proportion of body fat that exceeds recommended limits, usually 15 percent for men and 24 percent for women (Fox, Kirby, & Fox, 1987).

Overlearning: Requiring additional practice at the time of original practice.

Overload: Resistance greater than that which a muscle or muscle group normally encounters. The resistance (load) can be maximal or near-maximal (Fox, Kirby, & Fox, 1987).

Overweight: A condition in which the body weighs more than normal based on height-weight charts (Fox, Kirby, & Fox, 1987).

Oxygen Consumption: The volume of oxygen used for energy expenditure. Usually expressed in liters per minute or in a relative term, milliliters per kilogram per minute (ml/kg-min) (Fox, Kirby, & Fox, 1987).

Oxygen Transport: The cardiorespiratory system, which is composed of the stroke volume (SV), the heart rate (HR), and the arterial mixed venous oxygen difference.

Pairing Techniques: The matching or associating of a primary reinforcer with a secondary reinforcer so that the secondary reinforcer (that is perhaps more socially normal and acceptable) gradually replaces the primary reinforcer.

Paraplegia: Paralysis or involvement of lower extremities and trunk resulting from spinal lesion or neurological dysfunction.

Paraprofessional: Individuals who are not trained to teach physical education but who can assist the physical educator by administering screening tests, securing materials and equipment, and working in one-on-one situations with students who need more personalized attention (Jansma & French, 1994).

Pathobiomechanics: Study of the nature and cause of disease which involves changes in structure and function of the mechanics of the human system (Suro, 1994 from Taber's, Kreighbaum & Barthels).

Pathokinesiology: Study of the nature and cause of disease, which involves structural and functional changes in the ability of a human body to move (Kreighbaum & Barthels, 1981).

Peer Tutor: Student with or without a disability serving as an aid or friend in order to assist the individual with a disability.

Perception:
(a) Decoding the environment, (b) the process by which information is interpreted within the cortical areas of the brain, or (c) the process of obtaining meaning from sensation and thus having knowledge of the environment (Sherrill, 1993).

Performance Generalization:
The ability to utilize a performance in a broad array of contexts, (e.g., balancing . . . on one foot, . . . while moving, . . . on a beam, . . . without support, etc.).

Performance Sampling:
The practice of measuring representative factors of motor performance as a means for obtaining an overview of an individual's true ability.

Perseveration:
Persistence or fixation on a single feature or source of stimuli, manifest in repetitive behavior such as vocalizations, hand gestures and fixation.

Personality Disorders:
A broad category that characterizes individuals whose personality traits are inflexible and maladaptive and significantly impair social, leisure, or vocational functioning (Sherrill, 1993).

Phenylketonuria:
A recessive genetic disorder accompanied by an enzyme disorder interfering with food metabolism. If untreated, brain damage and mental retardation may result.

Physical Activity Reinforcement:
A systematic procedure in which a structured time to choose among various preferred physical activities is contingent on the individual's meeting of a predetermined criterion of behavior (Lavay, 1984).

Physical Guidance:
The most intrusive level of cueing or prompting for a student with a disability. Physical guidance can range from the touch of a body part, to the physical manipulation of the individual's limbs and body so that the individual can complete a movement sequence (Dunn, Morehouse & Fredericks, 1986).

Physical Restraints:
The use of equipment or personnel to control or reduce the freedom of movement a student has so as to prevent them from causing injury to themselves and others.

Physical Therapy:
Provides identification, prevention, remediation, and rehabilitation of acute or prolonged movement dysfunction. Treatment by physical means, evaluating patients and treating through physical therapeutic measures as opposed to medicines or surgery.

Physical or Psychological Aversive Strategies:
Application of a stimulus that the individual does not like that reduces the likelihood that the inappropriate behavior will be performed again.

Piaget's Theory:
A theory of cognition which emphasizes the process by which children acquire knowledge; the interaction between the individual and the environment is viewed as critical to assimilation.

Pictographs:
Symbols that look like the things they represent.

Positive Practice:
The individual is required to practice an appropriate behavior for an extended period. For example, if an individual becomes angry and refuses to shake hands with another person after a contest, the individual might be required to shake hands with several individuals. See Overcorrection.

Positive Reinforcement:
An increase in the frequency of a response (behavior) will occur when it is followed by a favorable consequence (Kazdin, 1980).

Positive Specific Immediate Feedback:
Information given to the individual immediately upon completion of the behavior that reinforces (increases the likelihood that it will be done again) a specific aspect of the behavior.

Positive Transfer: Occurs when experience with a previous skill aids or facilitates the learning of a new skill.

Post KR Delay: The interval of time between the presentation of KR and the next response.

Postural Reflexes: See Equilibrium Reactions.

Power: The product of an applied force and the speed with which it is applied; the quantity of work done per unit of time (Kreighbaum & Barthels, 1981).

Prader-Willi Syndrome: A congenital disorder characterized by excessive eating and mental retardation.

Preload: The load on the muscle at rest (Mohrman & Heller, 1986).

Premack Principle: A more preferred behavior by the individual is contingent upon the successful completion of a less preferred behavior. A high probability can reinforce a low probability behavior (Eichstaedt & Lavay, 1992).

Present Level of Performance: A statement of the individual's physical and motor fitness, fundamental motor skills and patterns, and skill in aquatics, dance and individual and group games and sports. This statement must be based on information obtained through assessment procedures designed to evaluate these aspects of physical and motor development (Dunn & Fait, 1989).

Primary Reinforcers: Stimuli or events that by their biological importance (food, water, warmth, etc.) can act as rewards and reinforcement to behaviors that precede them being given (Cooper, Heron, & Heward, 1987).

Prime Mode of Communication: The method of communication with which an individual with a disability is most comfortable and competent.

Primitive Reflexes: Those which appear during gestation or at birth and become suppressed by six months of age.

Problem Solving Techniques: A technique used with Guided Discovery, Divergent or Exploratory Teaching Styles to allow divergent responses and variations to the completion of any task or activity (Siedentop, Herkowitz, & Rink, 1994).

Professional Development Activities: See Staff Development.

Program Evaluation: A process by which program merit can be determined by measuring student outcomes, consumer satisfaction, and quality of program operations for the purpose of improvement, accountability and enlightenment.

Prompt: A cue or stimulus which occasions a response of the behavior, usually in the form of physical guidance to initiate a proper movement (Eichstaedt & Lavay, 1992).

Propriceptive Neuromuscular Facilitation (PNF): Series of therapeutic techniques designed to enhance the neural muscular response (relaxation or contraction) of a body part, based on neurophysiological principles (Anshel, 1991).

Proprioception: Sensory information arising from within the body, resulting in the sense of position and movement; similar to kinesthesis.

Prosthesis: Replacement of a missing part by an artificial substitute, such as an artificial extremity.

Proteins: Basic foodstuffs containing amino acids (Fox, Kirby, & Fox, 1987).

Public Accommodation: Equal access and equal services in the public domain. Making programs accessible and facilities architecturally accessible in the public domain as per the Americans with Disabilities Act.

Pulmonary System: The system of blood vessels that carries the blood between the heart and lungs (Hole, 1992).

Punishment: Any aversive event or consequence which decreases the occurrence of a particular behavior; remedial or a positive reinforcer.

Quadriplegia: Paralysis or involvement of all four extremities in the trunk, resulting from cervical spinal lesion or neurological dysfunctions.

Qualitative Aspects of Skills: Elements of the skill that relate to how the skill is performed rather than the outcome (quantitative) of the skill. Evaluation of the qualitative aspects of a skill is conducted using criterion referenced tests and assessments (Auxter, Pyfer, & Heuttig, 1993).

Quantitative Skill Teaching: Skill instruction where the emphasis lies in the final product (outcome or result) of the skill and not the process (the way) in which the skill was performed. Evaluation of this kind of instruction is done using normative assessment tools and objective assessment measures (Siedentop, Herkowitz, & Rink, 1984).

RPE: Ratings of Perceived Exertion.

Random Practice: A practice sequence in which tasks from several classes are experienced in random order over consecutive trials.

Ratio Reinforcement: Schedule of reinforcement based on the individual being rewarded for a certain number of occurrences of the target behavior.

Reaction Time: The interval of time from a suddenly presented, unanticipated stimulus until the beginning of the response.

Reality Therapy: Developed by Glasser, Reality Therapy is an approach to managing behavior in schools based on the need to give and receive love, and the need to have self-worth.

Reasonable Accommodation: May include (a) making existing facilities used by employees readily accessible to and usable by individuals with disabilities; and (b) job restructuring, part-time or modified work schedules, reassignment to a vacant position, acquisition or modification of equipment or devices, appropriate adjustment or modifications of examinations, training materials or policies, the provision of qualified readers or interpreters, and other similar accommodations for individuals with disabilities.

Rebus: Puzzle representing a word, phrase, or sentence by letters, numerals, pictures, etc., often with pictures of objects whose names have the same sound as the words represented; used as an alternate method of teaching reading.

Reciprocal Style of Teaching: A style of teaching where the teacher has the learner work with a partner. In working with the partner, they offer and receive feedback from the partner based on criteria prepared by the teacher (Mosston & Ashworth, 1994).

Reflexes: Automatic, stereotyped reactions to stimuli (Spence & Mason, 1992).

Refractive Error: Refers to problems of visual acuity associated with inappropriate bending of light rays before reaching the retina (e.g., myopia and hyperopia) (Sherrill, 1993).

Regular Education Initiative (REI): A term used to describe the goal of keeping as many students as possible in the regular education setting (Sherrill, 1993).

Regular Physical Education: Full spectrum of game, sports, rhythms, aquatics and fitness activities.

Reinforcement Event Menu: A list of highly desirable reinforcers are displayed for individuals to observe. These items can be earned by meeting a predetermined criterion of behavior.

Reinforcement Schedules: A set of rules or a plan that outlines the number of times a behavior must be performed before reinforcement is given to the individual performing the behavior. Used to strengthen the occurrence of a behavior.

Related Services: Supportive services as are required to assist a child with a disability to benefit from special education.

Response Cost: The withdrawal of a positive reinforcer as a consequence of the occurrence of an undesirable behavior. Examples would be fines or loss of privileges.

Response Programming: Involves organizing the motor system for the desired movement.

Response Selection: Involves deciding what movement to make given the nature of the environment.

Restitutional Method: The individual is required to remediate a disruption they have caused. For example, an individual who fails to put equipment back in its proper location would be required to put that piece of equipment away and then straighten and replace additional equipment.

Satiation: The elimination of the effectiveness of a reinforcer on a behavior caused by excessive application.

Secondary Reinforcers: Stimuli or events that have acquired reinforcing capabilities (e.g., money or tokens).

Self-Actualization: As proposed by Maslow refers to making actual or realizing one's potential; emphasis is on internal rather than external motivation and personal responsibility.

Self-Efficacy: A conceptual framework proposed by Bandura for changing fearful and avoidant behavior; a situation specific form of self-confidence.

Self-Monitoring: The ability to keep track of one's own behavior such as using self-recording and monitoring heart rate.

Self-Recording: The recording of personal scores on a log or publicly posted recording chart (Van Houten, 1980).

Self-Stimulatory: Refers to behaviors that are self-induced, repetitious, non-goal oriented and provide stimulation.

Sensory Integration: The theory that the inability to organize sensory information for use accounts for some aspects of learning disorders and that enhancing sensory integration will make academic learning easier.

Sensory Receptors: Devices sensitive to light, heat, radiation, sound, or mechanical or other physical stimuli (Taber's, 1989).

Seriously Emotionally Disturbed: A condition exhibiting one or more of the following characteristics over a long period of time and to a marked degree, which adversely affects educational performance: (a) An inability to learn which cannot be explained by intellectual, sensory, or health factors; (b) An inability to build or maintain satisfactory interpersonal relationships with peers and teachers; (c) Inappropriate types of behavior or feelings under normal circumstances; (d) A general pervasive mood of unhappiness or depression; or (e) A tendency to develop physical symptoms or fears associated with personal or school problems (Federal Register, August 23, 1977, p. 42478).

Shaping: Reinforcing small steps or approximations of the desired target behavior.

Short Term Memory: Thought to be workspace (also referred to as "working memory") where controlled information processing activities can be applied to relevant information; it is thought to be severely limited in capacity.

Short Term Sensory Memory: The most peripheral aspect of memory and involves processing in the stimulus-identification stage resulting in memory of the environmental sensory events that are stored for a maximum duration of about one-fourth of a second.

Short Term Objectives: Statements which explain how annual goals will be met. Written in behavioral terms, consisting of the following components: (a) performance/behavior, (b) condition, and (c) criteria (Eichstaedt & Lavay, 1992).

Shunt: Device implanted in the body to remove or drain excess cerebrospinal fluid (Anshel, 1991).

Social Imperception: Inability to gather information from the environment to utilize in determining the appropriateness of one's actions.

Social Reinforcers: Actions provided by the instructor of a social nature (physical contact, standing close to the student, verbal praise, etc.) that reinforce the desired behavior.

Social Values: Rules, morals and ethical standards that when exercised, reflect socially appropriate behavior.

Special Education: Specifically designed instruction at no cost to the parents, to meet the unique needs of a child with a disability including classroom instruction, instruction in physical education, home instruction, and instruction in hospitals and institutions.

Specially Designed Physical Education: Physical education programming for a special education class with minimal or limited adaptations (California Department of Education, 1993).

Specificity Hypothesis: A view of motor abilities holding that tasks are composed of many unrelated abilities.

Speed-Accuracy Trade-Off: The tendency for accuracy to decrease as the movement speed or velocity of a movement increases.

Staff Development: Any systematic attempt to change school personnel.

Standardized Instruments: Tests that specifically describe procedures for administration including set of conditions, equipment and instructions, (standardized administration) to which data collection must conform in order for the data to be considered valid.

Static Lung Volume: Lung volume measured during rest.

Statics: The study of factors associated with nonmoving systems (Kreighbaum & Barthels, 1981).

Stimulus Identification: Primarily a sensory stage which requires analyzing environmental information from a variety of sources, such as vision, audition, touch, and kinesthesis, to decide whether a stimulus has been presented and, if so, what it is.

Stimulus Overselectivity: Abnormally limited attentional scope; inability to select relevant cues and to see the whole.

Stroke Volume: The amount of blood pumped by the left ventricle of the heart in one contraction or beat (Fox, Kirby, & Fox, 1987).

Structure-of-Content: An approach to specifying curriculum content that uses a logical analysis of the subject matter and builds from a base of specific elementary content to a complex, comprehensive content.

Sturge Weber-Simumitri's Syndrome: Congenital syndrome characterized by port-wine stains; associated with mental retardation, epileptic seizures, and glaucoma.

Summative Evaluations: Measurement and evaluation of an individual's performance using a predetermined standard; usually at the end of an instructional unit or as in measuring progress.

Tactile Defensive: An individual who is hypersensitive to touch and/or pressure.

Tangible Reinforcement: An object or an activity that when given after the performance of a behavior increases the likelihood that the behavior will again be performed.

Task Analysis: The identification of subskills and intermediate progressions sequenced in a specific order that the student must learn in order to complete a more complex skill or task (Siedentop, Herkowitz, & Rink, 1984).

Task Description: An approach to specifying curriculum content that describes in a step-by-step progression the elements of a task; the outcomes generated by this task analysis process is a series of descriptions that follow the progress of a given task through its various component operations.

Task Style of Teaching: A teaching style in which the teacher determines the basic framework to the lesson (e.g., what tasks will be learned, in what order they will be learned, etc.) but where the students are permitted to make decisions on the pace at which they work and how the skill is to be executed (Siedentop, Herkowitz, & Rink, 1984).

Task Variation: See Random Practice.

Tay-Sachs Disease: An inborn error of metabolism.

Technical Aides: Computer based speaking and writing systems, e.g., laptop computers using standard hardware and customized software.

Therapeutic Recreation (TR): A helping profession which promotes wellness and improves the quality of life through leisure (Winslow, 1988). Professionals in this field are called therapeutic recreation specialists.

Thermoregulation: Ability of the body to regulate its temperature influenced by environmental conditions (e.g., sweating).

Time on Task: Time spent in the lesson where the student is actively engaged in the assigned activity (Randall, 1992).

Timeout: The removal of an individual for a period of time from a reinforcing environment. This is contingent upon the emittance of inappropriate behavior in an attempt to decrease that particular behavior (French, Lavay, & Henderson, 1985).

Token Economy Reinforcement: Tokens, checkmarks, points, or chips earned for meeting a predetermined criterion of behavior are later exchanged for items which are reinforcing and of value to the individual.

Top-Down Model: Envisioning where the student will be upon graduation and planning content the student will need in order to be successful in future settings (Block, 1994).

Total Communication: A combination of communication modes (e.g., verbal, gestural, pictorial) that offers the individual with a disability an extended range of communication capabilities (Cartwright, Cartwright, & Ward, 1989).

Total Inclusion: The practice of educating all students, including students with disabilities, in regular education and regular classes (Block, 1994). See Inclusion.

Touch Talker: An augmented device which allows the nonverbal student to directly select (point to) symbols (ranging from 8 to 128) to communicate their wants and needs.

Transdisciplinary Model: Breaks down traditional boundaries and encourages a sharing of information and cooperation among team members throughout the implementation of services to the individual.

Transfer of Learning: The gain or loss in proficiency on one task as a result of practice or experience of another task.

Transition Time: Lesson time spent in organizational, transitional and nonacademic type activities (Randall, 1992).

Traumatic Brain Injury: Refers mostly to closed head injuries caused by concussion, contusion, or hemorrhage that result in permanent damage (Sherrill, 1993).

Tuberous Sclerosis: A syndrome manifested by convulsive seizures, progressive mental disorder, adenoma sebaceum, and tumors of the kidneys and brain with projections into the cerebral ventricles.

Underweight: Body weight is lower than minimal weight calculated from skeletal measurements, body weight lower than the 20th percentile by height-for-age, and percent body fat is lower than 17% (McArdle, Katch, & Katch, 1986).

Utility (of Measurement Instruments): A desirable test characteristic referring to the usability of the data as well as the usability of the instrument (see also Administrative Feasibility).

Variable Practice: A schedule of practice in which many variations of a class of actions are practiced.

Ventilation: The movement of air into and out of the lungs (Fox, Kirby, & Fox, 1987).

Verbal Communication: Medium of oral communication that employs a linguistic code (language); through this medium one can express thoughts and feelings and understand those of others who employ the same code.

Verbal Directions: The least intrusive level of cueing or prompting that consists of the instructor verbally explaining to the student with a disability what they should do in order for them to respond and complete the task (Dunn & Fait, 1989).

Vestibular: Apparatus in the inner ear that provides signals related to movement in space (Sherrill, 1993).

Vocational Specialist: Provide vocational education services and programs to individuals with disabilities who cannot succeed in a regular vocational setting. These programs and services may include the following: special remedial instruction, guidance counseling and testing services, employability skill training, communication skill training, special transportation facilities and services (Meers, 1987).

Von Recklinghausen's Disease: Multiple neurofibromata of nerve sheaths. They occur along peripheral, spinal, and cranial nerves; may experience pressure and pain on the spinal cord or on the brain.

Wolf: A less expensive augmentative device which allows for direct touch selection or scanning to communicate. The wolf limits the amount of communication as compared to the Touch and Light talkers.

REFERENCES

Abbott, M., Franciscus, M., & Weeks, Z.R. (1988). *Opportunities in occupational therapy careers.* Lincolnwood, IL: National Textbook Company.

Alberto, P.A. (1990). *Applied behavior analysis for teachers* (3rd ed.). Columbus, OH: Merrill Publishing.

American Physical Therapy Association. (1986). *Definition and guidelines.* Rockville, MD: Author.

Anshel, M.H. (Ed.) (1991). *Dictionary of the sport and exercise sciences.* Champaign, IL: Human Kinetics.

Auxter, D., & Pyfer, J. (1989). *Principles and methods of adapted physical education* (6th ed.). St. Louis, MO: Times Mirror/Mosby.

Auxter, D., Pyfer, J., & Heuttig, C. (1993). *Principles and methods of adapted physical education and recreation* (7th ed.). St. Louis, MO: Mosby.

Ayres, A.J. (1981). *Sensory integration and learning disorders.* Los Angeles, CA: Western Psychological Services.

Barnes, M.R., Crutchfield, C.A., & Heriza, C.B. (1979). *The neurophysiological basis of patient treatment, Vol. 2: Reflexes in motor development.* Atlanta, GA: Stokesville Publishing Co.

Baumgartner, T.A. & Jackson, A.S. (1991). *Measurement for evaluation in physical education and exercise science* (4th ed.). Dubuque, IA: Wm. C. Brown.

Bigge, J.L. (1991). *Teaching individuals with physical and multiple disabilities.* New York: Macmillan.

Block, M.E. (1994). *Including students with disabilities in regular physical education.* Baltimore, MD: Paul H. Brooks Publishing.

California Department of Education. (1993). Program advisory clarifying adapted physical education program services. *Physical education framework for California Public Schools.* Sacramento, CA: State Department of Education.

Carlson, N.R. (1991). *Physiology of behavior.* Boston, MA: Allyn & Bacon.

Cartwright, G.P., Cartwright, C.A. & Ward, M.F. (1989). *Educating special educators* (3rd ed.). Belmont, CA: Wadsworth Publishing.

Cooper, J.M., Adrian, M., & Glassow, R.B. (1982). *Kinesiology.* St. Louis, MO: C.V. Mosby.

Cooper, J.O., Heron, T.E., & Heward, W.L. (1987). *Applied behavior analysis.* Columbus, OH: Merrill Publishing.

Cowden, J., & Tymeson, G. (1984). *Certification in adapted/special education: National status-update.* Northern Illinois University.

Craft, D. (1994). Inclusion: Physical education for all. *Journal of Physical Education, Recreation and Dance,* **65**(1) 22-23.

Dillman, D. (1978). *Mail and telephone surveys: The total design method.* New York: John Wiley & Sons.

Dreikurs, R., & Cassel, P. (1991). *Discipline without tears* (2nd ed.). New York: Penguin Books.

Dummer, G.M., Reuschlein, P.L., Haubenstricker, J.L., Vogel, P.G., & Cavanaugh, P.L. (1993). *Evaluation of K-12 physical education programs: A self-study approach.* Dubuque, IA: Wm. C. Brown.

Dunn, J.M., & Fait, H.F. (1989). *Special physical education* (6th ed.). Dubuque, IA: Wm. C. Brown.

Dunn, J.M., & French, R.W. (1982). Operant conditioning: A tool for special educators in the 1980's. *Exceptional Education Quarterly,* **3**, 42-53.

Dunn, J.M., Morehouse, J.W., & Fredericks, H.D.B. (1986). *Physical education for the severely handicapped.* Austin, TX: Pro-ed.

''Education of all handicapped children act of 1975'' (PL 94-142, 29 Nov. 1975), *United States Statutes at Large,* **89**, 773-796.

Eichstaedt, C.B., & Lavay, B.W. (1992). *Physical activity for individuals with mental retardation: Infancy through adulthood.* Champaign, IL: Human Kinetics.

Eichstaedt, C.B., & Kalakian, L.H. (1987). *Developmental/adapted physical education: Making ability count* (2nd ed.). New York: Macmillan.

Federal Register. (1990). Individuals with disabilities education act.

Fiorentino, M. (1981). *A basis for sensorimotor development—normal and abnormal.* Springfield, IL: Charles C Thomas.

Fisher, A., Murray, E., & Bundy, A. (1991). *Sensory integration: Theory and practice.* Philadelphia, PA: F.A. Davis.

Fox, E.L., Kirby, T.E., & Fox, A.R. (1987). *Bases of fitness*. New York: Macmillan.

French, R., Folsom-Meeks, S., Cook, C., & Smith, D. (1987). The use of electrical response devices to motivate nonambulatory profoundly mentally retarded children. *American Corrective Therapy Journal*, **41**, 64-68.

French, R., Henderson, H., & Horvat, M. (1992). *Creative approaches to managing student behavior*. Park City, UT: Family Development Resources, Inc.

French, R., & Jansma, P. (July, 1978). *Behavior management*. Unpublished manuscript, University of Utah.

French, R., & Lavay, B. (1990). *Selected readings in behavior management for physical educators and recreators*. Kearney, NE: Educational Systems Associates Inc.

French, R., Lavay, B., & Henderson, H. (1985). Take a lap. *Physical Educator*, **42**, 180-185.

Gabbard, C. (1992). *Lifelong motor development*. Dubuque, IA: Wm. C. Brown.

Gagne, R.M., & Briggs, L.J. (1979). *Principles of instructional design*. New York: Holt, Rinehart, and Winston.

Gallahue, D.L. (1989). *Understanding motor development in children* (2nd ed.). Indianapolis, IN: Benchmark Press.

Graham, G., Holt-Hale, S., & Parker, M. (1993). *Children moving* (3rd ed.). Mountain View, CA: Mayfield Publishing Co.

Harrison, J.M., & Blakemore, C.L. (1992). *Instructional strategies for secondary physical education*. Dubuque, IA: Wm. C. Brown.

Hellison, D. (1985). *Goals and strategies for teaching physical education*. Champaign, IL: Human Kinetics.

Henderson, H., & French, R. (1989). Negative reinforcement or punishment? *Journal of Physical Education, Recreation and Dance*, **60**(5), 4.

Hole, J.W., Jr. (1992). *Essentials of human anatomy and physiology* (4th ed.). Dubuque, IA: Wm. C. Brown.

Jansma, P., & French, R. (1994). *Special physical education* (2nd ed.). Englewood Cliffs, NJ: Prentice-Hall.

Kazdin, A.E. (1980). *Behavior modification in applied settings*. Homewood, IL: The Dorsey Press.

Kelly, L.E. (1991). National standards for adapted physical education. *Advocate*, **20**(1), 2-3.

Kelly, L.E. (1991). Is there really a national need for more adapted physical educators? *Advocate*, **20**(1), 7-8.

Kelly, L.E. (1991). [Developing outcome standards for adapted physical education]. Unpublished raw data.

Kelly, L.E. (1992). *National standards for adapted physical education*. (Grant No. H029K20092). Washington, DC: United States Department of Education, Office of Special Education and Rehabilitation.

Kelly, L.E. (in press). National needs assessment of adapted physical education roles, responsibilities and perceived training needs. Charlottesville, VA: University of Virginia.

Kreighbaum, E., & Barthels, K.M. (1981). *Biomechanics: A qualitative approach for studying human movement* (2nd ed.). Minnesota: Burgess Publishing.

Lavay, B. (1984). Physical activity as a reinforcer. *Adapted Physical Activity Quarterly*, **1**, 315-321.

Magill, R.A. (1993). *Motor learning: Concepts and applications* (4th ed.). Dubuque, IA: Wm. C Brown.

McArdle, W.D., Katch, F.I., & Katch, U.L. (1986). *Exercise physiology: Energy, nutrition, and human performance* (2nd ed.). Philadelphia, PA: Lea & Febiger.

Meers, G.D. (1987). *Handbook of vocational special needs education* (2nd ed.). Rockville, MD: Aspen Publishers.

Melograno, V. (1985). *Designing the physical education curriculum: A self-directed approach* (2nd ed.). Dubuque, IA: Kendall/Hunt.

Mohrman, D.E., & Heller, L.J. (1986). *Cardiovascular physiology* (2nd ed.). New York: McGraw Hill.

Moon, M.S., & Bunker, L. (1987). Recreation and motor skills programming. In M.E. Snell (Ed.), *Systematic instruction of persons with severe handicaps*. Columbus, OH: Merrill Publishing.

Morris, G.S.D., & Stiehl, J. (1989). *Changing kids games*. Champaign, IL: Human Kinetics.

Mosston, M., & Ashworth, S. (1994). *Teaching physical education*. New York: Macmillan.

National Association of State Directors of Special Education. (1991). Physical education and sports: The unfulfilled promise for students with disabilities. *Liaison Bulletin*, **17**(6), 1-10.

National Consortium on Physical Education and Recreation for the Handicapped. (1991). Summary of the NCPERH board meeting, Arlington, Virginia, July 20, 1991. *Advocate*, **20**(1), 4-5.

National Resource Center for Paraprofessionals in Special Education. (1988). *A training program for paraprofessionals working in special education and related services*. New York: New Centers Training Laboratory.

Nicolosi, L., Haryman, E., & Kresheck, J. (1989). *Terminology of communication disorders*. Baltimore, MD: Williams & Wilkins.

Orlick, T. (1982). *The second cooperative sports and games book*. New York: Pantheon.

Pangrazi, R.P., & Dauer, V. (1992). *Dynamic physical education for elementary school children* (10th ed.). New York: Macmillan.

Randall, L.E. (1992). *The student teachers handbook for physical education*. Champaign, IL: Human Kinetics.

Rimmer, J.H. (1994). *Fitness and rehabilitation programs for special populations*. Dubuque, IA: Wm. C. Brown.

Rink, J. (1993). *Teaching physical education for learning*. St. Louis, MO: Mosby.

Sage, G. (1984). *Motor learning and control: A neuropsychological approach*. Dubuque, IA: Wm. C. Brown.

Schmidt, R.A. (1988). *Motor control and learning: A behavioral emphasis*. Champaign, IL: Human Kinetics.

Schmidt, R.A. (1991). *Motor learning and performance: From principles to practice*. Champaign, IL: Human Kinetics.

Seaman, J., & DePauw, K. (1989). *The new adapted physical education* (2nd ed.). Mountain View, CA: Mayfield.

Sears, C.J. (1982). The transdisciplinary approach: A process for the compliance with Public Law 94-142. *The Journal of the Association for the Severely Handicapped*, **6**, 22-29.

Sherrill, C. (1988). *Leadership training in adapted physical education*. Champaign, IL: Human Kinetics.

Sherrill, C. (1993). *Adapted physical activity, recreation and sport: Crossdisciplinary and lifespan* (4th ed.). Dubuque, IA: Wm. C. Brown.

Siedentop, D. (1991). *Developing teaching skills in physical education* (3rd ed.). Mountain View, CA: Mayfield.

Siedentop, D. Herowitz, J., & Rink, J. (1984). *Elementary physical education methods*. Englewood Cliffs, NJ: Prentice Hall.

Snell, M.E., & Grigg, N.C. (1987). Instructional assessment and curriculum development. In M.E. Snell (Ed.), *Systematic instruction of persons with severe handicaps*. Columbus, OH: Merrill Publishing.

Spence, A.P., & Mason, E.B. (1992). *Human anatomy and physiology* (4th ed.). Minnesota: West Publishing.

Taber's cyclopedic medical dictionary. (1981). Philadelphia, PA: F.A. Davis.

Thomas, C.L., (Ed.). (1989). *Taber's cyclopedic medical dictionary* (16th ed.). Philadelphia, PA: F.A. Davis.

Van Houten, R. (1980). *Learning through feedback*. New York: Human Sciences Press.

Vogler, W.W., & French, R.W. (1983). The effects of a group contingency strategy on behaviorally disordered students in physical education. *Research Quarterly for Exercise and Sport*, **54**, 273-277.

Walker, J.E. & Shea T.M. (1991). *Behavior management: A practical approach for educators* (6th ed.). New York: Macmillan.

Wessel, J.A. & Kelly, L. (1986). *Achievement-based curriculum development in physical education*. Philadelphia: Lea & Febiger.

Williams, H. (1983). *Perceptual and motor development*. Englewood Cliffs, NJ: Prentice-Hall.

Winslow, R.M. (1989). Therapeutic recreation: Promoting wellness through leisure. *California Association for Health, Physical Education, Recreation & Dance Journal*, **51**(6), 11-12.

Wolfgang, C. & Glickman, C.D. (1986). *Solving discipline problems*. Boston, MA: Allyn & Bacon, Inc.